A Christian

COMING OUT

A Journal of the Darkest Period in My Life

To Mick,
Join me on the
journey!
Lou Anne

By
Lou Anne Smoot

A Christian COMING OUT
A Journal of the Darkest Period in My Life

ISBN: 978-0-9891033-0-5

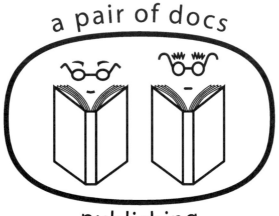

a pair of docs publishing
www.apairofdocspublishing.com
P.O. Box 972
Boiling Springs, North Carolina 28017-0972
704-473-0346

Printed by
BP Solutions Group, Inc.
Asheville, NC

"The book is a real page-turner. The narrative is warm, sensitive and courageous. The author captures the swirling of emotions engulfing her, making this a book full of life and the decisions each of us much make."
– Paul Parsons, Dean of Communications, Elon University

"Thank you for sharing this loving story with me. I laughed, and I cried, and I cheered. The story is powerful indeed."
– Dr. Tom Preston, Tyler, Texas

"There's enough angst in the first 200 pages for everyone to feel the pain of 'the mold that governed my life didn't fit.' And then in the last third ('I am finally getting to the point where I think I can talk without a box of tissues close at hand') there's comforting relief when love and relationship and normal daily life return to win the day. Well done!"
– B. Parsons

"I am reading parts of your book out loud to Joe, and we are marveling. He comes from a Baptist family – probably much like yours – and he understands it better than I. It seems to me that religion is the enemy, the very source of human pain – what kept you from finding the love you needed."
– Anne Williams, Tyler, Texas

Dedicated Posthumously To **Marilyn Hillyer**

whose Christlike example
led me safely through a very dark valley
and helped me bear sorrow I thought I couldn't
bear

With Thanks To **Alice Parrish**

who started me on my journey
through her words of love and acceptance

and to **Brenda McWilliams**

who supports me, encourages me,
and loves me.

A PERSONAL NOTE

The names of all the individuals in my book have been changed as I have no desire to bring hurt or discomfort to any. My story, however, requires "truth" in order for you to understand the journey I made during the year 2000 as well as the reason the journey was so long in coming and so very painful to complete.

If you recognize yourself in an incident you'd prefer to forget, I deeply apologize.

ACKNOWLEDGMENTS

Many thanks to my children: Billy, David and wife, Holly; Stephen and Laura, all of whom I love so very much and who continually returned that love to me as I began my "coming out" process. Their gift of unwavering love and support bolstered my flagging opinion of myself. Thank you to my two brothers, Bill and Paul (and wife, Mary Helen) for their love and support as I floundered in self pity.

As I began condensing all my notes into a book form, I shared my writing with Rev. Bruce Lowe of Dallas who insisted this book should be published. His "Letter to Louise" (which can be found at www.godmademegay.com) introduced me to a world where God loves me as His unique creation. Bruce was the first to take time to proofread my (at that time) almost 600-page book, offering specific suggestions for improvement. His gentle, loving, encouraging spirit has always been there to lift me up.

Many thanks to my friend, Troy Carlyle, who courageously published his own autobiography, The Remainder of My Life; and, by example, showed me it could really be done. Tom Preston and Shelley Thrasher devoted much time to reading and critiquing my book. Their suggestions brought about a great condensation and improvement of what I originally wrote. Thank you Tom and Shelley.

There were those who simply read my book and offered amazing support and reassurance. Without their encouragement, I might have given up.

This book would not exist without the rhetoric of Marilyn Hillyer known in this book as "Barbara." This gifted writer passed away in 2006, and I miss her so very much. "Janie" has blessed my life and remains my good friend and avid supporter.

I thank God every day for Brenda McWilliams who has been my partner in a covenant relationship since the end of 2000.

. . . I have come to believe that by and large the human family all has the same secrets, which are both very telling and very important to tell. They are telling in the sense that they tell what is perhaps the central paradox of our condition--that what we hunger for perhaps more than anything else is to be known in our full humanness, and yet that is often just what we also fear more than anything else. It is important to tell at least from time to time the secret of who we truly and fully are--even if we tell it only to ourselves--because otherwise we run the risk of losing track of who we truly and fully are and little by little come to accept instead the highly edited version which we put forth in hope that the world will find it more acceptable than the real thing. It is important to tell our secrets too because it makes it easier that way to see where we have been in our lives and where we are going. It also makes it easier for other people to tell us a secret or two of their own, and exchanges like that have a lot to do with what being a family is all about and what being human is all about. Finally, I suspect that it is by entering that deep place inside us where our secrets are kept that we come perhaps closer than we do anywhere else to the One who, whether we realize it or not, is of all our secrets the most telling and the most precious we have to tell.

Listening to Your Life by Frederick Buechner, pp 317-318.

A CHRISTIAN COMING OUT

August, 1999

Sunday. 6 a.m. As I slowly and quietly slid out of bed so as not to awaken my husband, Jim, little did I realize, as I slipped on my robe, that by the end of the day, my life would have changed irrevocably. The day began like any other Sunday morning as I took advantage of the quiet time to review the Sunday School lesson I would teach to a women's class at First Baptist Church in Tyler, Texas, an extremely conservative (fundamentalist) area of the state we call deep East Texas. The church, over 150 years old, is an imposing structure located downtown. Prior to accepting this assignment, I had occasionally worked with children, either in Sunday School or during Vacation Bible School. I found teaching adults more challenging as I lack confidence, and feel anxious about each week's lesson, despite the ladies' reassurances that I am doing a great job. To combat these feelings of inadequacy, I spend many hours preparing the lessons, certainly a lot more time than is needed, or expected.

The class is small. Quite small. Once seven attended, but three or four is the norm. Sometimes only one or two show up and once there was no one other than me. These loving, kind, supportive ladies in their 50's, having struggled the previous year without a teacher, refused to disband or to be absorbed into

1

another class. When I recently agreed to be their teacher, they welcomed me with open arms.

Upon arriving at church on this hot August Sunday in 1999, I climbed the stairs of the Education Building up to the Fourth Floor. At 60 years of age, I reminded myself that I should take every opportunity to climb those stairs because the time would come when I'd no longer be able to do so. I was always challenging my short, 5'4" petite stature to remain energetic, both physically and mentally.

This particular Sunday I was selfishly disappointed when only one class member arrived, and yet what happened to me that day would never have happened if anyone else had appeared. My first reaction was a feeling of frustration for the many hours I had spent preparing the lesson. Teaching only one person is very awkward, so I said, "Janie, it's difficult to teach a lesson to only one person, but if that is what you would like for me to do, then I certainly have a lesson prepared. Otherwise, we can use this opportunity to visit and get to know each other better."

"That's a great idea, Cheyne," she replied. Janie, always smiling and animated, was an enthusiastic type of person. All of that energy was bundled into a tiny body that weighed less than a hundred pounds. Although she was a regular attendee, I knew little about her and initiated the conversation by asking how many children she had. Among women in their 50's, this topic is usually an excellent means of getting to know someone. During the next 40 minutes we shared stories about our families, our lives, and our faith. We touched upon a variety of subjects, and my original opinion of Janie, that she was a very caring and tender-hearted person, was confirmed that morning.

As Janie began talking about her artist son, how caring and thoughtful he was, I felt certain he was gay--a homosexual. I can't explain the feeling, but there was really no doubt in my mind. Without thinking, I blurted out, "Is your son homosexual?"

My question took her completely by surprise and shocked her, but after a few moments of hesitation, she admitted, "Yes, he is, but that's just the way God made him, and God loves him just the way he is. We, too, should love and accept homosexuals just the way they are."

I was amazed. Dumbfounded. Here I was, 60 years of age and in all my life I had never heard a Christian say anything positive, loving, or accepting about homosexuals. Janie's loving, caring attitude broke through the wall within me--the wall I had carefully constructed to protect myself from the world. At that moment, the full impact of her words seemed to pass over me because I felt no forewarning, no hint whatsoever of the devastation, of the uprooting of my carefully planned life her words would bring.

When our class time ended and we stood up to leave, Janie reached over to give me a hug in parting. I had always avoided "touching," but Janie was a hugger, so I complied and put my arms around her and briefly held her close, letting her long, blonde hair brush against my face. Our bonding began that morning.

Returning home after the worship service, I prepared lunch for Jim, and for me. We had married in 1963 at a time when he was a junior high school teacher in Odessa, Texas, and I taught in one of the local high schools. Although we seemed to have much in common, our marriage had always been a struggle. Jim had earned his doctorate, risen in his profession, and now worked in the public school district's central administration after having both taught at The University of Arkansas and later served as a high school principal. His career choice required him to be authoritative, and when he used that same tone in the home, I sometimes yearned to rebel. But I tried very hard to be obedient and compliant–a good wife. For after all, he was a good man who loved his family and provided well for us. He was five years older than I, a fine-looking man of medium build with greying reddish hair.

After cleaning up the lunch dishes, and changing into more comfortable clothes, I returned to the kitchen to bake cinnamon bread. As I stood in our kitchen mixing up the bread, my thoughts returned to the conversation Janie and I had that morning. Life had dealt her some pretty damaging blows. As I thought about some of the personal problems she had shared, an all-encompassing, pervading sorrow swept through me. I was amazed at my reaction, at this feeling of pain for another person's problems. I have always prided myself in "being in control." I seldom feel deep emotion, especially regarding problems that are not even my own. I realized I had never before felt anything like what I was then feeling. Something peculiar was happening to me.

When I was only twenty years of age, I deliberately disconnected my emotions, buried them very deep within me. Over the years, I kept my emotions so subdued that I eventually convinced myself they no longer existed. Now, forty years later, I

4

took for granted I was in complete control. This was a mistake. A terrible mistake. I should have continued to be vigilant and watchful. I should have never assumed that just because my emotions had been dormant all these years they no longer existed.

I began having empathizing thoughts about Janie, feeling profound sorrow for her. My reaction to this emotion amazed me. I began to cry! Tears streamed down my face!

Soon another thought came to me--just bounced into my mind. "Perhaps Janie and I can be friends." I had lived my life avoiding close friendships. This was my way of protecting myself. Never to have a close friend. Never to confide in anyone. Never to feel anything. Consequently, I had gone through life confiding in no one, never unburdening myself to anyone else, not even my husband. But suddenly, I felt something in Janie that made me hope--that made me yearn for a friendship I had been missing. I saw in Janie a gentle spirit, an openness, and a loving attitude. I had really enjoyed talking with her. She had trusted me that morning as she shared personal problems. I thought, "If she trusts me enough to share those difficulties, then perhaps I had found someone with whom I could share my problems--someone who might actually understand me." My heart began to soar and dream of the possibilities of at last being able to open up and be honest about myself. I didn't realize until this afternoon what a burden I had been carrying all my life, the burden of secrecy.

"What would it be like," I thought, "to reveal myself to someone who would understand me, and hopefully accept me regardless of my flaw, my sin?" Would I really have the nerve to sit down and be open and honest with her?"

The more rapidly my mind jumped from one possibility to another, especially the possibility of having a real friend, my emotions suddenly changed directions-- again! Instead of feeling happy about a possible friendship with Janie, I experienced a terrible pain as if my heart were cracking open. Extreme emotional anguish flooded through me, as if I were being swept up in crashing torrents of agony. I had lived for too many years protectively keeping my past safely bottled up inside me. I was reconciled to always being "alone." So secure had I become that only occasionally did I bemoan the fact that my aloneness would go with me to the grave--that no one would ever really know who I was.

I've been at war with my body for nearly all of my life. Major battles some years; small skirmishes others. But always at war. Beginning when I was a teenager, I refused to face the truth about myself, in essence killing my soul, the being I was created to be. Denying my existence as a unique individual resulted in forming an untouchable, carefully guarded space within me that was kept private--even from myself. My emptiness grew as I blindly, and very successfully, played the role that society, church, and my family insisted was mine. But they were wrong. They didn't know me. How could they when I didn't even know myself? All I discerned was that the mold that governed my life didn't fit. It hurt. It made me miserable. Simple existence became my goal, not happiness because I was convinced I could never be happy. I often yearned for an early death as a means to escape.

Friends and family, looking upon me in this stage of my life, call me successful. My marriage has lasted for 36 years, my husband and I are respected members of the community and our four children are healthy, kind, intelligent, good-looking, and college educated. My outward life gives no indication of my inward misery.

Dormant for many, many years, my feelings suddenly came to life this Sunday afternoon. I was feeling emotion. Unwelcome emotion. Unexpected emotion. Caught by surprise, I was unprepared as well as inexperienced to handle it. I didn't understand what was happening inside of me. When I began to envision the possibility of unburdening myself to someone, of being open and honest as to who and what I was, instead of feeling happiness and joy, a feeling of sorrow cascaded over me, overwhelmed me. Tears streamed down my face as I stood in front of my stove. Grabbing tissues to staunch the tears, I was bewildered as to what was happening, where it was coming from. Just as raw flesh suddenly exposed to the air causes excruciating pain, so my emotions, suddenly released from captivity brought me a similar anguish. My being was on some type of emotional roller coaster ride. First, sorrow for Janie's problems, next the exciting hope in the possibility of discovering a friend in which to confide, then this inexplicably painful sadness. My emotions continued their wild swing that afternoon. I was no longer in control. What I felt next I don't even want to talk about. Thoughts I never dreamed I would ever have. Thoughts pushed so far back inside of me that I had even forgotten about their existence, their reality. I was devastated, shamed, embarrassed at what I was thinking.

Friday Evening, January 7, 2000

Five months later, when my husband had finished eating supper and we were both still sitting at the kitchen table, I gathered up all the courage I could muster and said, "Jim, I need to talk to you. I'm very unhappy. You have probably sensed this."

"Yes, something's going on with you."

And something was going on with me--ever since my Sunday conversation with Janie. The emotions that overwhelmed me that afternoon had taken control of my life. I was unable to sleep, had lost my appetite, and was constantly on edge. The only hope I had in regaining my sanity was to get out of my marriage. So I replied, "I guess I don't know any other way to say it. I just need to take a sabbatical, a leave from the marriage for awhile."

In shock, Jim replied, "I'm very, very sorry to hear this."

I continued, "I'm going to sleep in the other bedroom. I think I'm going to go to Lubbock (far West Texas) after church on Sunday and stay in Anne's apartment for a week or two to think through some things." (Anne is our beautiful, intelligent, tender-hearted 21-year-old daughter, a senior at Texas Tech University. I think of her as being tall because she is certainly several inches taller than I. Five days prior to this evening I had confided in her, told her the truth about her mother. Her immediate reaction was, "Mom, you've got to get a divorce." Every day since then, she has said, "Mom, you've got to do it. Don't keep putting it off. You've got to get a divorce.")

Jim asked, "Do you think that's the only solution? To separate?"

"Yes, I do. You know how many years we've tried to make this work. You would be much better off if you had somebody whom you could love."

"I don't want anybody else."

"You'd be better off with someone else."

"No, I'd be better off with someone who is . . ."

"a different person than I am."

"No, let me get in behind that wall. I've never been able to get in behind that wall. I miss it. A long time ago we had a talk; and I told you that you have a private side that I just can't get next to. This hurts. It cuts to the inner part of my soul because we've always said that no matter what, we'd make it work, that we were survivors."

"If you can't have some kind of happiness, then it's just not worth it."

"Oh, I don't agree with that. You've put forth a lot of effort in things that have made me happy. Now, I evidently haven't put forth enough to make you happy. Do you think it's absolutely irreparable? Is that how you feel it is?"

"Yes."

"Then if you feel that way, you're talking about divorcing!"

"That's probably what will happen."

Stunned, Jim stated, "I always said that if we ever got a divorce it would be that you left. I tolerated what I considered unhappy parts to the marriage in order to keep the family together. Can you say anything else other than the fact you are unhappy?"

"No, I don't think I can."

"Well, I've been unhappy for 15 years!" (We had come close to divorcing 15 years earlier, at which time I had placed some restrictions on our lovemaking.)

"Then why are we sticking it out? Why don't we try to be happy in other ways, separately? Why stick it out and both be unhappy?"

"Because I thought we made a commitment."

"We did, and we've stuck with it year after year and it's getting worse. OK? It's worse."

"You really think so?"

I stated, "Yes, there's a tension between us that you can cut with a knife. The children noticed it during Christmas."

"I didn't feel that. But if you have already made up your mind and there's not going to be a chance to sit down and try to reconcile and say, 'Honey I'll do this if you'll try to do this,' then let's just go ahead and get a divorce."

Jim continued, "Once upon a time I used to hope and pray that you would have an affair. Does that make any sense? So that I knew there was somebody in this world who could make you happy. Because I have tried so hard. Maybe if you had an affair at least I could say there was somebody you had found that really has touched those innermost strings that I have been unable to touch."

"Well, I didn't. And you didn't."

"I asked your dad one time, 'Has there been any kind of tragic experience with a man in Cheyne's life because there just seems to be a wall around her that I can't get inside of?' He said, 'No, not a thing.'"

10

The conversation continued, sometimes getting into hurtful incidents of the past. I was amazed at myself for actually initiating this conversation. I had married Jim almost 37 years earlier, married him believing I could make him happy, and that I myself could learn to be reasonably happy. We had both tried, put forth effort, but there was no spark there--at least on my part. Less than three years after we married, I realized I had made a terrible, terrible mistake. I wanted out of the marriage, but never said a word to anyone about it. I was miserably unhappy but had been taught by my parents and by my church that marriage is forever, a commitment not to be broken. The first time I considered divorce, our first son was only a year old and I reminded myself of how much he loved and enjoyed his father. And vice-versa--how proud Jim was of his son, his namesake. How selfish of me to separate these two! Then I thought of my parents. Dad was a school superintendent, a deacon in their local Baptist church, a pillar of the community. How hurt and embarrassed he and Mom would be to have their only daughter a divorcee. I couldn't do that to them. Then I thought of Jim's parents, loving individuals who had accepted me as if I were their own daughter. His dad was a Southern Baptist pastor, his mom a school counselor. They were so proud of me, and so loving towards me. Divorcing their son would be a terrible, hurtful blow to them. And then there were others who would be hurt by the divorce, siblings on both sides of the family. Each time I contemplated asking for a divorce, thoughts such as these always came to my mind. I always concluded that the only one who would benefit from a divorce would be me--and I considered that pure selfishness. I had been taught all my life not to be selfish. I couldn't break that pattern. It was ingrained into my psyche.

Now, however, as I think back through all those years, I realize the irreparable harm Jim and I inflicted on our four children by rearing them in a home where the parents didn't love each other. We were polite and considerate to each other--but unaffectionate. The blame falls on both of us, but more on me. I found it impossible to show affection when I didn't feel it. Jim shared with me one time that it took just a touch sometimes to "stir him." Hating intimacy as much as I did, I certainly didn't want to endure it more often than necessary--so I avoided touching him. There were nights in bed when I longed just to be held, nothing else. This was not possible.

My mind returned to our conversation as I heard Jim say, "I told someone the other day that the most awful thing in the world would be to grow old alone. I can't think of Hell having a worse definition. And quite frankly, I could always look forward to--it might not have been the Good Housekeeping Seal of Approval marriage, but at least we could have some companionship with each other. I'm not going to beg you. I don't know whether that's pride or reality. There are going to be a bunch of people surprised when we divorce. Nine out of ten people we know think we have a really great marriage. We've produced four fine-looking children that any parent would be delighted to have as children. There would be ten million others that would get a divorce before Jim and Cheyne did. I don't know what else to say. I keep thinking that the longer we talk, a bubble will pop and this dream will come to an end."

12

We talked finances for a few minutes and I said, "I'd like you to keep the house. You need the yard. (Jim spent many hours keeping our yard a real showplace in the neighborhood.) You need the workshop. (Upon purchasing our home eleven years earlier, we immediately had a beautiful brick workshop built for Jim. He equipped it with all the latest woodworking tools.) I just want a little place, that's all."

(When we moved to Tyler in 1988, we had purchased a nice, 3-bedroom brick home on about three-quarters of an acre of land. It was certainly the nicest home we had ever owned.)

"You're talking as if your mind is already made up."

"It is. It's made up." (When I began this conversation I believed my asking for a divorce would anger Jim. I expected ugly words, but I was wrong. He didn't get angry. All I was sensing was sadness.)

He said, "I have enjoyed being married--because it's a way to gain people's respect. It's just one of the things when you are looking for a job to say you're a good family man. My family has always been close to me. I admit I have thought it might have been a mistake that we didn't go ahead and divorce about fifteen years ago when we had decided to do so. We would have both been young enough then to have found someone else. You see, I don't think you will find somebody else. Now don't misread that. That's not to be perceived as a slap. I didn't mean it that way. I think you have the total ability to be satisfied just with yourself. Just, if nothing else, to live by that Walden Pond and never see anybody else. I can't do that. That's not meant as a putdown."

"I don't take that as a putdown."

13

Jim continued, "It's that private shield that has just ripped me apart. I can't get inside it. I sometimes wish I was having an affair so you'd have a reason to leave, because I can live with an affair. This is hard to wrestle with. I want to submit to cognitive power, but it won't submit to cognitive power. But we've talked it to death. I'll stop right now and say 'I love you,' and that's not a male effort to strum the emotional heartstrings because your heartstrings are not easy to strum. I just want to tell you I've been pleased, happy--that I wish things went differently.

"I've never told anyone I have an unhappy marriage. No one. Our son, Michael, realizes there's some tension between us. He thinks he'll never get married because if we can't make it, he certainly can't make it. It's a horrible thought that we're responsible for this thirty-year-old remaining single. And he's got all the 'gold and silver coins of the realm'--handsome sucker! He has so much ability that he makes me seem like an idiot. Well, is there anything else to say?"

"No, there's nothing else to say."

My heart was heavy as I stood up and walked out of the kitchen through the living room, and into the guest bedroom. I had actually asked Jim for a divorce, and he had agreed to it. I should have felt some type of happiness to have at last broken free of a relationship that had transformed me into a disconnected person-- detached from the person I knew myself to be. I no longer recognized myself. Denying who and what I was, accepting the role of a submissive wife, I learned to hate myself. For years I felt as if I were walking around as only a shadow of the real me. Sitting down on the bed, I felt numb. Almost in shock.

14

For days I had dreaded this evening, asking Jim for a divorce. Several days before I had promised myself that I would do it tonight--Friday night. I knew Jim would be out of town today, attending the funeral of his sister-in-law, Hazel. As Jim was dressing in his suit and tie this morning, I sat at the computer working on my Sunday School lesson. He came over to me and said, "I know you would be willing to go with me to Hazel's funeral, but I just see no need in it." Those were welcome words. Hazel and I had never had anything in common. We were certainly polite and kind to each other, but we were just very different human beings who seldom saw each other. She had suffered for years with cancer and had eventually succumbed to it.

Relief flooded through me to know that Jim didn't expect me to go with him to the funeral. The drive to their hometown would take hours, it would be an all-day trip, and I dreaded being in the car with him for such a long period of time--just the two of us. What would we talk about? I certainly didn't want to ask him for a divorce as we were driving down a highway. And how could I carry on any type of decent conversation with him, then talk divorce this evening? Besides I had always dreaded being alone with him for extended periods of time. We had little to talk about. Any conversation of substance would inevitably end up in some type of disagreement.

I hated disagreements. I hated his anger. I did all in my power not to upset him, but so often failed in that regard. I had learned over the years to be very careful of what I said, and how I said it. He so often took things the wrong way--took comments personally that I didn't mean personally. I taught myself to weigh

15

my words, to think before I spoke aloud, to ask myself, "Could he take this statement the wrong way?" Talking became such a chore that as often as possible, I opted to just be quiet.

I always reminded myself of the rare occasions when Jim became so angry with me that he would shout: "One of these days I'm going to declare you an unfit mother and take the children away from you!"

That was the phrase that frightened me half to death. I don't believe he ever had any inkling of how frightening that statement was to me. Years later, I reminded him of saying that to me several times when his anger just overpowered him. He denied ever having said it. I believe that it was spoken out of such anger that he really didn't recall saying it. There were other things he said to me in anger that I don't believe he was consciously aware of saying.

But his threat to declare me an unfit mother and take the children away from me was a threat that I, and I alone, knew could come to fruition. If there was one thing in this world I thought I succeeded at, it was being a good mother. But I also knew there was something in my past that could, in the courts of that day and time, condemn me as being an unfit mother--and conceivably cause my children to be removed from my care. Consequently, upon hearing those words, my heart froze. I reminded myself again how very, very important it was to guard my secret. To always guard my secret. Otherwise, I might lose my children.

Heated arguments that produced these hateful words were few and far between, but each time they occurred, a vise of fear squeezed my heart, reminding me of the importance of always being on guard and to never, ever share my secret with anyone.

And I didn't. Not even with a marriage counselor Jim and I saw for awhile. All I was willing to tell the counselor was that I didn't love Jim. He kept thinking there must be a third party involved, but I assured him there wasn't. And that was true. Only a memory of long ago. My fear kept me from openly confiding in the counselor because I felt certain that whatever I told him would be shared with Jim. I couldn't have that. I had to protect myself--and my children. So I kept my secret.

Our children are now grown. The threat of declaring me an unfit mother and taking the children away from me is no longer a threat. Nevertheless, I continue to guard my secret--from him. However, I've started weakening. I've now told two people--Janie and my precious daughter, Anne. Neither has turned their back to me. Both still love and accept me. How fortunate I am!

I slept little tonight, still in a state of disbelief that I had actually asked Jim for a divorce and was now spending the night in another room--on opposite ends of our house--bedrooms separated by the kitchen and living area. Part of me felt relief, part of me felt guilt, and part of me realized that the deep pain I had been enduring since that Sunday afternoon in August was not going away and that the divorce would do nothing to alleviate that pain.

As my thoughts recalled the various emotions I experienced that August afternoon five months previously, especially the crushing sorrow that exploded in my heart almost immediately upon becoming hopeful to at long last meeting someone who might understand me, I reminded myself of what I had learned the day following my emotional roller coaster. As I was driving to the grocery store the following day, Monday, I began surfing the radio channels and came upon a Christian talk show featuring an author. Having missed out on the beginning of the show, I didn't know the name of the speaker or the title of his book. But shortly after tuning to the program, I was amazed to hear this author describe what happens to a person who has lived for a long time without hope and suddenly experiences hope. He explained that this sudden intrusion of hope, as strange as it may sound, results in a tremendous sorrow. "The individual, so completely unprepared to experience hope, is submerged in painful sorrow."

Amazing! This is exactly what had happened to me--and I kept telling myself at the time it happened that it made no sense. Now, the very next day, I was hearing this phenomenon explained on a radio show I had just happened onto. I immediately gave thanks to God for guiding me into selecting this radio station.

These thoughts and others passed through my mind as I stayed in the guest room Friday night, knowing Jim would leave the house early in the morning. He and his friend, Milton, were driving to Dallas to attend an all-day woodworking seminar. Jim's being out of the house would give me the whole day to pack and to make preparations to drive to Lubbock the day afterwards, Sunday. When Anne and I had talked about the very real possibility of my asking her dad for a divorce tonight, she had suggested, "Mother, why don't you drive to Lubbock and stay in my apartment for a week or two. You'd have it all to yourself until my classes begin. I'll stay here until my Christmas holiday is over. Go stay in my apartment." Her suggestion was a good one. I liked the idea of getting away–of getting away from Jim, of getting away from the house, of getting away from Tyler. Yes, I decided to do as she suggested and go to Lubbock where she had one more semester before completing her degree at Texas Tech.

Anne came into the bedroom that evening to see how I was doing. We sat on the bed together and held hands. She knew I had asked her dad for a divorce. She had been sitting on the sofa in the living room while Jim and I had talked at the kitchen table. That put us about ten feet from each other. Anne was watching TV and didn't realize the substance of our conversation until it was almost over--because we had talked so quietly and calmly. No anger. No heated words. She eventually realized I was doing what I told her I was going to do that evening--talk with her dad. Therefore, soon after I walked to the guest bedroom, she joined me. I was at a loss as to what I was supposed to do next. I had just changed my whole life--in a 20-minute conversation. My life would never again be the same. But that change was nothing compared to the change I would make the end of next month. As Anne and I visited that evening, she said, "Mom, I want you to get some counseling. You need to talk to a professional counselor."

Her suggestion was hitting me at the right time. I had been telling myself that I needed to talk with someone. My life was in a mess. I was experiencing such sorrow and such pain that for the past three months I felt as if I were faced with only three choices: suicide, a mental institution, or divorce. These three choices had been going through my head constantly. About five days earlier, when I first mentioned my mental state to Anne, that's when she began urging me to divorce her dad. Not only did she know I needed to ask for the divorce, but she knew I needed professional help. And I knew I needed help. The divorce was just a stop-gap solution.

"I don't know anyone that I can talk with," I replied.

"I do, Mom. One of my classes at Texas Tech was led by a psychologist who is a professional counselor. He is great. I just love him to death. I'll call him right now and make an appointment for you to see him while you are in Lubbock. Would you let me call him right now?"

"Yes," I agreed. "I'll talk with him if he can see me."

Anne then located a number she had for Dr. Kerns and called him at home. His schedule was full, but he agreed to work me in for an hour's appointment on Wednesday, January 12. I made a note of the appointment, his name, and the directions Anne gave me to his office. This would be a "first" for me--telling someone the cause of all my pain. But I was ready to do so. I had to do it, for my own sake.

Saturday, January 8, 2000

When I told Michael, our handsome 30-year-old entrepreneur I had asked his father for a divorce, he asked, "Is this something you have been planning all along and were just waiting until Anne finished college?"

"No," I truthfully answered. "I haven't been planning this for a long time. And it has nothing to do with Anne's finishing college."

"Mom," he said, "you and Dad are just on different planes-- completely unable to communicate." He continued by admitting, "I can say something to Dad and it doesn't bother him at all, but if you say exactly the same thing, it just pushes his buttons. You're always pushing his buttons, you know."

"I know, Michael. You're right. That's one of the things I tried to tell your dad last night–that I had become afraid to talk with him for fear of angering him--that I felt intimidated by him."

As he hugged me, he stated, "Mom, I just want you to be happy."

Later in the day I visited with our eldest, J.W., our 34-year-old, single, elementary school teacher. He is his father's namesake and rightly so for he looks so much like his dad. He, too, was very kind, very loving, and very supportive. He said the same thing as Michael said, "Mother, we love you and just want you to be happy."

J.W. asked few questions. However he reminded me of his resentment in being "left out" when his dad and I first talked about divorcing in July, 1985. He was 20 at that time and was away at college when Jim called Michael and Josh into our bedroom. "Boys," he said, "your mother and I are planning to divorce because your mother doesn't love me anymore."

I couldn't believe he had said that–laid all the blame upon me. My mind is a blur about that evening. Michael would have been 16 and Josh, 14. I feel Jim informed them in order to hurt me, knowing how crazy I was about the children and how I so detested seeing them hurt. Anne, who was then seven years of age, was not at home either. She was spending a week with my parents in Little Rock, Arkansas. As I try to recall that evening, I remember feeling anger at Jim, a deep anger. In front of two of our sons, he was blaming me entirely for our marital problems; and I didn't feel I was entirely to blame. When we talked "divorce" at this time in our marriage, we were living in Austin, Texas, and the word was first used by Jim--stemming from the anger that overflowed when I decided to rejoin a church we had previously left. During a period of about five years, we had left three different churches. Something about each church angered Jim. When we moved to Austin, we joined Hyde Park Baptist Church--the largest Baptist church in the city--and an ultra-conservative church. Seven years after we joined this church, it made a decision to establish its own private school. I knew this upset Jim immensely. As a public school administrator, he was a strong supporter of public education. When Anne, our baby, was less than two years of age, and we were all sitting around the supper table one evening, Jim announced, "I'm sure you are aware that I will never again set foot inside Hyde Park Baptist Church. We'll locate another church to join." Jim continued, "None of my church contributions will ever be used to support a private church school. This school is being established to enable those prejudiced people with money to keep their children segregated from the minority. That's what it's all about despite the assurances of our Director of Education that they just want to take advantage of this opportunity to 'spread the gospel.' That's just not what it's all about, and I'll have no part of it."

Austin, Texas, at this time, was in the midst of a court-ordered busing plan. Jim and I supported integration and even chose to purchase our home in a racially-integrated neighborhood, despite the effect we knew it would have on the sales value of that house. We "put our money where our mouth was." We felt strongly about our children attending integrated schools--so much so that by the time we eventually moved from Austin fifteen years later, our neighborhood school was over 90% minority. In addition to Jim's strong feelings about integration, he believed that if the new church school were successful, he could conceivably lose his job. He was Austin's newest high school principal, having recently chosen to step down from a position in central administration. He felt if the church's high school were successful, Austin would need one less high school, and, as the newest principal, he would be the one to go. I felt his reasoning very faulty along these lines, but he had nevertheless concluded that his job, his standing in the community, and his livelihood were being personally threatened by his own church.

Thirteen years earlier, we had lived in Austin for the two-years it took Jim to earn his Ph.D. It was during this time that I made the decision to quit my full-time teaching job at The University of Texas in order to be a stay-at-home mom. Because I no longer worked outside the home, my church provided my primary social outlet. I actively participated in its programs, directed a fourth-grade Sunday School department, worked in their Mother's Morning Out program, played in their handbell choir and

23

enrolled our children in their choirs and children's missions programs.

When Jim made his announcement that we would not be returning to Hyde Park Baptist Church, not only was I upset, but the boys were upset. None of us dared stand up to Jim, to argue with him, to plead. Quiet prevailed around the table. Jim was the "head of the family," and we abided by his wishes. This was in 1980, and we began visiting churches. In a fairly short period of time we joined a neighborhood church, Windsor Park Baptist. I again became quite active and played in their handbell choir. I agreed to direct their fourth-grade Vacation Bible School.

When we had been members for less than a year, Jim was asked to serve on the church's education committee. The first meeting he attended was a disaster. When he returned home from that meeting, he said, "Would you believe that I sat in that meeting tonight listening to everyone knock down public education and discuss the possibility of establishing a private school?" Anger was in his voice as he continued, "They did nothing but run down the public school system. We aren't going back to this church ever again."

This time I spoke up and said, "I've already agreed to direct the fourth-grade department's Vacation Bible School. It's less than a month away and there isn't time to get someone else. Besides, I'm not going back on my word. They're depending upon me. Wait until Vacation Bible School is over, then I'll be willing to quit this church and hunt for another one."

Jim abided by my request. In the summer of 1981, as soon as Vacation Bible School was over, we began visiting other churches--all of us, that is, except Michael. Michael was twelve at that time and dearly loved Windsor Park because many of his school buddies attended and he was involved in an active youth group. He didn't want to leave, and became quite adamant about it. Jim told him, "We are a family, and we'll attend church as a family. Our family is not going to divide up on Sunday mornings."

I disagreed with Jim's decision; and when we were alone, I suggested, "Let Michael continue to go to Windsor Park Baptist. We ought to be happy he *wants* to go to church. Most boys his age have to be dragged into a church, but he enjoys going. If we force him to go with us, he may end up hating church altogether. I think we will make a terrible mistake forcing him to come with us."

"I don't agree with you at all. It's wrong for our family not to worship together on Sunday morning. That's what family is all about. Besides, how do you propose we get him to and from his church while we go somewhere else?"

"We'll drop him off on the way to whatever church we attend. This means he will arrive earlier than usual. It will also mean he will stay later than usual because he will have to wait for us to get there to pick him up. We'll explain this to him--and if he still wants to go to Windsor Park, then let's let him go."

Michael was more than willing to arrive early and leave late. Many a time, when we finally arrived to pick him up, he was standing all by himself in the parking lot. He never complained. However, the rest of us, J.W., Josh, Anne, and I, had to listen to Jim's griping every Sunday morning after dropping off Michael. "This is not right," Jim would say, "all of us not staying together on a Sunday. I don't know why I let you talk me into this because this is just not right. We shouldn't have a son attending a church different from the one we attend. This is just not right and I'm sorry I ever gave in and let you talk me into this."

Every single Sunday we listened to the same spiel from the time we dropped off Michael until the time we arrived at whatever church we attended that day. The atmosphere in the car was unpleasant every Sunday morning. We varied our churches, visiting differing ones. By the spring of 1982, we settled upon University Baptist Church, on Guadalupe, close to the University of Texas. After we had been members there for awhile, an incident occurred one Wednesday evening that instigated another church move. Our youngest son, Josh, who must have been eleven or twelve years of age at that time, was given a lead role in a children's choir performance based upon the life of David, the shepherd boy who killed the giant, Goliath. Josh was elated to be given this role. Never before had he been given an opportunity to "shine." To the contrary, he always had trouble "fitting in" because he was both extremely intelligent and socially immature--a combination that always caused him problems. His peers assumed whenever he used big words he was showing off. But that was just Josh--good-natured Josh who never had a mean bone in his body. He had no idea he was setting himself apart from his peers by the intelligent questions he asked, the correct answers he gave, the words he used.

When Josh proudly announced to me his part in the musical, he handed to me a paper listing the rehearsal dates-- every Wednesday evening--and the rules which clearly stated that a missed rehearsal meant being dropped from the performance.

I was therefore careful to take Josh (and Anne) to church every Wednesday evening. He attended all his rehearsals--except the last one--a specially-called rehearsal. A card arrived in the mail one day announcing the extra rehearsal--scheduled for Monday afternoon just prior to the Wednesday performance. As I showed the card to Josh and told him we needed to plan to attend this rehearsal, he quickly stated, "Mom, I don't have to go."

"Why not?" I asked, surprised at his statement.

"That rehearsal is for those who don't yet know their parts. I know my part. So I don't have to go," he explained--full of self-assurance.

"But Josh, they'll need everyone to be there."

"Not me. They don't need me. I know my part."

I should not have listened to him, but I did. I had other children needing my attention that Monday afternoon, and felt a sense of relief that I wouldn't need to spend hours of my time driving Josh across town in heavy traffic for the rehearsal.

Wednesday night arrived, and Jim joined us at the church for the meal and service--looking forward to Josh's performance. As we sat together in the Fellowship Hall finishing up our meal, the children were summoned to dress in their costumes. A few minutes later, Josh returned to our table--in tears, bawling--obviously heartbroken. Totally confused, I asked, "What is it Josh?"

"I'm not in the play anymore," he sobbed.

Shocked, I asked, "What do you mean?" not wanting to believe what he was saying.

27

"They took my part away from me because I didn't go to the rehearsal on Monday. I don't have the part any more. I'm not in the play."

Others in the room were becoming aware of the scene playing out at our table--and Jim was appalled anyone would treat a child this way. His anger overflowed, and he began to make a scene. I got up and ushered the children out of the room, with Jim following. Several church members came over to us to help smooth over the problem and one even went to talk with the choir director on our behalf. But the director was resolved to hold fast to the rules. Josh had missed a rehearsal, so he could not be in the play. However, as a peace offering, he offered Josh a minor role in the performance. Josh didn't want the minor role--and was, by then, in no condition to perform anyway.

Josh continued to cry. Our family sat down on some steps not far from the Fellowship Hall, watched the costumed children file into that room to perform, then walked out of the church as Jim informed us we would never again set foot in University Baptist Church.

During parts of 1984 and 1985, we visited churches. We couldn't seem to find a congregation we wanted to join, and I became fed up with our "rootlessness"--especially the absence of the children's participation in children's and youth activities. Contrary to my normal acquiescence to Jim's leadership, I decided during the summer of 1985 to return to our original church, Hyde Park, and to take 7-year-old Anne with me. One afternoon, as Michael, Josh, Anne and I were sitting on the grass in our front yard and visiting, I shared with them my decision--to return to Hyde

28

Park Baptist Church and to take Anne with me. (J.W. was in college by then--living in Waco.) I further explained to the two younger boys that they could choose what church they wanted to attend. Michael, who had continued to attend Windsor Park Baptist, quickly indicated that's where he wanted to go. Josh, hesitating a little, said, "Mom, since you are taking Anne with you, I'll go with Dad so he won't be by himself."

"That would be great, Josh," I replied.

The next step was to disclose to Jim my decision. So seldom did I "rock the boat," that I found it very difficult to broach the subject with him, but I finally garnered the courage to say, "I'm tired, Jim, of visiting churches and moving from one church to another. I'm going to return to Hyde Park where so many of my friends are, and I'm going to take Anne with me."

"You know I will never go back there. What you are proposing is to break up the family! This is the same as asking me for a divorce! Is that what you want?"

"No, all I'm proposing is to return to Hyde Park. But if you want to talk divorce, then we can talk divorce." Our discussions went downhill from that moment. When he began questioning me as to whether or not I loved him, I finally admitted that I didn't love him. I didn't want to say it, but I felt a need to be honest. That seems strange to me now, thinking back on how my whole life has been a fabrication--and yet I held honesty in such high esteem. It doesn't compute. And yet I always felt I was doing what was expected of me--what was the right thing to do. The fact that I was miserable all those years seemed like a punishment, a cross I had to bear--and I bore it alone, and silently.

When J.W. reminded me of his resentment in being "left out" of these first discussions Jim and I had of divorcing, memories of that period of time all flooded back.

Sunday, January 9, 2000

When I taught my Sunday School class this morning, seven members were present--a big group. The number had been growing and this pleased me. I didn't share with the group the personal trauma I was enduring, but I did inform them that I would be out of town the following Sunday and had already asked one of their favorite substitutes to step in for me.

As soon as I left church, I drove to Mother's apartment located in a retirement home. Mother was 89 years of age. She was a beloved resident of the facility, respected, and a humdinger of a bridge player. Tall and thin, she was regularly receiving compliments on her beautiful white hair. Mother never had any problems speaking her mind, or speaking out. I grew up in her shadow and now see myself very like her. Dad passed away almost four years ago, so two years later she left all her many friends and moved from Little Rock to Tyler, in order to be close to me, her only daughter. As I entered her living room, I got right to the point. "Mother," I said, "I've asked Jim for a divorce, and I'm now on my way to Lubbock for several weeks."

"You're getting a divorce?" she asked.

"Yes, I am, Mother."

She then amazed me by saying, "I know you've been unhappy for a long time. This doesn't come as any surprise to me. I just want you to be happy. When did you say you're going to Lubbock?"

"Now. As soon as I leave here. The car is already packed. I'll be staying in Anne's apartment. You have her phone number. I'll call home tonight to let everyone know I've arrived safely."

I had dreaded telling her. One of the reasons I had not asked for a divorce many years earlier was my desire not to hurt or embarrass my parents. I felt certain that having a divorced daughter would devastate them. I also dreaded enduring her attempts to talk me out of the divorce, and I felt certain this is what she would attempt to do. But, much to my surprise, that didn't happen.

A few more words were said, we hugged, she admonished me to drive carefully, and I left--my heart much lighter than when I had arrived. Her reaction pleasantly surprised me. My dread in telling her resulted from what she and dad had said in 1985 when Jim and I were serious about divorcing. Seven-year-old Anne had gone home with them for a two-week summer visit, and it was during this time that Jim told Michael and Josh we were divorcing. Only a few days into her visit, Anne became homesick and begged to come home. Because the drive from Austin to Little Rock is a long one--over 500 miles, we agreed to split the difference with my parents and meet them outside a cafeteria in Mount Pleasant (Texas). The day of that drive, 16-year-old Michael had other plans, so only 14-year-old Josh rode with us.

31

Prior to our arrival, we instructed him, "Josh, give us a few minutes to visit with your grandmother and granddad and Anne, then we'd like you to take Anne a little ways off and play with her so that your daddy and I can talk privately with your grandparents. We don't want Anne to hear of the divorce right now. We'll sit down and talk with her about it later."

"Sure, Mom," he replied. Josh, I knew, would do as we asked. All of us were quieter than usual that day. We didn't play our usual car games that make the time pass quickly and help keep the atmosphere light and happy. None of us seemed to have much to say.

We made excellent connections in Mt. Pleasant. Anne, of course, was delighted to see us, and kept clinging to me. But she was also delighted to see her brother, Josh, who was just as happy to see her. All the boys were crazy about her, and she felt the same about her three "big brothers." I eventually suggested to Josh that he and Anne could walk over to another area and play for a few minutes. Josh took Anne's hand and led her away. We watched as they happily played chase.

We then turned to Mother and Dad and said, "There is something we need to share with you. Jim and I are planning to get a divorce."

"What?" they exclaimed unbelievingly. "You're getting a divorce?"

"Yes. We've already talked with Michael and Josh about it."

"But I don't understand!" Mother exclaimed. "Why are you getting a divorce?"

"We think it's best" was about all I could come up with.

Both of my parents were shocked at our decision. They really didn't know what to say. Finally, Dad looked at me and asked, "Cheyne, does this decision make you happy?"

"No," I admitted. And the decision didn't make me happy. Although I wanted a divorce, I hated to break up the family. I dreaded telling everyone our marriage was over. I wasn't certain how in the world I would be able to support myself and the children. All I felt was misery, and guilt! Lots of guilt. I was breaking my marriage vow "until death do us part" although I had spent nearly every year of the marriage yearning for "God to just take me" so that I could escape the marriage. So when Dad asked me if the decision made me happy, I simply answered, "No."

Dad took that to mean, I suppose, that I was not in favor of the divorce--which was the farthest possible thing from the truth. He then looked at both of us and said, "You need to work this out. Find some way to work this out. Get counseling, but try to make a go of this marriage. You two don't need to be doing this." Dad was superintendent of the Little Rock Public Schools, used to making decisions and giving directions.

I didn't know what to say. I was forty-six at the time, and I had spent my life obeying either my father or my husband. If Dad told me not to divorce, and to try to make a go of it, then that's what I would do. I must have said something like "All right." Jim and I had little to say to each other as we drove home to Austin. Two of our children were in the car, and we didn't want to talk in front of them. We ended up not divorcing--primarily because each of us insisted the other contact a lawyer and start the proceedings.

Neither of us did that, so the decision just died for lack of any action. But we were both unhappy. Very unhappy.

Because of this earlier experience in telling my parents we wanted a divorce, I was delighted this Sunday afternoon with Mother's loving and understanding reaction. Actually, I was amazed. My assumptions that others would be condemning had been wrong. My daughter and sons were loving and supportive, and now my mother was reacting in the same way.

A little over seven hours later, I arrived in Lubbock, exhausted. Wiped out. After all, I had been awake since 3:15 that morning, had taught a Sunday School class, and had then driven 400 miles. Climbing into bed, I felt a desire to read! I had brought library books with me on the legal aspects of divorce and the financial decisions that need to be made in regard to divorce. I also brought some books I thought would help me better understand myself and the deep emotional pain I was suffering.

I chose to read Mel White's *Stranger at the Gate*. I read, and I cried. I placed a box of tissues beside me on the bed and every few minutes stopped to wipe away tears. I had never before read a book like *Stranger at the Gate*. For the first time in my life I discovered other people exist who are like me, have feelings similar to mine, and have suffered in much the same way. This was news to me. I had always believed I was unique, one of a kind, atypical. I cried and cried for the lost years, for all those lonely years of silence and fear. I cried for the years of repression and the unwarranted guilt I carried all my life for something I couldn't help. I discovered other people are like me, people I never knew existed. People who experienced the same passions and

34

fears, the same feelings of separateness, the same feelings of self-condemnation and guilt. Never before had I cried like this. A purging was taking place, an emptying. The tears kept coming. After reading a page or two and learning something that applied directly to me, the tears would start up again. Reading, sobbing, reading, sobbing. I released repressed emotions and learned I wasn't the terrible sinner I always thought I was. Finally, at 11:30, I cut off the light and slept for awhile.

Monday, January 11, 2000

As soon as I awakened, I picked up White's book and continued to read--this time I took time to note page numbers enabling me to later on summarize the points I considered most important to me.

White's words excited me. Words like, "Doing justice begins by walking away from the churches and the synagogues, the preachers, priests and rabbis, who use God's word to condemn us and into churches and fellowships where we are loved and respected as God's children who happen to be . . . (different). "[1]

Another passage said, "When we act in faith, there is enough light in this world to conquer the darkness. As we journey together, let that light so shine in us that the darkness will be driven away and this long, dark night will end forever."[2] I knew I was in the midst of a long, dark night, had been for most of my life, and now I was seeing a light through the words I was reading. Mel White expressed my feelings exactly when he stated, "Feeling abandoned by God, by the church, and by society, I longed to end my life."[3]

"Misusing the Bible to support old prejudice is not a new phenomenon,"[4] White wrote as he gave documented examples. Everything he said "hit home." All of my life, I had avoided reading about my problem. "By not paying any attention to it, it will just go away," I thought. The only information I ever gleaned on the forbidden subject came from either the Ann Landers column or the Dear Abby column. Thank goodness their comments were sensible ones, without the prejudice I normally heard from Christians and family.

As I took a break from reading this Monday morning, I thought back to the previous day when Janie lingered for a few minutes after I completed the Sunday School lesson. She was the only one in the group who knew I had asked Jim for a divorce as I had called her on Saturday to tell her of the events the night before. She, along with Anne, had been encouraging me to take this step. I can hear her saying, "Cheyne, this is something you just have to do." Over and over she encouraged me to get out of the marriage. Each time she said it I knew she was right, but doing what is right can sometimes be very, very difficult. After the other class members left, Janie asked, "Are you all right, Precious?"

"Yes, I'm fine," I replied, although I was probably still in a state of shock. She then handed me a little gift bag containing a book which she had wrapped in gift paper and tied with a bow. "This is a book I want you to read," she explained. "I didn't think the other members of the class needed to see it so I wrapped it up like a gift. But it's a book I had at the house, and I want you to read it."

Thanking her for loaning me the book, which was Bruce Bawer's, *A Place At The Table*, we visited a few minutes about my asking Jim for a divorce. I commented, "One of the things Jim said to me as we discussed the divorce was that there had always been a wall between us. He didn't realize how right he is."

"Cheyne," she replied, "he knows what it is. He just doesn't want to admit it, but he knows."

I think she's wrong. I don't believe he knows, and yet a part of me wishes he did know so I would never have to explain it to him. Then a wave of fear passed through me. What if he found out prior to the finalization of our divorce? Would this anger him to such an extent that he might make the divorce difficult? "I must continue to guard my secret," I told myself.

After a trip to the grocery store this morning, I climbed back into bed, propped myself up as I snuggled under the covers, and continued to read. I also called Josh, the only son with whom I had not yet talked. Josh will be 29 next month. He and his wife, Sandy, live in the Houston area. He works for a company that sub-contracts with NASA and is involved in preparing experiments that are taken up in space ships. His comments mirrored what my other children said, "Mom, I just want you to be happy." However, he did add, "I can't help but selfishly wish our baby could have the same family togetherness that I had as a child." He and Sandy have been married for four years and are expecting a baby in July.

Wednesday, January 12, 2000

Today I met with Dr. Kerns, the therapist Anne recommended. Upon arriving at his office, I was asked to complete a long form detailing the problems I am experiencing as well as the expectations I have of this visit. When I read the question, "Tell me in what way you think I will be able to help you," I wrote, "Frankly, I don't think you can do a thing to help me." When Dr. Kerns read my statement, he laughed. "You really don't think I can help you?" he asked.

"No, I don't think there is a thing you can do for me. There's nothing anyone can do for me." My problems, in my mind, were insurmountable, unsolvable. The only reason I kept the appointment was to bare my soul, something I had never done. And that's exactly what I did this afternoon.

I confided I married Jim knowing I was not in love with him. I felt pressure to marry–to fit in. Mother often "fixed me up" with a blind date whenever I came home from college for a visit. She knew I had turned down numerous marriage proposals and she was concerned about my future. I dated some really nice guys–good marriage material–but I never fell in love with any of them. When I was 22, I said to myself, "I'm never going to fall in love with a man. Just face facts. Quit waiting to fall in love. Find a nice guy and marry him. Just get it over with and do what everyone expects you to do." It never entered my mind I could go through life and never marry. Marriage was a given, at least in the society in which I grew up. Any talk of my future included the assumption I would marry and have children.

38

Soon after I made the decision to marry without love, I was introduced to Jim who seemed to fit all my criteria. Five years older than I, he was a school teacher with ambitions to become a school administrator. He was Baptist (and the son of a Southern Baptist minister). He was a very nice person, he loved me, and he loved children. What more could I ask for?

Once I made my choice and married him, I attempted to be the perfect wife despite the misery I experienced in this role. Although I despised the person I had become, I experienced great pride in my children and showed Dr. Kerns a picture I brought of the six of us. I wanted him to know what a lovely, handsome family I have. I told him everything--the pain and misery I was now experiencing, the reason for it, and the hopelessness of my situation. I mentioned Jim's extreme prejudice against people like me, of hearing him say (as a high school principal) that he would never allow (people like me) to teach in his school because they have no business being around children. His attitude made it impossible for me to be open and honest with him.

"Do you think there is any chance he can have a good attitude if you were to explain to him 'the wall' that is between the two of you?" he asked.

"No," I responded. "No way in the world."

As I poured out my heart to him that afternoon, I cried continually. A dam had broken, one that had been closed for the past forty years. The tormenting anguish was all pouring out. He placed a box of tissues next to me as I sobbed for most of the hour, gut-wrenching cries of hopelessness. Several times he became so concerned about me that he left his chair to sit beside me, patting me on the back. Several times he asked me, "Do you believe God loves you despite (your problem)?"

"Yes," I sobbed. "I know He loves me, but I don't know why He made me the way I am."

"If Jesus were to walk into this room right now, do you believe He would put His arms around you and tell you how much He loves you?"

"Yes," I admitted. "But I don't understand this heartbreak. I don't understand why I am hurting so many people. Why I will have to go through the coming torment of disapproval by others. None of it makes any sense unless . . . unless God has had a plan all along for me to use my life experiences to help someone else. That thought is all that keeps me going."

"You do have difficult times ahead of you," he agreed. "But you don't have to place an ad in the paper about it."

"You need to make some definite plans prior to returning to Tyler," he suggested. "Be specific. Decide before you leave here where you will spend the night, where you will eat your meals, whom you will see, and whether or not you will attend church. Make these decisions ahead of time."

When our session was over and I stood up to go, Dr. Kerns said, "I don't normally do this, but would you mind if I prayed?"

"No, of course not," I answered.

Dr. Kerns held my hands as he prayed a beautiful prayer asking God to watch over me and bring comfort to me. At no time during the session did he even question my decision to get a divorce.

Thursday, January 13, 2000

Although I didn't turn out my light last night until 11 p.m., I was wide awake this morning by 5, probably 4:30. I decided to splurge and eat breakfast at IHOP. My weight continues to drop, and I don't need to lose any more pounds. I entered the doors of IHOP at 5:30 a.m. and received wonderful service so early in the morning. The food was good, but I had no appetite. I ate almost half an omelet, a small biscuit, and drank half a glass of orange juice. When I couldn't push any more down, I paid my bill, got in my car, and drove the loop around Lubbock. I set the speed control, listened to Beethoven's Piano Concerto #1 in C Major, and drove a practically empty highway lit by street lamps and a sprinkling of stars in a dark sky. It took 24 minutes to go around the city. Upon returning to Anne's apartment, I climbed back in bed as I was feeling headachy. I must have slept for just a little while.

After supper, I called Mother. I'd been feeling guilty about not calling her. I tried to keep the conversation upbeat to hide how depressed I was. At one point, she said, "I awoke before five this morning thinking of Jeff Tatum."

"What in the world made you think of Jeff Tatum?" I asked. Jeff and I had dated in college, he had asked me to marry him, had even bought me an engagement ring, but I had turned him down. Jeff was a nice guy, a really fine fellow. Despite the fact he had fallen in love with me, my feelings for him never went beyond friendship.

41

Mother's answer to my question amazed me. "I figure he's probably the one you've been thinking of, the reason you have decided to leave Jim."

"Oh, Mother!" I exclaimed. "I can't believe that thought ever occurred to you!"

"Isn't he the one who drove out to Big Spring (where they lived when I was in college) to give you a big diamond ring?"

"He offered me a diamond ring while we were at Baylor University! I bet you're thinking of Allen Adair. He drove out to Big Spring to see me."

"Yes, I remember him. He's the one that gave you that pretty sweater from Germany. I remember all those fellows, but I'm sure I wouldn't recognize them if I saw them."

"One you probably wouldn't recognize is Duane Morris. I went steady with him my senior year in high school. Remember Duane?"

"He used to work at that restaurant in Austin."

"Yes, the Nighthawk Restaurant. That's the one. He worked in both of their restaurants, the one on the south side as well as the one on the north side of the city. He used to be tall and skinny when I dated him. He's now a big man. He owned a car dealership in Austin. He and his wife, Wendy, own a ranch--close to Kyle, I think. His wife and I used to be in the same Sunday School class at Hyde Park Baptist."

"Well, I figure it's one of those fellows you're thinking about."

"Mother, you're wasting your time. Quit thinking. And that's all I'm going to say on the subject. You're worrying about something that's not happening."

"Oh, I'm not worrying about it. It's not a problem with me."

Friday, January 14, 2000

I awoke at 3:35 a.m. recalling the questionnaire I completed at Dr. Kerns' office. Listed at the bottom of the questionnaire, in rather small print, were perhaps up to a hundred various "problems" I might be experiencing. I was asked to circle all that applied to me. I circled quite a few. The ones I recall circling were sadness, marriage, suicidal, depression, sexual problems, and sleep disorders. I was then asked to mark the two that I considered the more important problems. I marked "depression" and "marriage."

At some point during the interview, after I had expressed my long-standing desire to die and the many, many times I considered suicide, Dr. Kerns asked, "Why have you never committed suicide?"

"Because of the children," I replied. "I've longed for death for most of my life, have looked forward to it, but I knew the children needed me. Suicide would be so unfair to them, and to my parents. But I've always wanted to 'just get life over with.' The pain is always with me, the hopelessness I've always lived with."

At that point, we discussed my specific problem and the fact that because Dr. Kerns works for a Christian counseling service,

43

he has had little contact with my particular problem. We spent a few minutes discussing it in very general terms, then I said, "That's where the hate comes from, you know. From Christians."

"Yes, you're right," he agreed.

Tonight Mother called again. She began the conversation with, "I think I've figured out who you are interested in. When you asked for that good smelling hand lotion for a birthday gift I decided I knew then who it was."

My heart began to pound, because the hand lotion did have a direct bearing on the person who had captured my heart. Fear set in. I didn't say a thing, but she continued, "It's Frank Smitherman, isn't it?"

I laughed—with relief along with the ridiculousness of her conclusion. Frank and I had taught together, shared a classroom for several years. We supported each other in that environment, were certainly friends, but our relationship never went beyond that. Besides, he was at least 15 years younger than I, maybe 20 years younger. "Mother," I said, "your imagination is working overtime. I can't believe you are sitting around trying to figure out who I am interested in. I'm not interested in Frank Smitherman for goodness sakes!"

"Well, it dawned upon me that when you asked for that expensive hand lotion, you were interested in someone. If it's not Frank, then it must be someone at the church."

"Why would you think that?"

"Because you're always going to the church for meetings, so it must be someone at the church!"

"Mother, you're wasting your time. I told you that last night, and I'm telling you again right now. You're wasting your time. Quit thinking! It's not going to get you anywhere. I'm not interested in anyone."

"Well, I figured you want to be free to be with someone else."

"I don't have someone waiting for me. There is no one. Quit thinking about it."

We talked awhile longer as she asked about the children and told me she had found a new hairdresser. I closed the conversation by saying, "I can hardly wait for your next phone call to see who in the world you have thought of next!"

Several hours passed after our phone conversation and the more I thought about mother's "meddling questions," the angrier I became. Memories flooded back from my teenage years when she put me through "the third degree" after every date. "Where did you go? Who was with you? Did you kiss?" Oh how I hated her questions. How I dreaded walking into the house after a date, knowing I'd be required to endure her inquisition. Her "guessing" who I was interested in rekindled unpleasant memories. What right did she have to ask me such questions? The nerve!

Monday, January 18, 2000

Jim called this morning. This was our first conversation since I asked him for a divorce more than a week earlier. He couldn't have been nicer--no pleading for me to change my mind.

None. He said, "I'd like for us to keep everything friendly. You're welcome to stay at the house until you find a place to live. I want us to find time to sit down together and go over the financial details of the divorce. There's no reason we have to get involved with lawyers. I think the two of us can work everything out in a friendly way."

"That sounds wonderful. I really appreciate your attitude about all this. I brought financial information with me and plan to spend some time studying it so I can make some suggestions as to how we can divide everything up so that both of us will be able to maintain, for the most part, the same standard of living."

"I hope you're right."

"I think I am. I'll have it all written down so that we can have a starting point for our discussion."

"I talked with Brad Albritton (Jim's Sunday School teacher who is a lawyer) and he said there is a 60-day waiting period between the filing of the petition and the granting of the divorce."

"That's not long. For some reason, I thought it would take longer than that."

"I'd like to continue to help you out with your car--maintain it for you. (He had always changed the oil, installed new brake pads, and carried out various car maintenance projects.) Perhaps you could repay me with a nice meal or two."

"Sounds good to me. I'll be glad to cook some meals for you."

"I've talked with Josh and Sandy and told them that when they come to visit, especially after the baby is born, that both you and I will be present in the house and it will be all of us together."

46

I thought this a rather odd scenario, but I was delighted to hear Jim being so nice and friendly, so I quickly agreed and stated, "I'll be glad to come over at that time, and cook for all of us."

His desire to have all of us together for visits made me realize the divorce would be easier than I had expected. I also felt his plans for family gatherings would be short-lived because once he became interested in someone else, he certainly wouldn't be inviting me over. Nevertheless I was delighted with his attitude and told myself, "We'll cross that bridge when we come to it."

January 27, 2000

This is the first day I have felt like getting out for almost a week. I returned home from Lubbock with some type of virus, and went straight to bed. Today I located a small apartment in a gated community for seniors for only $470 a month. I was delighted to have found a place so quickly and easily as my strength was gone.

One of the questions I regularly ask myself during this time is, "What do I think I'm doing, getting a divorce? . . . making a mess of my life at the age of 61 (I had a birthday in December)? I'm giving up everything I know me to be and stepping out into an unknown world as a single person. A divorcee, for goodness sakes! Me! Do I really want to do this?"

The answer that quickly resounds in my mind is, "What's the alternative? Do I want to stay married for the rest of my life?"

"No," I tell myself. "That's an impossible situation. I cannot, absolutely cannot, stay married. I have no choice. I must get a divorce."

"Will getting a divorce solve my problem? Make me happy?"

"No. It won't solve my problem. My misery will continue. But getting a divorce will help."

January 31, 2000

Jim and I came to an agreement today on dividing up the money. I felt we were both happy with the decisions we made. No, happy is not the right word to use. I was satisfied that I could live on the smaller portion I had asked for. I think I was able to show Jim how he would have enough to provide for his needs, to continue the house payments, and to maintain his standard of living. We had always lived on a strict budget, which I had drawn up. I therefore prepared Jim's budget for February--something he could use as an example. I wanted him to understand how his portion of the money would meet his needs.

The budget was my responsibility--because I enjoyed it. Jim abided by it, but he didn't enjoy it. He never complained, however, because he knew his money was being spent (and saved) wisely; and I believe he was thankful I was careful with it. But finances were my forte, and I even completed our tax returns every year. The divorce would force Jim into financial areas that would be new to him, and I hated to leave him unprepared. I promised to balance his checkbook at the end of February, then took time to show him some of those basic steps before I headed to a bank to open an account in my name.

Jim called a lawyer to check on the cost of handling the divorce: $400 plus a $150 filing fee. Jim and I agreed to split the cost. Even if we file right away, it will be April before the divorce is final.

February 1 - February 22, 2000

Tuesday, February 1: Moving day. Having been ill for almost two weeks, I did little preparation to move from the house into the little apartment. Consequently, my goal was to move only a few bare essentials, to get partially settled, and to pick up additional items from the house in the next few days. Jim was very helpful, and we both worked hard all day. As he assembled the bed for me, I silently said, "Thank you, God," for Jim's willingness to help and his generous attitude. We completed the last load after dark, and when I made no move to get back in the car with him, Jim said, "You are coming back to the house to sleep, aren't you?"

"No, I plan to stay here."

"But you don't have anything set up here."

"The bed is put together. That's all I need. I can find some sheets to put on it. I'll be all right. Really. I want to stay here tonight."

Reluctantly, Jim left me alone in the apartment. Later, after 9 p.m., I drove to Wal-Mart to purchase shelf paper and a few food items.

Wednesday, February 2: Jim and our handsome 30-year-old son, Michael, both called to check on me today. I stayed very busy putting things away. One of the passages I read today was, "The most powerful yearning is for a past one never had."[5] This fit me to a tee. I have constantly yearned for a life I denied myself when I was 20–and always wished for something I could never have.

Saturday, February 12: The past ten days have been busy in making my apartment livable. Now, for the first time in weeks, I'm experiencing an overwhelming sadness. Tears are ready to fall constantly. I'm not certain what has caused this. I think the catalyst was going through a box of old letters and notes--many written to thank me or praise me for something or another. (Aren't those the letters people save–the uplifting ones?) I noticed for the first time that many were from Barbara Lawrence, a friend from church. Barbara was about my age, actually a year or two older, and always struggling with her weight, trying to lose about 20 pounds. Barbara's intelligence amazed me, and I admired the way she always seemed to know what was going on in the church. Her father, now deceased, had been pastor of The First Baptist Church in a neighboring town, so she was well grounded in scripture and was regarded by all as an excellent Sunday School teacher.

50

Her numerous contacts with me emphasized the tremendous effort she has exerted to be my friend--and yet I have done so little for her in return. Guilt crept over me. I have treated her rather shabbily, and yet I know why. It was purposeful--that old promise to myself to never again have a close friend. I looked at the evidence of Barbara's perseverance--notes, gifts of books, help with Sunday School lessons, invitations to lunch, and written encouragement. She was always there for me, willing to be my friend. An overpowering urge is coming over me to unburden myself to her. How strange that I should even consider such a thing, and yet I feel a need to explain my aloofness, my pulling away from her offers of friendship. I imagine her reaction to hearing of "my secret." I can picture total amazement on her part, perhaps a revulsion, or maybe just a smile as she says something like, "I kinda figured that." Who knows how she will react! I felt a churning deep inside, an uncomfortable churning of not just stomach, but of spirit. My whole being was sad.

Sunday, February 20: I'm enjoying my little apartment and especially the freedom in doing what I want when I want to do it. More than that, I'm able to relax knowing I no longer need to weigh my words prior to speaking. Yes, I get lonely. But I've always been lonely, even around people. I continue to live in a fantasy world, thinking about a person I have no right to think about, or yearn for. It's getting worse. I feel as if I am digging my own grave in this regard. It makes no sense that I am so completely infatuated with an individual who is so very different from me. I dream of our being together, just day after day being together. I realize that the emotions, the longings I feel are worse when we are apart. Sometimes I think I will just explode! That's when the tears come. I remind myself it is just an infatuation. But knowing this to be true doesn't lessen the pain. I'm too old to be feeling this type of emotion. I'm like a teenager with my first crush! I find the pain indescribable, unbelievable, incredible, and devastating as it develops within me a terrible feeling of hopelessness that pervades all my being with despair. Yes, hopelessness, because there is no chance of my fantasy coming true. The person I love is "off limits," in the same way a parish priest would be off limits. That type of love is wrong in the same way my love is wrong, sinful. But I continue to live in my fantasy world where the two of us are always together.

Tuesday, February 22: I awoke this morning at 3:30 a.m. and just couldn't go back to sleep so I finally arose at 6. My weight is still dropping and I'm down to 110. I've lost my appetite. I realize my emotional state is affecting my physical condition.

Monday, February 28, 2000

I shall always remember this date because of an e-mail Jim sent to me late last night and the decision I made when answering it. I had heard little from him since I asked for a divorce almost two months earlier. Consequently, when I began reading his long letter, my heart began to pound as I realized what he was asking. Here is his letter:

"Cheyne: I feel certain you were aware I could not walk over and speak to you this morning before Sunday School. . . . To the best of my ability I want you to know and try to understand feelings that have built up during the last several weeks.

"During January and early February I experienced feelings of sadness, grief and hurt; asking why did the request for divorce happen. I was determined to help you move and get established in your new apartment, even though it took great effort to sublimate my feelings. I was determined to keep communications open for the sake of our children. That approach seemed to work for the first 5-6 weeks.

"But about two to three weeks ago a real anger began to permeate my very being. I thought for awhile that surely it would have been easier to cope with your death than it would with this awful thing called divorce. I felt anger because you have turned my world upside down and I do not know why. It was an anger emanating from the fact I've lost my help-mate of thirty-seven years and I do not know why. It was an anger growing from the reality that I had worked so hard for thirty-seven years to raise a family with you (and I've told you many times that you deserve most of the credit for the way they have turned out) and I was really looking forward to the next twenty years when we would have $1500 or so extra each month to do some of the things that we had denied ourselves through the thirty-five years of raising four fine children. Now, I am forced against my will to divide our retirement income and maintain two households, which leaves both of us with less. And, the most pervasive source of anger was that I still feel a deep love for you and now that love has been rejected. You have left a gigantic hole in my heart that simply hasn't had time to heal. You, of all people, know that I have never been as good as you are at hiding my emotions. I wish I could be telling you 'thank you' for doing what I did not have the courage to do, but that is not the case right now. When I saw you at church this morning my whole body flushed with anger and resentment on the one hand and on the other a wish I would suddenly awaken and realize the days since January 7th have been just a bad dream. I have considered leaving the church to see if 'out-of-sight, out-of-mind' would be hastened. But I do enjoy the men in my class and it is getting easier to face the group each week.

"The closest answer to 'why' goes back to the conversation we had on Friday night, January 7th, when I returned from an emotionally draining day with *(my brother)* Mark. If I recall correctly, you said you were miserably unhappy. As I've laid in bed at night during the last several weeks thinking about that statement, I've allowed myself to think selfishly about the many times in the last thirty-seven years when I was unhappy with your behavior or lack thereof. And I ask myself why didn't I ask for a divorce. You know the answer to that . . . divorce wasn't and isn't my path to solving problems. I've even had the thought that your asking for a divorce was a selfish act on your part and that did not make sense, because you were always the most unselfish person with your time, talent and resources. That was particularly true of your behavior toward my family members. In addition, you could always share so unselfishly with people who were mere acquaintances.

54

"Finally, I guess the real source of anger is why didn't I see this coming and why I didn't know you were so miserably unhappy. To help me reach some sort of mental and emotional closure on this phase of my life, I really need to know specifically why this is happening. Would you do me the courtesy of sitting down at your computer and sharing with me the specific things over the last several years (or last 37 years) that have caused you to ask for a divorce. And, if your answer still comes up 'unhappy,' please identify the ten or so things that contributed to your unhappiness. This request is not aimed at providing me with a list of behaviors that I can seek to correct and attempt a reconciliation. The Rubicon has been crossed and there is no turning back now. I simply need to know why, so I can understand specifically and accept those reasons as a closure to the anger that is eating at my very soul.

"In the meantime I hope you will find something, somebody or even the fact that you are away from the major source of your unhappiness and can finally grasp the peace of mind you are seeking. I mean this from the bottom of my heart. Jim"

When I finished reading his letter, I said to myself, "I must tell him the truth. It's not fair to keep him in the dark. He's hurting as badly as I am--in a different way, of course, but he's still hurting. It would be cruel to withhold the truth from him." But even as I had these thoughts, other thoughts began taking over, such as "He won't want to hear what I need to tell him. The truth may infuriate him to the point that he may retaliate by delaying the divorce, or by causing problems with the division of money." With those thoughts in mind, I asked myself, "Should I wait until the divorce is final to be truthful with him?"

Our divorce would not be final for almost 6 weeks. "I can't wait that long to answer his letter. After all, what I will tell him may bring about some type of relief for him to know that I accept responsibility for the problems in our marriage."

I sat at my computer and wrote Jim the following letter: "Jim, you said in your e-mail that you 'really need to know specifically why this is happening.' Well, it all relates to the 'wall' you have referred to so many times, the wall you could never penetrate. You've always been right. There is a wall. I've wanted many, many times to explain that wall to you, but have always felt that 'discretion was the better part of valor.'

"I've spent my life trying to be something I'm not. I've finally come to terms with the fact that God just made me to be different, and I've got to quit feeling guilty about it. For years I prayed that God would fill me with a deep, passionate love for you. Desperately wanting to be the wife I knew I should be as well as the wife you wanted, I begged God, I pleaded with Him. But it was not to be.

"When that prayer wasn't answered in the way I wanted, I then began to pray that I could just die. I have had suicidal thoughts off and on for over 40 years. I have begged and pleaded with God to 'just take me' because I didn't want to live. When these thoughts came to me after the birth of the three boys, I realized what a selfish prayer that was--to leave our wonderful boys with no mother. So I changed my prayer, bargaining with God to

56

let me live just long enough for the children to be 'on their own.' Then I'd be ready to go and to please take me then.

"That time has come. The children are on their own, and I've had more suicidal thoughts in the past 5 months than I have ever had before. I have fought a terrible, terrible depression. Janie Robbins perceived my unhappiness. After I admitted that I was unhappy in my marriage, but that 'I was reconciled to it,' she knew there was a much deeper cause for my depression. Finally, she just asked me, 'Are you gay?'

"Never before had I ever admitted this to anyone, and yet I admitted it to her because I knew her to be non-judgmental, someone who accepts people just the way God made them without expecting them to conform to someone else's guidelines When I answered, 'Yes,' I felt my very soul was bleeding. But she kindly reached over and patted me on the hand and said, 'It's O.K.' Arguing with her, I again heard her say, 'It really is O.K. That's just the way God made you, and He loves you just the way you are.' She has been a pillar of strength for me. (And I think you need to be assured that she is definitely heterosexual and in love with her husband, Charles.)

"Her first reaction was, 'You've got to tell your husband.' But I couldn't do it. I knew how it would hurt you, and I have a pretty good idea of how you are hurting right now. I've tried for many years to soften your views on homosexuals, but have been unsuccessful. I recall one time when you said you would never knowingly allow a homosexual to teach in your school. (Jim was for many years a high school principal.) I was devastated that your prejudice was so deep. The only difference between hetero-

57

sexuals and homosexuals is their sexual orientation which is mysteriously imprinted upon each of us by God.[6] Other than that, we are just like everyone else.

"I started off to make this a very long letter wanting to explain what it is like to be gay in a bigoted world and to always long for something you can never have. I also thought about spending time refuting those six biblical passages which are always used to condemn homosexuality. But this is not the time for all of that because you are hurting and confused. I don't fit the stereotype of what you have always perceived to be 'homosexual.' That's because the only ones you hear about are the oddballs. The rest of us are so afraid to 'come out of the closet' that no one knows who we are. 'We're the teachers, lawyers, doctors, business people that you interact with day after day and never dream that we are gay. We are rich and poor, young and old, parents and grandparents, children and grandchildren. We come from every possible race, religious and ethnic background. We're not a menace to the country. Quite the contrary, we are a powerful, loving, gifted, creative presence. Most people who condemn homosexuals are not wicked. More often, they're uninformed. Not unintelligent--on the contrary . . . they are often very intelligent--but uninformed.'[7]

"There's a book I recently checked out of the library that I wish you would read. I think it would answer a lot of your questions. It was written by Mel White who served as a ghostwriter for such leaders of the Religious Right as Jerry Falwell and Pat Robertson. He was also a ghostwriter for Billy Graham, W. A. Criswell and other well-known religious personalities. The title is

Stranger at the Gate. He talks about what it is like to be gay and Christian in America.

"I realize you will need to talk with friends about this letter, and that's fine with me. You might even want to talk with (our pastor) Bob Watson. I'm so very, very tired of living a lie that I'm almost anxious for it to all come out. It wouldn't surprise me at all to be asked to give up my Sunday School class and even leave the church. So, hang in there with your church buddies. I probably won't be around much longer.

"By the way, you can talk with Anne (our daughter) about all this. She knows. Janie urged me to tell her. Actually, Janie thinks Anne 'hung the moon.' She sees her sweet, sweet spirit and instinctively knew she would react lovingly and understandingly. It was as Janie predicted.

"I'm so sorry to have hurt you like I have. I never intended for it to end this way. We are both victims of the homophobia present in today's society that tells gays 'to just get married and the problem will go away.' But it won't go away. I can't decide to be straight any more than you can decide you are going to be gay! We have both suffered needlessly because of society's bigotry and prejudice. But I continue to cling to the promise in the Bible that 'all things work together for good to them that love the Lord.' Despite the years of suffering, we have produced four wonderful children. We have lovingly served not only our families, but public school systems, churches, and various facets of society. We have, in essence, been productive members of society--and will continue to be.

"If it eases the hurt at all, just know that I accept all the blame for the failed marriage. I always knew you loved me. I always knew you were faithful to me (and I was always faithful to you). We both did our best."

The die is cast. The secret I have protected all of my life is no longer a secret. My life is changing, and I am not certain what is about to happen. All I know is that my heart feels lighter and is no longer bound by that all-encompassing vise-grip of fear.

A second e-mail from Jim quickly arrived. It said:

"Cheyne, . . . I noticed your reply to my need for more explanation.

"I do not want to discuss this matter over the Internet. It may surprise you, but I have known deep down in my heart that this might have been the problem. As soon as I can eat and go get my exercise done, I would like to come by and visit with you. Please know that the deep love I expressed last night in my e-mail is still present for the person I thought was the most beautiful girl I had ever met. Jim"

When Jim arrived about 9 a.m., he took me in his arms and began crying. Our emotions overflowed so I placed a box of tissues on the sofa close to where we sat down. I answered whatever questions he had, and allowed him to vent the anguish he had experienced in never being able to get close to me--the futility and the heartache he had experienced.

Having given Jim permission to "tell," I knew this was probably news that would spread rapidly. I decided to send to both Anne and Barbara Lawrence copies of both Jim's letter to me as well as my reply to him. Barbara was bound to hear about this from someone in the church. She has been too nice to me to allow her to be broadsided by the news so I felt the need to warn her as to what was going on. About 8 p.m. I e-mailed to her copies of both Jim's letter and mine. I began the e-mail by first welcoming her back from her trip to Italy, then said, "If you are reading this late at night--don't. It's quite long--and emotionally draining. So just save it until tomorrow.

"This is something I ought to say in person, but I think it will be more considerate to let you first 'learn of it,' then, if you want, we can talk. I feel I will definitely catch you off guard, and that's unfair of me to do that in person.

"As you already know, the divorce I am getting is long in coming. To be quite frank, I have wanted a divorce since 1966. That's a long time to live with someone you are not in love with.

"My request for a divorce caught Jim off-guard even though he has been aware for a long time that we did not have a good marriage. I'm sure you are wondering why in the world I am telling you this, but I'm having a hard time deciding exactly how to do it. Let me start by copying and pasting the letter Jim sent to me last night. Here goes"--(and I copied and pasted Jim's letter to me).

Then I said, "I wanted you to know what Jim wrote so you can try to understand why I have ended up telling him something that I have kept secret all of my life, actually secret until this past November. I've always thought he would be better off not knowing, that it would be less painful for him, but I decided late last night that the pain he is now experiencing in 'not understanding' may be worse. Therefore I sent him the following letter:" (and I copied and pasted my reply to Jim). Following my pasted letter, I wrote "Jim received the above letter this morning and came over to visit for over 3 hours. There was lots of crying on both our parts. He has amazed me with his kindness. I would have never believed it of him. I think, no, I know, that this has been a relief to him--to at last know the reason we did not have a good marriage, a loving relationship. He plans to tell the three boys right away as well as my mother. He has urged me to tell my friends.

"Because he will start sharing this information, I feel certain it will spread quickly. Therefore, because of your friendship I didn't want you to be caught by surprise.

"Barbara, I have spent my life trying not to have a close friend--always fearful that I would feel something toward her I shouldn't feel. I have done little (at least to my way of thinking) to encourage our friendship, and that's why. I relegated myself to 'aloneness' when I was about 20. Right now I'm concerned about Janie Robbins because we have developed a close friendship; and I'm so worried that when my sexual orientation becomes public knowledge, people will assume things about Janie that just aren't true. As I repeatedly have warned her not to publicly acknowledge that we are friends, she keeps telling me she's not worried. I haven't worried so much about you. I figure you can handle it.

"If you have questions, or want to talk, that's fine. If not, I certainly understand. No problem. Cheyne"

Tuesday, February 29, 2000

Jim called again, asking "May I come over for another visit?"

"Sure," I told him. "Come on over."

As we sat together on the sofa, Jim related to me his visit last night with Michael. "He had a tough time accepting it," Jim said. "He knows you are a good mother, a good cook and all that, and he still loves you very much, but he just doesn't understand."

"Please get Mel White's book, *Stranger at the Gate*," I urged. "I want both you and Michael to read it. I really think it will help you understand what is happening."

"Michael is concerned about all of this being known. He asked me some very pointed questions last night," Jim continued. "Questions that have made me stop and think. He asked me, 'Why are you wanting everyone to know about this, Dad? You know how you are--you have this habit of always jumping in and taking over. Why are you wanting to go out and tell everyone about this. This is a family matter.'"

"After Michael asked me this, I began to wonder why I want others to know about this," Jim stated.

I quickly jumped in and declared, "Don't tell anyone for **my** sake!"

"But in your letter you said you were relieved to no longer have to be living a lie and that you were ready for it to all come out."

"That's true. I will probably tell some friends. And you are welcome to talk with your friends. But there is no need for you to tell anyone 'just to tell them,' or to do it for me!"

"Why would I want to talk about it?"

"Don't you have a desire to just share things with others, just to have someone to talk with?" I asked.

"I unburdened myself to Milton Herrington that Saturday on our way to Dallas for the woodworking workshop--the day after you asked me for the divorce. He has been a great friend to me."

"Then tell Milton. He probably needs to know just so he can understand you better. Tell Milton and tell whomever else you want to know about it. But don't go around telling people just because you think you are doing me a favor. I'm quite capable of telling whomever I want."

I continued, "I've given thought to your planning to tell Mother. I don't want you to do that. I'll do that. Deep down she knows the truth. She's known it for a long time. And when I tell her, she ought to have guilt feelings; and I hope she does!"

"She never hurt you on purpose."

"No, I know that. She just did what her society and her religion demanded. I know that. Nevertheless, I want to tell her. I owe her that."

Jim then stated, "I plan to drive to Houston to tell Josh and Sandy. I'll take Anne with me when she comes home on her spring break. We can go together."

Although his statement bothered me somewhat, the fact he was the one telling the children, I made no comment. Jim then asked me, "Is your sexual orientation something you thought about every year during our marriage?"

I exclaimed, "Every year? It was more like every day!"

To which he commented, "It must have been a miserable life."

Truer words were never spoken, but I didn't say that. In fact, I made no comment at all, because he couldn't have been more accurate in his appraisal of the situation.

When he stood up ready to leave, he put his arms around me and kissed me, saying, "This is something I want the kids to see."

I meekly replied, "O.K.," not knowing what else to do at that point.

Later in the day, I listened to a phone message from Gwen Patterson who works with me on the Task Force involved in organizing a local Christian Women's Job Corps to train and further educate women presently on welfare. This type of organization is dear to my heart--helping those who really need help and doing it in a way that does not involve a monetary handout but a training program preparing them to obtain decent-paying jobs. Gwen, aware of my divorce, invited me to join her for dinner. Calling her back, I said, "Gwen, I'm just not up to meeting in a public place."

"Cheyne, would you like to talk about it?" she asked.

"Not over the phone," I said. "I'm not certain it's something you want to hear. I think I will just explain it by e-mail. Then, if you still want to talk, give me a call."

"Cheyne, please be assured that I am your friend."

"You might not be after you read what I plan to send to you. I'll just wait to see if I hear from you."

My emotions were so raw. For days, I had been "sleep deprived" plus the constant emotional turmoil I was enduring. Regularly I told myself, "Keep your head on straight, Girl. Don't lose it."

Anne called about 2 p.m. "Hi, Mom. Just called to see how you are doing. Now be truthful with me."

"It's been pretty rough, Sweetie. I've told your dad the truth about me. He has taken it much better than I expected. But others are finding out that I'm different, and I'm not going to know from one day to the next who knows and who doesn't know. I'm afraid my emotions are not holding up very well."

Tenderhearted Anne began crying, and I assumed she was experiencing a sadness for herself and the upheaval in her life--her mother moving out of the house, her parents divorcing, and now others finding out she has a gay mother. That would upset anyone. "Are you going to be all right?" I asked. "I'm so sorry you are having to go through all this."

"Mother, I'm crying because of *you*! I'm so *worried* about you. Are *you* going to be all right?"

"I'll be fine, dear. It's a little rough right now, but I'll make it. Please don't worry about me. I want you to feel free to share any of this with your friends. You need someone to talk with about all this, and I just want you to know you have my permission to talk to anyone you want to talk to about anything you want to talk about. I'm through trying to keep all this a secret."

"I had thought about talking with my friend, Kristy, but was afraid she might tell someone else, so I didn't say a word. I haven't talked with anyone about it."

"Please feel free to talk to your friends. I really don't mind at all. You need someone to share all this with."

Late that afternoon, the e-mail arrived from Barbara that I had anxiously been awaiting all day. With a mixture of trepidation and excitement I read:

"Dear Cheyne, I love you. I frequently say 'I love you' to men and no one ever seems to think I'm hitting on them, so I figure you'll read this as a statement of fact and not a proposal." (By now I was smiling as relief surged through my body. I continued to read.)

"The difference between Janie and me is that she wasn't afraid to ask, and I have been, though I've wondered for a good while if perhaps this was not the case. I've known for a long time you were in pain, and I thought that pain would be intensified if the question were off-base. You know that I sometimes ask questions about stuff that really isn't my personal business of people I care about but I thought that question might not just push the envelope, but rip it right open, and I didn't want to fracture my friendship with you.

"I value you for the person you are, and I grieve for the pain you've endured and for the rough time I'm sure you still have ahead of you. I can't imagine not being friends with you for any reason other than your choice. I'd love to talk to you some time, any time-- and I'll probably ask you more questions that are none of my business. Remember, you don't have to answer them. It's rather hard for me to understand how you feel, pretty much in the same way that I've never been able to put myself in the shoes of someone who wants to climb mountains or go into space.

"I can't imagine your being asked to leave the church, although if you find someone with whom you want to have a relationship I can imagine it getting rather uncomfortable for you there. But you haven't said anything about that, so I suspect you haven't, as yet.

"Whatever. I'm your friend, always have been, always have thought we have much in common. It certainly helps me understand your desire to take as little as possible from your marriage with you into your new life, so I'll quit pulling that chain.

"I would love to see you any time. Call me!

"I'm an oldest child, born to be bossy, so I will say that I think it would be a good idea for you to send the entire thing you sent me to Bob (our pastor). (She included his e-mail address.) Your letter and Jim's explain your situation quite clearly, and it is a good thing to read it quietly instead of having to try to remember what's been said and respond with what's in your heart immediately.

"As I said, I love you. Call and we'll set a time to visit/eat Chinese food. Barbara"

As soon as I received her e-mail, relief flooded through me, a sense of joy pervaded my being, and I got just a glimpse of the terrific friendship she was offering to me. Sitting at my computer, I whipped out a quick response that said, "Thank you. What else is there to say? You amaze me. I do want to talk, but I don't think I am ready to handle this subject in a public place. My emotions

68

are raw right now. Maybe you can come here or I can visit in your place.

"I just don't know Bob (our pastor) well enough to approach him, either by e-mail or otherwise. The idea of doing so just throws me.

"You are one in a million, Barbara--a special gift from God. Cheyne"

Just a few minutes later, another e-mail arrived from Barbara. "Want to come over Thursday or Friday? I'm free both days--tomorrow, too, to be truthful, but I think I need a down day for my brain to return to Texas time after our overseas trip.

"About Bob--here's my thinking. You may not feel that you know him well, but he's your pastor. He's going to hear about this from heaven knows where, and it would be a mercy if he had the facts from the source, even if you don't want to talk to him yourself. With e-mail you don't have to talk to him yourself. I don't want him to hear only what Jim can say as there's no way he could know what it's been like to walk in your shoes. I could, of course, forward that e-mail to him, but I certainly won't without your permission. Nor, by the way, will I be initiating a conversation with anyone other than my husband about it. But I am so grateful to know, instead of hearing a third-hand report from somewhere. I think Bob would be, too. Think about it."

In the midst of these e-mails back and forth with Barbara, Gwen Patterson with the Christian Women's Job Corps called and asked to drop by for a visit. She arrived soon afterwards. I had sent her "the letters" Jim and I sent to each other which "outed" me. I knew the visit with her would be emotionally draining. I also recognized that she was one of the most fundamental, legalistic Christians I would talk with about my sexual orientation. For that reason, I shared with her more of my past than I have with anyone else. I wanted to see her reaction, to learn how bad it might be for me. Gwen stayed for an hour and a half. I wanted her to realize this was not something I had "chosen" as most fundamentalist Christians believe. I wanted her to be aware of the frustration I've experienced in dealing with prejudice and bigotry, and the lifelong decisions gays make in marrying because that is what is expected of them. I felt a need to stun Gwen with the agony of 37 years of unnatural heterosexual sex from a homosexual's viewpoint.

I also took time to relate an incident that occurred in one of the meetings of our Task Force. About eight members, prior to the beginning of the meeting, began talking about "Angels in America," a controversial play to be performed at nearby Kilgore College. Negative opinions about this play were rampant throughout East Texas and a form of political blackmail resulted when Gregg County Commissioners rescinded $50,000 in support of the college's Texas Shakespeare Festival. The play was about homosexuals and that evening nearly all of these Task Force members began venting blatant prejudice toward homosexuals--so obtrusive that I was dumbfounded. I sat there not moving, not saying a word. I wanted to get up and walk out of the room, but I didn't. I wished I had had the nerve to say, "I find this talk very offensive." But I just sat there, silent. I was the secretary, and they were depending upon me to take the notes. So I remained quiet and listened to so-called Christians voicing horribly prejudicial statements as they advocated banning the play.

70

In visiting with Gwen, I said, "What I heard that night was obscene bigotry." Then I added, "I'm not certain I can fit into a group like that."

Gwen's reaction to all I said was, "I just don't know what to say."

"I understand completely," I replied. "Don't worry about it."

"I hope you are not still battling suicidal thoughts."

"No, I'm really not. I haven't given it serious thought since I asked for a divorce almost two months ago."

"I still want to be your friend, Cheyne. Feel free to call me any time."

"Thanks, Gwen. I appreciate that."

"Would it be all right if I pray for you?"

"That would be wonderful. Of course you can."

And Gwen prayed a beautiful prayer. She is truly gifted in intercessory prayer. I've never heard anyone else pray such beautiful prayers.

Wednesday, March 1, 2000

Jim wanted to tell the three boys about my sexual orientation, but I wanted to tell Josh, and his wife, Sandy. That way Jim would have told two of our children, and I would tell two. That sounded fair to me. So I sent the "two letters" to Josh because I believe this is the best way to explain it all. It explains why I decided to "come out," and it gives the receiver of the letters privacy as they read and try to assimilate the position in which they are placed. I don't have to sit and watch their reactions, which may not be positive at the outset but hopefully will improve as the shock wears off.

Next I e-mailed Jim to apprise him of those I had told-- Barbara, our pastor, Gwen Patterson, and Josh and Sandy. In that letter I also told him that I had not told Mother, but whenever I did, I would let him know. I knew it would probably upset him that I had told Josh because he had planned to drive to Houston to do that in person. Although I normally avoided angering Jim whenever possible, I just didn't care what his reaction might be in this regard.

This afternoon, I received the following response from my pastor, Bob Watson: "Dear Cheyne, I was moved to tears by your e-mail of yesterday. I have been broken-hearted at the news of your separation from Jim, and have desperately wanted to express my care in some appropriate way. Thus, in a way, I was relieved to receive your letter. Upon reading it, I so much appreciate your entrusting such heartfelt matters to me. I trust you know they will remain in confidence.

"Your response to Jim showed so much courage and care. It grieved me to know of your long struggle in coming to grips with your sexuality. Furthermore, I know it wasn't (and won't be) easy to share such a delicate understanding of who you are. I am grateful that Janie was there for you. It doesn't surprise me. I consider her a person of perception, sensitivity and intelligence.

"I want you to know that you matter to me. If you need to talk or even just vent, please don't hesitate to do so. I realize that the issue of sexual preference is such an emotional, misunderstood and volatile subject. I do hope and pray that we can be the church for you in this time, in the best sense of the word. To that end, pray diligently and lean on brothers and sisters-in-Christ like Janie and Barbara, and others, including me. Please know of my thoughts and prayers. Your brother-in-Christ, Bob Watson"

I rejoiced in this letter from my pastor--to think he was moved to tears by reading what I had sent to him. I was convinced few Baptist pastors would have passed up the opportunity to condemn me for what they perceived as a "chosen sexual orientation." The fact that Bob heaped no condemnation upon me made me feel truly blessed to have him for my pastor.

A little later in the day, I received an e-mail from my eldest son, J.W., who is in his twelfth year of teaching elementary school. He's a hard worker who supplements his teacher's salary by driving a school bus every morning and every afternoon. He wrote, "Yesterday as I was arriving at the bus barn, Dad called my cellular and said that he needed to come over to the house later and talk with me. Of course, I began to wonder what it could be about. When I got to the house (and saw what a mess it was in!!), I called him back to suggest that I drive over there; but he was insistent that he needed to come here. 'You'll understand when I get there,' he said.

"Boy, that put my mind to wondering. I came up with two possible scenarios. First, I decided that he was having a giant garage sale and selling everything out of the house (and the house) and was preparing to move somewhere far away. The other scenario was that he'd already found someone, and she was already living at the house.

"I'm glad that you had the courage to be so honest with him and with all of us. Now I'll admit the idea that my mother is gay may take awhile to get used to. But it really doesn't change anything about how I feel about you. You're still the same mother I've loved for 34 years. To me, the divorce brings more changes to my life (no more family dinners at the house), than news of your sexual orientation.

"I hope and pray that people will be loving and accepting of you as you are.

"I love you and that's never going to change."

I immediately replied,

"Thanks, J.W.. Your words did my heart a lot of good. Although all four of you children have affirmed your love and acceptance of me, your two brothers are having a much more difficult time about this than you and Anne. I love you so very much. Surely you know that. Whenever I talk about you, I refer to you as my missionary son. God has used you in so many precious ways. You are special to me and your letter reaffirms what I already knew about you. Again, thanks so much. I needed that. Love, Mother"

Coming out to my family and close friends keeps my emotions at a high pitch. I cry at the least little thing and constantly fight depression and loss of appetite. Josh's sweet wife, Sandy, called and visited with me by phone for almost an hour. Despite the fact she was extremely kind, loving, and non-condemning, I kept crying off and on throughout the conversation. "Mom," she asked, "I want you to talk Josh out of driving to Tyler tomorrow (260+miles). Your news has hit him rather hard and he feels he needs to talk with you personally. He's in such an emotional state, I don't want him making that long four-hour drive."

"Put him on the phone," I replied and then proceeded to quash his plans by promising to make the drive myself tomorrow afternoon after my visit with Barbara.

After getting off the phone with Sandy, I shared with Barbara, via e-mail, copies of J.W.'s sweet note as well as our pastor's reply to my communication with him. . . . to which she replied with the following note: "Big surprise--your son loves you and your pastor recognizes your courage and care! I trust you recognize that as whatever you'd call the keyboarding equivalent of tongue in cheek--thumb in palm? Bob's caring response and J.W.'s loving one do not surprise me in the slightest. It's not that you've actually changed, Cheyne, it's just that you're letting us know you better."

Thursday, March 2, 2000

When Barbara opened the door for me this morning, I felt such a mixture of emotions that the tears immediately began falling. For two and a half hours, I explained who and what I was, I cried, I tried to avoid the subject that was causing me such extreme pain and anguish, and I confessed to feelings and relationships I had previously kept only to myself. Barbara does that to me. She brings out my innermost feelings because she's gutsy enough to ask the questions--and intelligent enough to know what questions to ask.

I confessed it all. Barbara's interest spurred me to "start at the beginning" as I first reflected on an evening in 1953 (or 1954) when six or seven of us high school girls went to a drive-in movie. We were all squeezed together in the car, laughing and having a great time. I sat in the back seat, behind the driver and next to the door. Sitting next to me, actually "squeezed" next to me was Jean, a senior I admired. I liked her and, as a 14-year-old sophomore, I looked up to her as a role model. However, that night, aware of her close physical presence, thoughts entered my mind that amazed me, shocked me. I wanted to kiss her. I imagined how wonderful it would be to put my arms around her and passionately kiss her. As soon as these thoughts came to me, I dismissed them, saying to myself, "How strange! Why in the world am I thinking such things?"

Confused and troubled by such embarrassing and shameful desires, I never mentioned it to anyone, certainly not to Jean. Instinctively I knew that what I was feeling had to be kept private-- that these were unacceptable feelings and desires. One other occasion arose when Jean and I were together. After an out-of-town football game, we sat beside each other on the school's band bus as we made a long trip home that night. We were tired, it was late, and I was sleepy. Jean knew I was exhausted and said, "Cheyne, if you want to lie down and put your head in my lap, that's fine with me."

I did. Put my head in her lap. I thought nothing of it until Jean held my hand, probably as a means to keep us balanced so I wouldn't fall on the floor. She probably thought nothing of it, but holding Jean's hand set my heart to hammering. I was immediately wide awake, having lost all desire to sleep. I was ecstatic. That was the most wondrous thing that had ever happened to me.

I was in the mode of confessing everything to Barbara and continued my story by explaining, "I never felt anything special towards any other girl until I got to college. (I attended Baylor University in Waco, Texas–the largest Baptist university in the world.) There I fell in love with Karen, one of my roommates. It all started so innocently. We were just kids, both being 17 years of age. (She had skipped a grade, and I had started first grade when I was five years of age.)

Having just entered college from opposite areas of the country, neither of us knew anyone in the school or even in the town. Consequently, when we first met as suite mates (and later became roommates), we were drawn toward each other because our other suite mates had friends at the school--someone to run around with. We didn't. Perhaps that instigated our bonding. We had a common need, a loneliness which the other filled. How? By talking. We loved to talk. The subject matter was immaterial. Whatever was mentioned, we discussed, we argued, we debated. We tossed our ideas and opinions back and forth. Hour after hour we shared our thoughts, our beliefs, our ideals, our hopes. If we both agreed about an issue, one of us deliberately pretended to disagree just so we could have fun debating the subject. Never before had I found someone with whom I so enjoyed talking and sharing confidences. I suppose it was her intelligence that first drew me to her.

Having no sisters, I'd never had the opportunity to really confide in anyone. I'd had many friends, had always been one of the popular leaders in school, but the conversations with those friends had never been deep, thoughtful, weighty conversations. They were just typical teenage girly talk. Karen introduced me to a different type of conversation, and I thoroughly enjoyed it. Loved it. She was an only child who had been sheltered from the mainstream. Our backgrounds were different as she was from Chicago, and I was from a small Texas town. But these differences only provided fuel for our conversations. We delighted in each other's company.

Our love of conversing was the catalyst in instigating our physical relationship. Baylor was very strict in those days. As freshmen, we had to be in our rooms by 8:30 p.m. Monday through Thursday. Visiting with our suite mates next door was even prohibited after 8:30 in the evenings unless we "happened" to both be in the bathroom at the same time. (Six of us shared one small bath.) Lights had to be turned out by 10 p.m. sharp! These rules were rigorously enforced by hall monitors.

Karen and I would often be in the middle of a good discussion at 10 p.m. and were not ready to be quiet and go to sleep. Our freshman year the dorms were so crowded that three girls were placed in rooms designed for only two—a pair of bunk beds and a single bed. Three of us divided up space in two chest of drawers and two small closets.

Our third roommate was always ready to go to sleep by 10 p.m. Therefore, when the lights were turned off, and all talking and visiting was to cease, Karen and I climbed into one of our beds and

78

continued to converse in whispers. Side by side we lay, not touching, enjoying the opportunity of entering into each other's minds and thoughts. Like an elixir to our needs for companionship, our whispered conversations sometimes continued for hours.

After a few weeks, I began yearning to hold her hand as we lay side-by-side talking. The longing to touch her, to just hold her hand dominated my thoughts. I ached with desire as I worried about doing something she might find repugnant. Needing to "test the waters," I allowed my arm to rest on the bed between us, next to her arm but not touching it. My heart raced as I gradually, very gradually moved my hand so that it "accidentally" touched hers. I held my breath waiting to see if she would move her hand away from mine. She didn't. Our hands rested side by side, just barely touching. Dare I hold her hand? Yes. A few minutes later, I gently clasped her hand in mine. Neither of us verbally acknowledged the hand holding as we continued our whispered conversation.

That was the start. First, the lying in bed side by side, then the holding hands. From then on, whenever we continued talking in bed after lights out, we held hands. It was just "understood." Neither of us ever said a word about it. Nothing changed in our relationship. We never touched each other at any other time--just held hands in bed. But it wasn't long before holding hands made me ache for more. I began to imagine what it would be like to kiss her.

One night, when our "third roommate" was gone for the weekend, Karen and I still climbed into the same bed to talk. By now it was habit. This night we were on the top bunk, just next to the hall door. I have trouble recalling the progression of events that night, but we went from hand holding to cuddling, then I recall propping up on my right elbow and leaning down and lightly and gently kissing Karen on the lips. She indicated no displeasure with my action, but explained, "I've never kissed a boy. How do you kiss?"

She knew I had kissed boys as I had dated regularly all through high school and had even "gone steady" my senior year. She considered me the "expert" in this field. I explained, "Just part your lips slightly. You'll find it a very natural thing to do."

She followed my instructions, and we kissed lovingly and tenderly, then longingly, desperately, feverishly. We each discovered a passion neither of us realized we possessed. After about an hour, Karen said, "We need to talk over what's happening to us--what we are doing."

"Yes," I agreed, "we should." Although excited by the pleasure I was experiencing being with her, I was frightened by it and worried about the possible consequences. We climbed down out of that upper bunk, donned our robes and house shoes, quietly opened the door, and walked down the deserted hallway to the basement stairs. A small prayer room was located in the basement of the dormitory, and this is where we went. We sat about four feet apart in straight-backed chairs facing each other.

Karen began the conversation by saying, "What we just did is wrong."

Agreeing, I stated, "Yes, it was." And yet I don't believe I had ever actually felt it was wrong. It was so natural, and felt so good. I had never brought to the surface of my conscience the thought that what I felt for Karen was wrong. That view of "wrongness" had been a dormant thought, one which had always hidden itself from me. But when she frankly stated that it was wrong, a part of my being knew she was right, so I agreed with her. I had always been the "perfect daughter," doing the right things, saying the right things, being the individual others looked up to. I had never before done anything truly "wrong." I felt my world crashing down upon me this night.

Karen continued, "The Bible teaches against this. There are a lot of verses prohibiting what we feel towards each other, especially in Leviticus." Karen had been brought up an American Baptist; I, a Southern Baptist. Her father was a professor of Old Testament in a seminary. My parents were both Sunday School teachers in a Southern Baptist church. The instructions and admonitions of the Bible were familiar to both of us. We had had the rules drilled into us from childhood. This particular subject, however, was never openly discussed. I didn't even know a word to use for it, and yet a part of me acknowledged that this was a wicked thing we had done. The love I felt for Karen was forbidden. "But how can love be evil?" I asked myself. I knew I loved her with all my being, all my soul. How can love be wrong? But, yes, according to the Bible, our love was wrong. In God's eyes, we were sinfully breaking His law.

As we sat in those chairs facing each other in that little prayer room, we acknowledged to each other that what we had done was wrong. Karen then concluded, "Then we need to stop what we are doing."

"Yes, we should," I agreed. Then, hesitating just a moment, I continued, "But I don't want to stop." At that point I looked at her and smiled.

"Neither do I," she quickly replied as a happy, goofy grin spread across her face.

"I'm in love with you," I confessed.

"And I'm in love with you," she responded.

As we openly declared our love for each other, our faces radiated happiness. These were "our marriage vows" as no others were allowed to us. Our fate was sealed. She has always been "my other half." Even though I haven't seen her in over forty years, she's still a part of my life. I explained to Barbara that falling in love with a girl stunned me. Even though I had dated quite a few boys, I had never fallen in love with one. I began to question in my own mind *why* I was drawn to a girl. Why had I fallen in love with a girl? Trying to make some sense out of my predicament, I recalled my desire to kiss my high school friend, Jean, as we sat next to each other at the drive-in movie. When that happened, I never gave it a second thought because I had never heard the words "gay," "lesbian," "homosexual," "queer," or "fag." Not one time in my life had I heard these words. The only word I had ever heard was "sodomy," and it was always spoken in such hushed tones that I had concluded it was something nasty that men did to each other. I couldn't even imagine what that "something nasty" was! I was very naive. Very. Sex just wasn't discussed openly. I was totally ignorant of the possibility of two people of the same sex falling in love with each other. Perhaps if I had been aware that this could happen, I would have avoided lying in bed with Karen as we conversed in whispers each night. If we had never gotten in bed together, as innocent as it was in the beginning, would we have fallen in love anyway? I don't know. I've often wondered about that.

Christmas vacation separated Karen and me for the first time. Thanksgiving, I had brought her home with me to Big Spring as there was not enough time for her to visit her parents in Chicago. But Christmas was another story. We went our separate ways. I saw her off on the train, knowing I was going to miss her terribly. But I wasn't devastated because I was confident I would see her again. This was not to be the final parting that we knew would eventually come. We never deluded ourselves about the future. We were in a bittersweet time--enjoying each other on a temporary basis. There was no future for us. We couldn't spend our lives together. Occasionally we alluded to the possibility, but common sense always took over. Two girls just didn't spend their lives together. At least we knew of none who did. We assumed it would be difficult for us to hold a decent job if we stayed together. We might even find it difficult to purchase a home together. Society had set up too many barriers for us. Neither of us knew of anyone else in our predicament. We knew of no one with whom to share our problem. We knew of no books to read on the subject. We assumed no one else faced what we faced. Our decision-making was based solely upon our religious upbringing, especially the admonition to "Honor your father and your mother."

We therefore knew there was no "as long as you both shall live" in store for us because neither of us wanted to embarrass our parents. They expected us to marry and have children. This was our lot in life. We knew that. Our parents were highly respected individuals and neither Karen nor I intended to hurt or shame them. For this reason, our relationship had to remain a secret--from everyone.

My parents had always wanted me to be a teacher. Both my parents were educators, and this was the field they chose for me. I felt my career opportunities were limited to teaching, nursing, secretarial work, or airline stewardess. In my mind, those were my options. Nothing else had ever been mentioned to me. I now wish I had taken my math skills seriously because I enjoy math. Nursing appealed to me--helping others. Airline stewardess appealed--traveling all over the world. But I chose secretarial work because I excelled in typing and shorthand. Being organized is one of my attributes--and secretaries need to be organized. I thought I would enjoy being a secretary and running an office.

My parents however, without prohibiting my interest in this field, continued to encourage me to "at least get your teaching certificate." "You may never have to use it," they explained to me, "but it's the best insurance policy you can ever have. If something ever happens to your husband, you could always support your family by teaching." Even as they recommended my career choice, they were also letting me know they assumed I would marry and have children. It wasn't until I was in my third year of college that I began to take their admonitions seriously and started taking education courses.

Regardless, though, of what careers Karen and I chose to follow, we would put those careers in dire jeopardy by living together.

We missed each other terribly that first Christmas vacation, so much so that we wrote long letters to each other every evening. Warning bells told me not to mail a letter to Karen every day, so I saved up three or four days worth of letters before putting them in an envelope to mail. Even so, my parents became suspicious of my behavior. Dad was a sociology major and had been introduced to the possibility of same-sex love. One night he told Mother, "I think we have a problem with Cheyne. Her writing to Karen every day, those long letters she writes, indicate she may have fallen in love with Karen." Mother was aghast. "Surely not, oh surely not!"

"Yes," he replied. "I think that's what has happened. You need to go in and talk with her about this."

And one night, as I was propped up in bed writing a letter to Karen, that is just what Mother did. As she sat down on my other twin bed just a couple of feet away from me, she haltingly broached the subject of same-sex love. She mentioned a relative she believed had gone through life with his male companion. Her words made it clear that such a relationship was sinful and that Karen and I needed to separate. I don't recall her ever using the word "homosexual." I don't believe that word was in vogue, but I'm not certain. The conversation was pretty much one-sided as she wanted me to "confess" to a relationship with Karen. I was speechless. Embarrassed that she and Dad knew. Devastated. At one point she asked, "Which one of you is the male in your lovemaking?"

I was speechless as I had no idea what she was talking about. "What do you mean?" I asked.

"Normally, one of the girls plays the role of the male. Which role do you play? Are you a top or a bottom?"

Her question shocked me. My mouth probably flew open as I had no idea what she was talking about. Karen and I played no "roles." We just loved each other . . . mutually. The longer she talked to me, the more condemnation I felt. I was terribly embarrassed at having been "found out," but another feeling was also present--an overwhelming desire for her to "understand my predicament," to sympathize with me. After all, Karen and I had not planned to fall in love! I was heartsick about it. Our situation was devastating as I had fallen deeply, everlastingly in love with someone I could never live with . . . someone I would eventually have to part from. We'd never be able to marry, to have a family, to simply share life. How much worse could it get? The feelings of guilt that Mother heaped upon me were the same feelings of self-recrimination, self-hatred, shame, and embarrassment with which my conscience constantly tortured me. What I yearned for, what I wanted, what I desperately needed from my mother was for her to put her arms around me, to tell me how sorry she was that I was suffering in this way, and to offer help. If she had done that, I would have unburdened myself to her, shared everything with her, but that didn't happen. Consequently, I never shared any of my feelings with her, never admitted anything.

I loved Karen with all my heart, with all my being, and there was not a thing I knew of to suppress that love, to make it disappear. How much better if I had fallen in love with a boy-- someone my parents would approve of and someone I could marry and with whom I could have children. However, I had fallen in love

86

with a girl. I was shown that evening the condemnation society would display if Karen and I were careless in keeping our relationship a secret. We had always been careful, but now fear entered my heart, a fear that only grew as time passed.

The next day I called Karen to tell her that "Mother knew about us." Karen was as shocked as I that my parents were aware of our relationship. "Have you saved all the letters I have written to you?" she asked.

"Yes. They're in a shoe box in my closet."

"You shouldn't have saved them. Burn them immediately. I bet your mother has read them. Don't save any of my letters!"

The possibility that my mother might read my letters never crossed my mind, but I did as Karen ordered, and burned her letters. I so hated to destroy those letters, to never again be able to read her letters filled with wonderful words of love, but I burned them. All of them. I never knew if Mother had read them. I never asked, and she never mentioned the letters. Perhaps she didn't even know the letters were in my closet, but I burned them anyway, just in case.

After Mother's confrontation, I became much more secretive with my writing and with the mailing of my letters. I was so upset with Mother that I didn't speak to her for days. I was angry with her, angry that she had confronted me, angry that she knew, angry at the condemnation she demonstrated toward me, angry that she showed no understanding of my situation, angry that she wanted to separate Karen and me but most of all I was angry at her lack of sympathy for my situation. I believe at that point in my life I hated my mother. I was anxious for the holidays to end so that I could return to the dorm, and to Karen.

Somehow she and I continued our affair with a third roommate in the room with us, and three suite mates next door. I don't know if we were unusually discreet, if the others were just dumb, or if they had some idea of what was going on. No one ever said a word to us about our relationship. The summer after our freshman year was a long, long summer apart from Karen. I missed her terribly, but I stayed busy working at Cosden Oil Refinery where I substituted for various secretaries when they took their two-week summer vacations. Just a week or two before time to return to Baylor, I received a letter from Karen which dealt me quite a blow. She informed me she was not returning to college in September, but would remain at home for the fall semester. She had decided we should end our affair. By her staying home the first semester of our sophomore year, this should give us time to make a clean break.

I wanted her to be happy; and if she felt that our being together was wrong, then I was willing to go along with her plan to end our relationship. I didn't argue with her about her decision. Instead I told myself, "If she can make the break, then I can, too." We had always been burdened by feelings of guilt, convinced that the deep love we felt for each other was sinful. We had always known our relationship could never be permanent. So I told myself that the three months of summer plus the four months of the fall semester would give me time to heal and to overcome my desire to be with her.

I spent the fall semester telling myself I could live without Karen, convincing myself I never again needed to touch her. And, by January, 1958, when Karen returned, I felt I had succeeded in my goal. With both of us determined to end the affair, we could do it. After all, we had both known from the beginning we had no future together. We were just separating a little sooner than we had originally thought necessary.

When Karen returned to Baylor, I was rooming with April Crider, an art major. She and I had little in common, but we got along fine as roommates. Karen, upon her return, was assigned to a very small room with no roommate. Although the room contained bunk beds, it was considered a single room because of its small size. Karen had come by my room to greet me, but we had gone our separate ways the rest of the day. Evening came, and I went to bed. My roommate, April, went right to sleep. My bed was very close to the hall door, and as I dozed off, I suddenly awakened with the realization that Karen was in the room kneeling down by my bed. Touching my hand she asked, "Aren't you coming to my room?"

"I thought you decided we should stay apart," I whispered. "I've thought about it a lot, and I'm willing to give it a try," I explained. "If we both work at it, I really think we can make the break."

Her reply amazed me. "You're the only reason I returned to school. If we can't be together, then I'm leaving on the train tomorrow and going back home. I came back to be with you. I love you so very much. Don't do this to me."

By then she was grasping my hand, imploring me to come with her to her room. My resolve melted--because it was a resolve based on doing what I thought she wanted. Now I was learning that I had either misread her, or she had changed her mind without letting me know. Whichever it was, I knew at that moment that nothing on this earth would make me any happier than going with her to her room. All the mental anguish I had gone through convincing myself that our intimate relationship was over was all for naught. Although our long separation provided a perfect opportunity for the two of us to end our affair, that reasoning vanished as she knelt by my bed, pleading with me to come with her. I would have done absolutely anything for her. Certainly anything to make her happy. With only a moment's hesitation, I climbed out of bed and followed her to her room.

The next day I asked the dorm mother if I could change rooms and be Karen's roommate. "No," she replied. "That room is too small for two people."

"We don't mind," I assured her. "We really would like to room together."

"Is there a problem with the girl you are now rooming with?" she asked.

"Not at all. She's very nice, and we get along just fine. It's just that Karen and I are good friends and enjoy being together. We really do want to room together."

The dorm mother then turned to Karen and asked, "Is this something you want? Are you in agreement with this request?"

"Yes," Karen replied. "I'd really like Cheyne to room with me."

90

"Well, the room is too small for two people, but if both of you want to stay in it together, then I'll assign both of you to that room."

We were elated. Some of Karen's and my happiest times were spent in that tiny dorm room which we kept the rest of our sophomore year and all of our junior year.

I continued to date boys on a fairly regular basis, and during my junior year I dated a senior named Eric McGill whose father was a Baptist preacher in West Texas. Eric had little money. He struggled to make ends meet, and worked in one of the dining halls in order to pay his bills. The only reason he could afford to attend Baylor University was because of the allowance available to P.K.'s (preacher's kids). Consequently, when Eric and I dated, it was always a very inexpensive evening such as walking around campus, having a coke, attending a free campus event, and occasionally, a movie. We seldom ate out.

One evening as we were walking across campus he said, "You're one of the few girls I have ever dated that doesn't require a lot of money be spent on a date. You and I have fun just walking around and talking. You don't realize how much I appreciate it. I just don't have the money to take you out to eat and go to expensive places, but you never have made me feel that was necessary."

"It isn't necessary, Eric. I enjoy going out with you." And I did enjoy going with him--up to a point. The point was always reached when I sensed the fellow was falling for me and wanted to hold and kiss me, or even worse, to marry me. Then I was ready to turn him loose and look for someone else to date. But until Eric made the comment about inexpensive dating, I had never thought about it, one way or the other. What we did together was not that important to me.

I do, however, recall one evening when we double-dated with his roommate, Jeff Tatum. (This is the Jeff Mother had been "thinking about" when I told her I was divorcing Jim.) After that double-date, Jeff became interested in me and asked me out. (I discovered later that Jeff had first asked Eric's permission to ask me out.) I accepted, and we dated a few times. Then Eric called. "Cheyne, I like you a lot, and I'd like to continue dating you, but I just want to make it clear that if you prefer going with Jeff over going with me, I understand and will step aside. I'll do nothing to stand in your way."

His call rather stunned me, as I had not thought about Eric in any kind of serious way. But he obviously had thought seriously about me. It was probably good that he was willing to "back off," and allow me to date Jeff. I replied, "Thanks, Eric. I do like you, but I need to think about this. You are really a great guy."

He stated again that if I chose Jeff over him he would not stand in our way. "I wish you the best," he stated. Eric was nice. Very nice. I appreciated his attitude, and Jeff and I ended up dating rather exclusively. But Eric remained in the picture as the three of us worked together in helping to establish a little church just outside of Waco. I'd play the piano when no one else was available to do that, and Jeff and Eric would take turns preaching and leading the singing. We met in a family's small three-bedroom home. Bedrooms became Sunday School classrooms, and the den and kitchen area was the "sanctuary."

92

One of the tragedies of being gay and having to keep it a secret is the hurt you bring upon others. Jeff fell in love with me, deeply in love with me. He was a wonderful guy, and I liked him a lot. But there was no way I could fall in love with him. I had no desire to spend my life with him. I was in love with Karen.

Jeff asked me to marry him. This was not the only proposal I turned down--certainly not the only heart I broke. How much better if I could have been open about my different sexual orientation. So much suffering could have been avoided.

While I was dating Jeff, Karen had become interested in a senior in her psychology class. His name was Russell Hampton. I became accustomed to hearing, "I'm heading to the library to study. I think Russell may be there. Don't wait up for me."

Returning from the library, she was either "down," because Russell had not shown up, or elated because he had. Occasionally, she would be in the clouds because he had asked her to the Student Union to have a coke with him.

I felt no jealousy toward Russell. After all, I dated boys and had dated boys all the time Karen and I were together. But Karen had never dated. She saw herself as overweight and therefore undesirable to boys. The truth was, she was inexperienced in being with boys and had no self-confidence along that line. Her mother had convinced her no boy would pay any attention to her until she lost some weight. The more critical her mother became, the more Karen ate. The battle between the two of them was constant whenever they were together.

Karen's mother had succeeded in convincing Karen she was unattractive. She wasn't. Her skin was unblemished, her makeup flawless, and her hair carefully coiffured. She was a large-boned blonde of German descent who probably weighed 135 to 140 pounds. I really didn't know, and I didn't care. I just knew that I loved her with all my heart and soul and yearned for her to feel good about herself.

Although I felt no jealousy toward Russell, I began to dislike him because he never asked Karen out on a date. He would hint to her after their class that he "might" study in the library that evening, and "maybe" they could study together. That's all it took for her to spend the evening sitting in the library, hoping he would show. And sometimes he would come, and sometimes he wouldn't. Helplessly, I watched her infatuation with him take control of her emotions. The more he took over her thoughts, the less she wanted to be with me. She finally informed me, "I'm in love with Russell. Your and my relationship must end. I don't want us touching each other any more. I realize this will not be easy for you, especially with us rooming together, but the time has come for our relationship to end. I don't want us to even hold hands any more."

I was devastated. She was my very life, and she was rejecting me. Just a year before I had been willing to halt our relationship, had really thought I could handle it, but at that time she begged me to come to her room to resume our relationship. I put aside all my resolutions, went to her room, and resumed our partnership. Now, the shoe was on the other foot, and I couldn't handle it. I was so used to cuddling with her at night, to sleeping next to her in that single bunk bed, that I now found it impossible to go to sleep by myself. I thought constantly about her, about

94

being with her, about touching her, about sleeping with her. When we turned out the lights each night, I'd be in the bottom bunk, she just above me in the top bunk. I wanted so much to hold her, and yet once she told me not to touch her again, I didn't. I never forced any attentions on her, but it wasn't because I didn't want to. I loved her so terribly, so completely, and I was living in abject misery.

This was my first experience in being rejected, totally rejected. I lowered myself one night to begging. I was beside myself. Karen ignored me. Her rejection drove me over the edge, and I told her I was going to kill myself. She didn't take me seriously, so I headed for the bathroom and found her bottle of sleeping pills. I emptied the bottle and swallowed all thirteen pills. "That's not going to kill you," she chided. "Those pills aren't strong enough to kill you."

She was right. With a lot of effort on her part, I awakened the next morning. "Wake up," she kept saying as she shook me. "You've got to get up. You have a date to the football game and you need to get up and dress."

I felt absolutely awful, like I was in a stupor. I could hardly hold my head up, but it never occurred to me to cancel my date. Whatever dates I made, I kept. I dressed, but not with any wisdom as I wore a sweater when the weather turned out to be warm. My date brought me a corsage, and I had great difficulty pinning it to my sweater. The heavy corsage drooped down from my loosely knit teal blue sweater. I knew it didn't look right, but I couldn't very well change clothes with my date standing there ready to go.

The game was a blur. I had a terrible time just staying awake. I was miserable. Ill. Hot. Uncomfortable. The corsage didn't look right on my sweater. I recall nothing of the game. Even less of my date. He never asked me out again.

During this period of time when Karen wanted nothing to do with me, I quietly cried myself to sleep most nights--those nights I was able to get to sleep. I was so accustomed to snuggling close to her that I found it impossible to sleep alone. I finally devised a plan that provided me a few hours sleep. After we turned out the lights, I waited until Karen was asleep, then I quietly crawled up into her bunk bed and curled up at her feet. Just barely touching one of her feet, I was able to sleep. I awakened before she did in the mornings and returned to my bed without her knowing I had slept with her. At least I assumed she never knew I did this.

Our little dorm room was so very tiny, probably 10 x 10. Besides the bunk beds, it contained a chest of drawers and a small desk and chair. We had our own little bath which was a distinct advantage. The larger dorm rooms were separated by a bath shared by those in both rooms--up to six girls to a small bath. Our little room was designed to be used by a hall monitor. Hence, the private bath.

We had spent many happy hours in that little room; but now, as we shared this tiny space mid-way in the first semester of our junior year, we avoided touching each other. We both felt the strain. My love for Karen continued unabated. I hated Russell. If he had shown a normal interest in Karen, I don't believe I would have disliked him. I wanted her to be happy. I wanted that more than anything in the world. We were convinced happiness would be found in marriage and family, so I wanted Karen to find someone to marry, someone to be good and loving to her. But

Russell didn't fit that bill. He never asked her out on a date. Never took her out to eat. Never took her to a movie. Never took her to any campus gathering. In no way did he "show her off" as someone special to him. All he did was rather furtively meet her at the library and occasionally buy her a coke. This was not a normal courtship. I knew that. Karen didn't. She was smitten.

I was the wrong person to tell her that Russell was not treating her right. I knew what he was doing to her, and I hated him for leading her on. Karen had led such a sheltered life that the little bit of attention Russell showered upon her was more than sufficient to cause her to "fall in love." This was her first beau. Occasionally I'd try to warn her about his intentions, or lack thereof; but I couldn't afford to do so very often or she would think I was just being "a sore loser." I stayed very concerned.

This next part of my story I didn't share with Barbara. But now that my mind is on Russell, I think I'll finish up the story about him.

Christmas of my junior year (1958), was a time I was dating both Eric and Jeff. Both these fellows gave me a ride home to Big Spring for that long holiday period as Jeff was going to spend the holidays with Eric whose family had recently moved to Big Spring. I recall sitting in the front seat of the car between the two of them with the three of us laughing and talking and just having fun being together. Then I heard Eric say, "I bet Russell is excited about now."

"Yeah. It's been months since he's seen his fiancee, Donna. They have a lot of planning to do over the holidays," Jeff added.

"Isn't their wedding planned to take place two weeks after he graduates?" Eric asked.

"Yeah. He sure is crazy about her," Jeff continued. "Talks about her all the time."

I was appalled at what I was hearing and asked, "Are you talking about Russell Hampton?"

"Yes."

"Are you saying he is engaged to be married?" I asked.

"Yes. He's been engaged for years. He and Donna plan to marry just as soon as he graduates in May."

"But I have a friend who likes him. She has no idea he is engaged!"

"Oh, I know," Eric replied. "He's told us he is just experimenting with her. It's part of that psychology he is studying. We've been telling Russell he shouldn't do her that way, but he won't listen to us."

I think this was the first time I realized these three fellows roomed together. I knew Eric and Jeff roomed together, but it never occurred to me that Russell was also their roommate. Years later it dawned upon me that Eric and Jeff probably planned that conversation because they felt sorry for Karen and the way Russell was treating her. But at that time my mind could not take in anything other than the fact that Karen was being duped, used, and treated unmercifully by the person with whom she had fallen in love.

My immediate reaction was disbelief, but then I reminded myself that Russell had never asked Karen out on a real date. I was astounded that anyone would treat another human being in such a callous, cruel manner. Karen was picturing wedding bells with Russell! She was convinced he cared for her. What he was doing to her was unforgivable.

I don't recall the rest of that drive. I was practically in shock. The cad! All I could think about was Karen and the heartbreak that was ahead for her. Should I tell her, or should I not? Obviously, I had to tell her. If the shoe were on the other foot, I would want to be told the truth. I couldn't allow Karen to continue to be hurt by someone who cared absolutely nothing for her feelings. But how was I going to tell her? Would she hate me for doing so? It didn't matter whether she hated me or not. She had to be told for her own sake, for her own self-preservation. From then on, I began mentally writing the letter to her, working on it, revising it in my mind, thinking of what to say and how to say it.

Several days passed before I actually set pen to paper, willing my words to be as tender, as kind as possible, yet knowing that regardless of the wording they would cut deeply into her heart. Russell had fooled her, had strung her along, had taken advantage of her naivete, and had cared nothing for her feelings. My letter, despite my efforts at being kind, would tell her she had been fooled and that the person she was crazy about cared nothing at all for her. Without having to spell it all out for her, I would reveal Russell's cruelty.

That letter was written forty-two years ago. I wish I could recall exactly what I wrote, but I can't. I do remember stating something like this: "Karen, being good friends usually means sharing happy times together. Occasionally, however, being a good friend requires one to be honest about a truth that will bring hurt and pain. Please know that what I am about to tell you brings me no joy, no happiness, only sorrow and anguish. I say these things with tears in my eyes knowing how much my words are about to hurt you."

I then related to her what Jeff and Eric had told me about Russell and about his engagement to be married as soon as he graduates in May. I stated it as kindly, as gently, as considerately as I possibly could, concluding with words like these, "I'm aware of the terrible hurt you are now feeling and will understand if you feel anger toward me for being the bearer of such unwelcome news. I certainly hope you don't dislike me for this, but I have chosen to be truthful with you regardless of the consequences. Please know how very much I care for you and how sorry I am to be the bearer of such terribly painful news."

During the remainder of that holiday period, I heard nothing from Karen. Today, I would have picked up the phone to check on her, but in the 50's, long-distance calls were rarely made, at least not in our home. Calling her was not an option. Besides I didn't know if she would even talk with me. I had no idea how she was taking the news about Russell or whether or not she even believed me. Would she think I was just trying some devious scheme to win her back? No, she wouldn't think that because we had complete trust in each other.

When the holidays were over in January (1959), I "hitched a ride" back to school with Jeff and Eric. They lived in an off-campus apartment, and needed to return a day or two early because of their work schedule. When I accepted their offer of a ride, I never thought to check my information packet to see if the

100

dormitories would be open. I just assumed they would be. But they weren't. We were all surprised. Here I was, in Waco, Texas, with no place to spend the night. The only alternative was to go to the downtown hotel, or at least that is the only alternative that occurred to any of us.

Eric and Jeff carried my luggage into the hotel lobby and I checked in. Jeff then asked me for a date for that evening. He wanted to take me out to eat, then to a movie. I accepted. I had a little over an hour before he would be back to pick me up, so I headed to my room to freshen up from that long 290-mile drive. In those days, boys didn't go up to a girl's hotel room, so I had arranged to meet Jeff in the lobby at 6:30, which I did. As we were about to leave the hotel, I was startled to see Karen walking in. "What are you doing here?" I asked.

"My train arrived today, and the dorms are not open. I'm staying in the hotel tonight."

"Me, too. Eric and Jeff gave me a ride back. I never dreamed the dorms wouldn't be open. So here I am!"

"Where are you going?" she asked, looking at Jeff and me.

"Out to eat and to a movie."

"Come see me when you get back. I'm in Room 342."

"O.K."

I wanted so much to visit with her right then, to immediately go up to her room, to see how she was doing, to find out how she took the news about Russell. I was mad at myself for having made the date with Jeff; but, of course, I had no idea when I made the date that Karen would be in the hotel. I resented the evening with Jeff. The dinner seemed to take too long, and the movie took even longer. Even then, he wasn't ready to take me home. Finally, about 10:30 p.m., I told him I was tired and really needed to get back to my room. He reluctantly returned me to the hotel. Upon entering, I headed immediately to Karen's room and knocked on her door. She opened the door right away and commented, "You certainly weren't in any hurry to get here!"

"I'm sorry, Karen. I had made the date with Jeff before I knew you were here. I just couldn't back out on him at the last minute."

"I know. I've just been anxious to see you." She was in her pajamas and robe and climbed back in bed, propping herself up with pillows against the headboard. I followed the rules she had set--the no-touching rules--and sat down on the floor, leaning back against the bed. Soon after I sat down, she gently placed a hand on my shoulder as she said, "Thank you for the kindest letter I have ever received. I read and reread your letter and realized that despite the horrible news you had to tell me, you did so in the most loving way possible. I even showed your letter to Mother. She agreed that it was the kindest letter she had ever read and told me how lucky I am to have you for a friend. She's right. I'm so lucky to have you for a friend. Thank you."

Delighted to feel the touch of her hand as well as hear her loving words, I explained, "I hope you realize it's a letter I never wanted to write. You know I never liked Russell and the way he led you on, but I felt nothing but sadness when I learned what he was doing to you. I'm so sorry. I'd do almost anything to keep you from being hurt like this." And tears were in my eyes and in my voice.

"I'm all right," she explained. "Yes, it hurt. It hurt very badly. But I'm over it. I really am." Then she touched me on the cheek and asked, "Would you stay with me tonight? I want you to spend the night with me. I'm so sorry for the way I've treated you."

What glorious words. Joy flooded my total being. She wanted me back! And the setting was ideal--a hotel room that afforded us complete privacy. Rising from the floor, I turned and leaned over and kissed her, then lay down beside her. Touching her, holding her, kissing her brought heaven down into my heart. After a short period of time, she suggested, "Go get your things from your room and move in with me."

"Are you sure?"

"Yes, I want you with me. I've treated you terribly and I'm so sorry. Please forgive me. I love you so much. Hurry now. Don't take long. I want you back here soon."

"I'll hurry," I promised.

Going to my room, I gathered up my luggage, mussed up my bed to make it look as if I had slept in it, then quickly returned to Karen's room. That was a marvelous night for us. We stayed in each other's arms throughout the night and long into the morning.

That last semester together was a bittersweet time for us. Karen's dad planned to spend the next year overseas and invited Karen to go with him. The opportunity was too good to pass up, so plans were made for her to complete her degree out of the country. We talked little about our future together. There was no future. We knew that. Had always known that. Consequently, the subject rarely came up. We had learned to treasure the time we had together and accepted the fact we would part in the very near future. Whenever I face something unpleasant, I avoid talking about it. I suppose I think that if I don't talk about it, don't acknowledge its presence, it will disappear. That's the way I treated Karen's and my eventual separation. We each kept our feelings about the future close to our hearts and seldom mentioned the inevitable farewell. For two individuals who delighted in discussing each and every subject, this was a subject we avoided.

This last semester of my junior year, Jeff was becoming quite serious about me, and sent me a bouquet of red and white carnations for Valentine's Day. I realized this was quite a splurge for him as he was on a very tight budget. He proposed to me, and I turned him down. Nevertheless, he continued dating me. Several weeks before he graduated, we were parked in some remote area and he asked me to lie down beside him on the front seat of the car. "No," I replied, "I don't want to do that."

"I promise not to do anything funny. You can trust me. I just want to feel you lying down beside me. That's all. That's all I want."

I already felt terribly guilty for not accepting his proposal of marriage, so against my better judgment, I did as he requested. I felt quite uncomfortable lying beside him. I was stiff as a board, waiting to see what was going to happen. True to his word, though, he didn't try anything funny. He just held me and kissed me. I continued to feel uncomfortable and could hardly wait "to get it over with" and sit back up. When we did sit up, he said, "I know you have already told me you won't marry me, but I just have to show you what I have already bought for you." He then reached in

104

his pocket and handed me a little box. Opening it, I saw a diamond engagement ring. I wanted to cry for him. I knew exactly what it was like to love someone and not have that love returned. I could well imagine how miserable he was, but I knew I would be miserable married to him. I wished I was in love with him as he would have been a wonderful person to marry. But I wasn't in love with him, and probably did him a big favor by turning down his proposal.

Then I explained to Barbara that two and a half to three years after that night, when I was a high school teacher in Odessa, Texas, Jeff called me. Explaining that he was now living in California, but presently visiting in West Texas, he asked, "May I stop by and see you tomorrow?"

"Of course," I said. "I'd love to see you. Come on by."

He came to my apartment, kissed me, and we sat down and visited. After asking how I was doing, he said, "I'm engaged to be married to a girl I met in California. However, I wanted to come by and see you first, to see if there was any chance at all of your changing your mind about marrying me. Because if there is any chance at all, I will not marry this girl."

"No, Jeff, there's no chance I will change my mind. I'm sorry."

"I am, too. But I tell you what! I need to buy a pair of shoes for my wedding. Will you go shopping with me?"

"Sure!"

So off we went to downtown Odessa, Texas, going in one store after another to look for just the right shoes for Jeff to wear to his wedding. As we walked down the sidewalk, he held my hand. Every chance he got, he held my hand. I thought, "How strange. He's buying shoes for his wedding, but holding *my* hand." But I figured it wouldn't hurt anything to let him do that, so I didn't stop him. He eventually found the shoes he was looking for, made his purchase, took me back to my apartment, and left. I didn't see him again for many, many years. His marriage lasted for quite some time, but they eventually divorced and he remarried.

But back to my junior year in college. Soon after the school year ended, I took a train to Chicago to spend the summer with Karen. Because Karen was going to be out of the country all the next year, my parents relented and let me spend the summer with her. But not without first laying some groundwork. From all the indications, they informed Karen's parents of our relationship and asked them to keep an eye on us and to prohibit our being together privately.

Although I had met Karen's dad when he made a trip to Texas, I had never met Karen's mother, who, upon seeing me for the first time, exclaimed, "Oh, how beautiful you are! What a tiny waist! I've never seen such a tiny waist. It must not be more than 18 inches!"

"Oh, it's more than 18 inches," I said. "Probably closer to 24 inches."

"Oh, no. It couldn't be! It doesn't look any more than 18 inches."

I was embarrassed, not just for myself, but for Karen. I knew how important a small figure was to Karen's mother who was a small-boned woman, unlike Karen. I knew that the more compliments she piled upon me, the more she was trying to draw

Karen's attention to her need to lose some weight. I was 5' 4" and weighed about 110 pounds whereas Karen was 5' 5" and weighed about 140 pounds. But we were built differently. Trying to compare the two of us was most unfair. "You're just like Scarlett O'Hara!" Mrs. Mundt exclaimed. "A real Southern belle!" Her mother's delight in my appearance was her way of saying to Karen, "Look at her! Why can't you look like that?"

The comparison between the two of us made for a very uncomfortable atmosphere. Karen told me that evening, after she and her mother had a few moments to talk, that her mother said, "No wonder Cheyne chose you for a friend. She knows you'll never give her any competition with the boys."

"Karen," I said, "you know that's not true. Don't give her words a second thought. They are just not true and you know it."

"I know, but still it hurts."

"Of course it does. What she said to you was very, very cruel. I can't believe a mother would say that to her daughter. I just can't believe it."

Karen's bedroom, which contained twin beds, was just off the living room. When time came for everyone to go to bed, Karen's mother began bringing covers and pillows into the living room and putting them on the sofa. She then told us, "You two girls leave your bedroom door open tonight. I'm going to sleep on the sofa so I can keep an eye on you."

That's when I knew Mother was bound to have called and told Karen's mother about our relationship and asked her to keep us separated. Knowing we were being watched was an uncomfortable feeling. Embarrassing. We did as we were asked and left the door open. We each stayed in our own bed and made no effort to touch each other. However, I was aware that Mrs. Mundt got up several times during the night to check on us. She just peered into the bedroom, then went back to her bed on the sofa. Nothing else was ever said about our relationship.

Karen and I were determined to do nothing to arouse suspicion. We were perfect and never broke the "unspoken" rules. After less than a week, Mrs. Mundt returned to her and her husband's bedroom. Karen and I continued to leave the bedroom door open, and continued to stay apart. Even during the day, we sat cross-legged on our individual beds to visit and talk. We were determined to do nothing that might result in my being sent home. The only times we touched each other were when both parents were out of the apartment, and even then we stayed alert and were very careful.

I suppose our exemplary behavior convinced Karen's parents that what they had been told about us was untrue, because they eventually left for a month's-long stay in their small cabin in the woods of Northern Michigan. Karen was taking a summer-school class at Northwestern University, so we couldn't accompany them at that time; and I was doing temporary work in various offices to help pay my expenses. Her parents, I'm sure, were needing some time alone prior to the upcoming year-long trip Dr. Mundt and Karen would soon be making overseas. Karen's mother would remain in Chicago as a public school counselor, and they were probably dreading the long separation.

When Karen's parents departed for Michigan, we were ecstatic! We had the apartment all to ourselves. Within fifteen

108

minutes from the time the Mundts walked out the door, Karen and I impishly grinned at each other and headed toward her parents' bed. We were like two kids left alone in a candy store, delighted at our good fortune. Those weeks we were alone in that apartment were like a honeymoon. We bought each other flowers and strawberry cheesecake (which I had never before eaten). Our days together were idyllic. Wonderful days together. We took long walks along Michigan Boulevard and sometimes even held hands, not caring who saw us. On days when I was not working, I accompanied Karen to Northwestern University and sat on the shore of Lake Michigan reading while she attended class. We went shopping, rode the subway and "EL", went to movies, visited the zoo, ate out at restaurants, went to museums, and enjoyed every minute we had together.

One day Karen met some of her former high school friends for lunch, eager to introduce me to them. My southern accent intrigued them as they kept asking, "Say something. Anything. Just talk." And I'd comply with their request. Naturally, I thought their accents a little odd, but they sounded just like Karen; and, by then, I had become accustomed to her speech. I happily entertained her friends, saying whatever came to my mind.

When Karen's class was completed, her parents called and instructed us to take a bus and join them in their cabin, situated on a small lake. The rustic cabin was quite small, but nice, containing a living room, a downstairs bedroom with a loft bedroom just above it, and a tiny kitchen. No electricity. No running water (but it had a water pump next to the kitchen sink). The Mundts used the downstairs bedroom. Karen and I had the loft which opened onto the living room.

Our days together in the Michigan woods were wonderful. We took long walks every day. Never before had I seen a birch tree, and I was amazed at the color of the bark and how one could peel it off. I marveled at what I considered very unusual and very beautiful trees, so unlike the trees I was familiar with in Texas. The woods afforded solitude and privacy to Karen and me. We often held hands as we walked through the woods. We used a small rowboat to explore the tiny lake. Then in the evenings, as a hush fell across the land, Karen, her parents, and I would gather in the living room to read, to visit, or to play games. Often I'd sit crosslegged on the floor and play my flute.

Neither Karen nor I seemed to comprehend that these days together in the Michigan woods were our last days together. We never discussed it. When we returned to the city, we returned to our mode of leaving the bedroom door open at all times, of never touching each other whenever a parent was in the apartment. Everyone began concentrating on preparations for the upcoming trip for Karen and her father. Purchases needed to be made, so Karen and I shopped a lot during that period of time. Doctors' visits were necessary in order for Karen to receive the required vaccinations. I accompanied her everywhere and assisted her in packing. Still, as we worked together in these travel preparations, neither of us voiced the question that remained buried below our conscious thoughts: "Will we ever see each other again?"

I look back on those days and wonder why we never addressed this question. Even now, tears come as I think about

110

seeing her off on the plane and not realizing how empty my life would be after that moment. I wished her a safe trip, a happy year- -the type of goodbye I would say to anyone. My heart was numb as I voiced my farewell at the same time Karen's mother voiced her farewell to her husband. I recall only a numbness, an emptiness, as Mrs. Mundt and I stood in O'Hare Airport until the plane was off the ground. Then, without a word, we turned and left the airport. She, I'm certain, had her own sad thoughts. After all, she was going to be totally alone for a year. Even though she would have her job to keep her occupied, she would be coming home to an empty apartment every night. I imagine she was dreading the loneliness she faced.

My thoughts? I don't know. I seemed to have no feelings, no thoughts. I couldn't afford to let my emotions show to Karen's mother, so I remained stoic. This was the beginning of my training in detaching myself from my emotions. I became quite adept at this.

Mrs. Mundt took me out to eat that night, then to a movie. We saw "The OK Corral" with Kirk Douglas. It was a new release. I've never had a desire to see that movie ever again. The following day Mrs. Mundt drove me to the train station, and I headed home.

Barbara asked, "Did you ever see Karen again?"

"Yes, several years later I saw Karen, but we were surrounded by others and were restricted to a public conversation. We never really had an opportunity to talk."

"Where is she now?" Barbara asked.

"I have no idea. I don't even know what country she lives in. The man she married, Louis Vanmeter, is from British ancestry

111

that had settled in South Africa, then moved to Israel. So I don't even know what country she is living in. No idea at all. I don't even know if she is still living, or how many children she has. I know that her firstborn was a boy, born a year and a half after my firstborn; and I know his name. But she and I broke off contact a long time ago."

"Why did you break off contact?"

"For about twelve years, we corresponded on a fairly regular basis. Then, in 1971, at a time when I was especially unhappy in my marriage, I said some things in my letter to her that I shouldn't have said. Our letters were always 'generic,' letters which could be shared with anyone. I usually shared her letters with Jim, and she had told me she always shared my letters with her husband, Louis. I knew this, and yet in this particular letter I bemoaned how unhappy I was in my marriage. I concluded by saying, 'I'm glad that I at least was able to know what love really is.' I shouldn't have said that. I knew after I mailed the letter I shouldn't have said that. How would she explain to Louis why I would say such a thing to her?

And I was right because I never received a reply. "When no letter from her was forthcoming, I decided not to write again. From all indications, Karen had a happy marriage. I was pleased for her, glad that she was happy. My letter could have instigated problems in her marriage, and I regretted making things tough for her. I also knew that my unhappiness would never disappear and the time might come when I would again say something to her that I shouldn't say. I told myself, 'I will never try to make contact with her again.' And I have kept that promise.

112

"But I miss her, Barbara. I've always missed her. When I'm in a crowd of people, I often look around, thinking that just maybe I will see her. I sometimes dream about her, dream of our being together. A dream I had just the other night had us meeting on a public street and yet we greeted each other by hugging, kissing, and holding each other close, oblivious to passers-by. When I awoke, I thought, 'We never showed any affection toward each other when others were around. We didn't even do what female friends normally do--hug or give an affectionate kiss on the cheek-- no, we never touched each other. We were very careful about that. So to have a dream in which we were publicly affectionate seemed antithetical to reality. It also told me how much I continue to miss her, even after 40 years."

Barbara then caught me by surprise when she asked, "Is there someone else in your life now?"

Tears started again, and I didn't answer.

"You don't want to talk about it, do you?"

"No," I mumbled as I shook my head.

So we went to another subject for a few minutes, then Barbara surprised me by asking, "It's Janie, isn't it? You're in love with Janie, aren't you?"

I had never intended to tell anyone this horrible secret I now harbored. But Barbara had guessed it; and as I sobbed anew, the answer was obvious.

Barbara then said the kindest thing to me. She said, "If I were you, I'd be in love with Janie, too."

She was so kind--this woman who had been born and bred Baptist, whose father was a Baptist minister--so kind to me. Of all the things I expected to come from her mouth, from any and all Baptists' mouths--condemnation and judgment--Barbara showed loving kindness toward me. How truly fortunate I am. How blessed to have a friend like her.

"I know I shouldn't be in love with Janie," I explained. "I don't want to be in love with Janie. It's wrong. I know it's wrong. She's happily married. She's heterosexual. I'll never touch her, never.

"Does she know you are in love with her?"

"Oh, no!" I stated emphatically. "I don't want her to ever know! It would just kill me if she ever found out. It's terrible, my being in love with her. I've never been so miserable in all my life."

The sobbing started anew as I explained, "I did everything right. All my life I did everything right just to keep something like this from ever happening. I've spent my life avoiding close friendships. After Karen, I never again allowed myself to have a close friend. I've been so lonely, but I was so terribly afraid that I might fall in love with a friend that I never had one. I made a point of not touching other women. When women began hugging each other, I stepped away. I avoided physical contact with women. Even with Janie, I did nothing wrong. Not a thing. I don't know why this happened to me. It's so unfair. If I had done something wrong, then I'm getting what I deserve, but I didn't do anything wrong. It just happened. It was as if someone were standing behind me with a wooden 2 x 4 and just slammed it into my head with all the strength they could muster. It hit me that suddenly and that powerfully. Just hit me completely out of the blue. I was just standing in the kitchen on a Sunday afternoon, and, wham!, I

114

started having these terrible thoughts about Janie. I didn't do anything wrong. It just happened," I wailed.

Barbara moved over close to me to help comfort me. I was in agony. I was admitting an unforgivable weakness that I never wanted to admit to anyone. I was ashamed of myself for having fallen in love with Janie. Terribly ashamed.

After a few minutes, Barbara suggested, "You need to give up teaching your Sunday School class, at least for a few months."

"I just can't do that," I replied.

"Why not?" she asked

"I have to be able to see Janie every once in a while. I couldn't stand it if I didn't see her occasionally."

"Cheyne, you've got to quit teaching that class. It doesn't have to be a permanent change. Just temporary. I'm teaching a class on that same floor, some younger ladies that I think you would enjoy being with. Come visit our class for awhile."

"No, I just can't." But her words did start me to thinking about it. I told myself I'd go ahead and teach the class this coming Sunday and then just see how things went.

After explaining to Barbara how long I've been unhappy in my marriage, I talked about the birth of each of our four children. I stated, "When the first child was a boy, I was delighted, as was Jim. We both wanted a son. My second pregnancy ended in a spontaneous abortion after four and a half months. Then I became pregnant with our second child. At this time, I begged God to give me another boy. At the same time, Jim was reminding me of how much he wanted a daughter. But I didn't want a daughter. I didn't trust myself with a daughter. I realize now my fears were ridiculous, but all I knew was that I had 'strange feelings' toward girls. I didn't understand *why* I had those strange feelings. I didn't know there was a name for people like me. I kept my head 'buried in the sand' by never reading about homosexuality, never discussing it with anyone. I remained ignorant on the subject. All I knew at that time was that I didn't want to take a chance on having strange feelings toward a daughter. I therefore constantly begged God for a son. And my prayer was answered. Our second child was a boy. A little over a year later, I again became pregnant. Jim definitely wanted a daughter this time. I never told him how desperately I was praying for another boy. 'Please, Lord,' I begged. 'Please give me another boy. Lord you've just got to give me another boy. Oh, please, Lord, make this child a boy!' Over and over, throughout the pregnancy, I voiced this prayer.

"Thank goodness, we had a third son. Jim was terribly disappointed, and guilt poured over me for having begged God for a boy. I was convinced then, and am convinced now that our three boys resulted from my prayers. Despite Jim's disappointment, I was secretly delighted to have a third son. Ecstatic!

"I've always thought of my inability to love a man as 'God's Dirty Trick' that He played upon me. That's what I've always called it. God's Dirty Trick. At the same time, I would tell myself, 'God has tried to make up for the dirty trick He played on me by blessing me in numerous ways--one being the granting of my request for sons!' God truly blessed me in many different ways. By all outward appearances, I had a good life.

"The years passed, and as the children began to grow up, I realized the time would come when Jim and I would be alone in the home, just the two of us. I wasn't ready for that. The children had always served as a buffer, as a means to avoid being alone with Jim. I wanted another child just to prolong that buffer a little while longer. However, I was reaching an age when few women continued to have children. The time had come to make a decision.

"I approached Jim and asked, 'Would you like to have another child? A fourth child?'

"'Yes, I would,' he replied. 'I'd love to have a daughter!'

"Realizing the likelihood we would have another boy, I warned him, 'We can't go into this wanting a daughter. The doctor told me our chances of having a daughter are one in eight. We either go into this wanting another *child*, regardless of whether it is a boy or girl, or we don't do this at all.'

"Jim immediately replied, 'I want another child. Yes, I'd like to have another child, regardless.'

"So Jim and I began trying to start a baby. I didn't get pregnant immediately. It took about a year, so that when our fourth child was born I was almost forty years of age. My thoughts about this child were different from the other three as I began considering the possibility of having a daughter. So many years had passed since I had felt anything special toward a female that I considered myself 'all right.' I began picturing how nice it would be to have a daughter with me in the kitchen, a daughter with whom to share thoughts and ideas, a companion. The more I thought about having a daughter, the more I wanted one. And I began asking God, 'I'd like to have a daughter, Lord. I believe I'm all right, that I don't need to worry about any kind of bad feelings I might have, and I'd like to have a daughter this time. If it be your will, Lord, please send me a girl. And, Lord, I promise that I will never, never do anything to this girl to hurt her physically or emotionally. If I ever begin feeling anything toward her that I shouldn't feel, I'll get out of her life. Immediately. I'll just get out of her life. I'll stage my own death, or whatever it takes, but I'll remove myself from her life. Lord, I promise I'll never do anything to hurt her in any way.'

"I know now that my fears regarding a daughter were ridiculous. But at the time, those fears were very real. I simply didn't understand myself at all. Lots of people have always thought our fourth child was an 'accident.'" I laughed as I said, "They have no idea how hard we worked to have Anne!"

By the time I left Barbara's this afternoon, I had been through a very emotional two and a half hour conversation and still had a four-hour drive ahead of me to Houston in order to visit with Josh and Sandy. Worried about my safety and well-being, Barbara stated, "I really don't think you need to get on the highway at this time. Wait and make the drive another day."

"I'm all right, Barbara. Really I am. I'll play some music and I'll be just fine."

"I don't think you are 'just fine' at all. I really don't want you to make this drive."

"I promised I'd come. They're expecting me."

"If you are intent on going, then come pick out some books on tape to listen to. I have quite a collection and you are welcome to any of them."

I accepted her offer and selected four or five books on tape, told Barbara goodbye, and drove away. The book on tape I listened to as I drove to Houston that afternoon was Janet Fitch's *White Oleander*. The story completely escapes me now, but I recall there was something in it about suicide because I told myself, "You don't need to be listening to this tape right now." But I listened to all of it and thankfully arrived safely at Josh and Sandy's house where I spent two nights.

March 3 - March 30, 2000

Friday, March 3: Sandy and I had some long conversations in which I shared with her some of the same things I had shared with Barbara. Sandy is a wonderful wife to Josh, intelligent, hard working, and loving. She's an inch or two taller than Josh, but that doesn't bother either of them. Josh is so proud of her. Sandy listened, asked a few questions, and very thankfully made me feel loved and accepted. I'm so fortunate to have a kind daughter-in-law.

This evening, Josh and I went out to dinner--just the two of us. Sandy thought we needed some time together. She knew Josh was finding it difficult to come to grips with the fact he has a homosexual mother. Our conversation drained me. When Josh is convinced of a certain truth, it is practically impossible to argue another point with him. Not only does he possess a logical, well-ordered mind, but his college degree is in bio-engineering! He therefore has more than a smattering of knowledge about the body, including genes. He is convinced people could not possibly be born with a different sexual orientation. "All behavior is learned," he stated.

"Josh, we aren't talking about behavior because there has been no 'behavior' on my part since I was in college. This is not behavior we are talking about. It's the way I am, the way I feel. Me! I've tried all my life to change, but I just can't change."

"But Mom, something has caused you to be this way. Environment, perhaps. But you just can't convince me a person is born this way."

"Josh, all I know is what I am, what I have experienced. I know this is not something I chose. No fool would choose to be homosexual. That's the most ridiculous supposition I can imagine. Just think about that for a minute. Why would anyone 'choose' to be gay?"

"Are you trying to tell me that the baby we are expecting in July could be gay?"

"Yes, that's what I'm telling you, and SO WHAT!" By then I was feeling frustrated because I had no facts with which to uphold my position and even if I had, I couldn't have held my own against Josh. His brilliance has always amazed me. Angry at myself for being so impotent in our argument and angry at Josh for his persistent logic, I said, "If your baby turns out to be gay, you'll treat it just like you would if he wasn't gay. Just love him or her and accept it the way it is without making it feel guilty!"

By then, Josh was becoming upset. "Well, I can't accept that. I can't believe there is a chance our child could be gay."

"I hope it's not, Josh. But if it is, just love it. That's all. Just love it."

Saturday, March 4: When I returned home, I checked my e-mail messages and read one from Gwen Patterson with the Christian women's group. She said, "I've really been thinking about you and praying for you. The pain you are suffering is so beyond my abilities to address that right now prayer is my only knowing action to do. You are a very dear person and I value you and your friendship. I was thinking about our conversation Tuesday and realized that I really never answered your question about coming to the task force meetings . . . At this time, I do not see wisdom in your participation. I don't think this is a surprise to you, and considering the conversations of the members concerning the play (that the members wanted to ban because it was about homosexuals) . . . I am concerned that you would feel uncomfortable. I cannot speak for the others, but if you are uncomfortable, I would think others in the group might be also. Cheyne, I don't want our friendship to end. I do need to ask you to bear with me while I pray for guidance . . .Can we walk as friends? Blessings, Gwen"

Now that I've "come out of the closet," I'm no longer welcome as a member of the Task Force for this group. That's the way I took her letter. It didn't upset me because that is what I expected. I sent her a quick reply, "Gwen, yes, we will remain friends. I appreciate your caring attitude as shown by your willingness to pray for me. The honesty you shared about remaining in the Task Force does not come as a surprise. I had already decided that was how you felt and perhaps also how I felt. No problem there at all. We can always talk as friends. Whatever questions you have, I will try to answer. Cheyne."

I shared Gwen's letter with Barbara who wrote back, "It's good that the friend from the Christian women's group is still a friend, more (in my somewhat biased view) for her good than for yours. I know that ultimately you are going to be okay though I also think you've just begun a part of your journey that is likely to take you places you can't foresee. That's true of all of us, though, to varying degrees. The good part is that if we're all following Him, allowing Him to shape us into what He created us to be, we'll all be heading in the same direction.

"I've always thought of the word 'valiant' when I thought of you, Cheyne, and I've never known why. Now I understand that association more, even though your emotions are overwhelming at the present time, I see valor. (Did you know that valor has its roots in a word that means worth, by the way?)"

I replied to Barbara, "I found it interesting you used the word 'valor' in talking about me. Anne and Janie have both used the word 'courage.' To be quite frank, I feel so much the opposite. I sat down about an hour ago and described my feelings in a long paragraph which could be quickly summed up as being scared to death of the future and the fact that I haven't yet faced the 'tip of the iceberg' in what will inevitably come to test my emotions, my resolve, and my ability to make the right decisions. It's as if I am teetering on the edge of a cliff, not knowing which way I will fall. There are times I feel as if I am taking it one day at a time, and other times when I feel it is an hour at a time. I keep telling myself it will get better, but I know in my heart it will get much, much worse before it ever starts getting better. I just keep telling myself to hold it together for a little longer."

Barbara and I kept up a running e-mail correspondence today. As soon as one wrote, the other answered. Barbara's answer to my last e-mail was "Which is to say, 'it' will doubtless get much worse, if 'it' means people hearing about you and responding out of ignorance and habit, rather than out of a caring commitment to decent treatment for every single person on the planet, if only because they're persons. On the other hand, 'it' should get easier, if 'it' means you become comfortable with yourself and God's love for you to such an extent that you don't have to allow other people's opinions to determine what you think you're worth. Time will just have to pass for your emotions to become less volatile-- which is connected to your need for more rest and better nourishment and a modicum of tranquillity. About valor--people think John McCain is a hero because he endured less than five years' captivity and torture. You endured almost 37 years; and, I believe, you're still working your way out of captivity. I suspect the next few months for you will be a bit like aging with some things getting better and several getting worse. Still, it beats the heck out of the alternative!"

I then took time to write to J.W., my eldest son, affirming the fact that he is free to tell anyone he wishes that he has a gay mother, but asking him to keep me abreast of who he has told so that if someone gives me a funny look at church tomorrow, I'll know why!

Sunday, March 5: When I awoke about 5:30, I was delighted to have an e-mail from J.W. who updated me on those he had told. One of his friends, he said, made the comment, "Your mother really has a lot of courage." He says he has yet to get a negative reaction.

The Sunday School lesson went well today. Our group was much larger than usual--eleven were present, even with two of our regulars missing. Many went out of their way to compliment me on the lesson I taught.

Janie walked with me to the parking lot, also complimenting me on the lesson. "Your lessons are so good, Cheyne. You really ought to tape them. You do save them, don't you?"

"Yes, I save them, but they aren't that original. I just gather material from lots of different sources and put it all together. I can't really claim any originality in the lessons I teach."

Janie has always been my most staunch supporter, always heaping praise on me. She herself recently received a nice award for volunteer efforts in a state organization and received a nice write-up in our local newspaper. As I complimented her on her recent recognition, she failed to pay attention to where she was walking among the cars in the church parking lot and ran into a rearview mirror. She received quite a jolt, and probably a bad bruise. My unthought-out reaction was to exclaim, "Oh, honey! Are you hurt?"

She didn't seem to react abnormally to what I said, but I knew I had goofed in my exclamation. I hope she doesn't give it more thought later on.

After we parted, I again reminded myself that I have to "get over" my feelings for her, and yet I can't imagine living my life without ever seeing or talking to her. My fantasy world returned as I thought how wonderful it would be to drive somewhere with Janie beside me. It would be a dream come true, just to have her by my side, enjoying life together.

Sunday, March 12: When I attended the Sunday services tonight, preceded by a snack supper, the Graysons, friends of both Jim's and mine, came by the table to greet me. They are being kind to me and probably don't know that I know that they know about me. It's like a game we are playing. But I felt a different reaction from Josh's friend, Charlie. (He was part of a "singles group" that learned about me from J.W.) Charlie walked right by me, and I knew he had no intention of speaking to me. I therefore looked him right in the eye and said, "Hi, Charlie!" He mumbled an embarrassed response as he continued walking. Normally, he would have stopped and asked, "What have you heard from Josh? How is he doing?" But he did none of that tonight. He seemed embarrassed to have to look at me.

Monday, March 13: I slept little last night. I called Janie this morning, and we talked for over an hour. "I hope Jim finds someone special," she said, then added, "Cheyne, you need someone in your life, someone to love. I hope you find someone special real soon." Thoughts of Janie raced through my mind as I mumbled, "Yes, that would be nice." She's right, of course. If someone else came into my life, this would be a means of subduing my feelings toward her. I definitely need to get over her. The divorce will be final in three weeks. I look forward to that time when I can truly feel free--except to belong to God.

Tuesday, March 14: I surfed the Internet this afternoon and ended up on a web site that contained all kinds of horrible, despicable comments about homosexuals. Unspeakable things were said. Why are people so mean and cruel? How could any human being say such unkind, nasty things about another?

I'm ready for an upward swing in my mood. I've been down in the dumps longer than usual this time. I just want to crawl into bed and stay there and count the hours until I see Janie tomorrow.

Wednesday, March 15: I awoke this morning at 3:30 a.m. and napped a little until I finally got up around 5:30. All day I've experienced an overwhelming feeling of sadness, the kind that's hard to put my finger on. This is the fourth straight day of constant sadness. Anne and I had lunch with Janie today. She had a funeral to attend this afternoon, so was wearing a black dress. She looked lovely. She thinks so highly of Anne, so the two of them conversed most of the time. I found myself tongue-tied not knowing what to talk about so I listened. After lunch, Anne left to go shopping. That's when Janie shared with me recent personal problems resulting in such a feeling of hopelessness that she felt an overwhelming need to turn to God for comfort.

I keep asking myself if I have ever truly turned to God in my own hopeless situation. I talk with Him. I beg Him. I plead. I call out in desperation "Help me God!" but I keep wondering if I have truly surrendered my complete self or if there is a fear within me that if I do, He will tell me how sinful I am and how I must completely deny the existence of my sexual orientation, a denial I don't believe is possible. I think that's what it is all about--this fight that I'm having with God. This fear that He may say the same thing the "Christian Community" is saying, that I truly am a sinful, sinful person.

Friday, March 17:   Despite my belief I have finally made some right decisions with my life in freeing both Jim and me to find true happiness, these "right decisions" have introduced me to the most tremendous misery I believe I have ever faced. And to make matters worse, I have fallen in love with someone who is happily married. How can that happen?

Perhaps I need to make some kind of conscious move toward finding a partner. This would perhaps be the solution for "getting over Janie."   But I have absolutely no idea how to go about finding someone else. No idea at all. Sometimes I feel a desperate yearning to put my arms around a woman and just hold her.

Saturday, March 18:   Anne, who has been visiting with me during her Spring Break and was getting ready to leave, said to me, "Mother, I love you just the way you are. I wouldn't change one thing about you."

I reiterated, "Surely there are some things you would prefer were different about me."

"No," she stated. "Not a thing. I'm real proud of you."

This afternoon I attended a shower at Janie's house. I was convinced some of the ladies attending would now know about me, and might say something to me. By the time I left my apartment, I was feeling quite ill. My stomach was churning. Pure dread.

That's all it was. I was so convinced someone would speak unkindly to me that I felt terribly nauseous driving to Janie's. I was determined, however, to face whatever was thrown at me. (I do wonder though if that's true that I can take it. Otherwise, why do I feel so ill when I anticipate the bad things that might be said?)

After arriving, I began to relax and actually enjoyed the gathering. Janie's home is so lovely, so beautiful, so filled with expensive artwork! Once I caught her reflection as she stood close to a large mirror which reflected greenery and flowers surrounding her reflection. The sight almost took my breath away. I wanted to just stare, but forced myself to look away. I didn't want her to see me looking at her. But I do believe that's the prettiest I have ever seen her. She was radiant.

When the shower ended, the honoree's father arrived. Within my hearing, he informed one of the guests that his wife insists I am the best Sunday School teacher at First Baptist Church! Then he turned to me and began complimenting me on how nice I looked and how much he liked my dress. I was speechless. He's always been nice to me, but he was extremely nice this afternoon, overly complimentary. The Lord really does move in mysterious ways. I dreaded the occasion so much that I felt physically ill as I drove to Janie's; but when I left for home, wonderful compliments made my heart sing.

Soon after arriving back at my apartment, Janie called just to visit. I was delighted, as well as dazed. We talked for an hour about all kinds of things--a happy conversation. She has two weddings to attend this evening! I know she is absolutely exhausted after being on her feet all afternoon, plus all her preparations for the shower. "Janie," I said, "I just don't know how you are able to do all this."

At church Sunday evening, I again saw Charlie, Josh's friend. He's been avoiding me. He still won't look me in the eye. I again spoke directly to him, forcing him to reply. But it was almost more than he could handle and he scooted away as quickly as he could. Too bad.

Wednesday, March 22: Janie called to tell me about a conversation she had at one of the weddings she attended. Jim's friend, Milton, made a point of walking over to Janie and saying, "Thank you for being such a good friend to Cheyne. I know how difficult and painful it is for her at this time, and I appreciate your standing beside her and helping her out."

As Janie shared Milton's words with me, my mind seemed to shut down--from amazement. Their conversation must have been an extended one, but I recall little of what else she related. I regret this. I do recall Janie told Milton, "I'm sure this is also a difficult time for Jim." Milton agreed, and yet returned to the subject of me and the "brave step" I have taken. What really amazed me about the whole conversation is the fact that Milton is probably Jim's best friend, the one with whom Jim went to Dallas the day after I asked for the divorce. Since neither Milton, nor his wife, have spoken to me, his sympathy and understanding came as a welcome surprise.

Thursday, March 23: It's hard for me to explain, even to myself, why I am amazed at the loving and kind reactions I have received from Barbara, Janie, Anne, J.W., Milton, and a few others, like our pastor, Bob Watson. I think it is all related to living with a feeling of guilt all of my life. It's such a part of me that I don't understand why everyone else isn't following my example and heaping additional feelings of guilt and sin upon me.

I have so many emotions that rush around inside of me now, some colliding against each other and bouncing off to head in different directions that making them stand still long enough to truly analyze my feelings is impossible. I simply know that I expected different reactions than what I am getting. It's as if I wish someone would haul off and beat me to a pulp and get it all over with. I think that's what I'd like to do to myself. The physical hurt appeals to me--like a cleansing. Or like something I deserve.

The one truth I continue to hang onto is that I know God loves me. Beyond that, I get all mixed up inside. I came across a very interesting verse the other day: Romans 9:20, which says, *But who are you, O man, to talk back to God. Shall what is formed say to him who formed it, 'Why did you make me like this?'*

Saturday, March 25: I haven't felt this heavy a load of depression for a long time. I'm not certain I can even explain it. I think it started with attending the funeral of an acquaintance. The funeral was more of a celebration of a life well lived, certainly not a sad affair. Nevertheless, this longing to die came over me--wishing I could just "go" and escape this world.

After the service, I stood in line to speak to the widow and the daughters. Several members of my Sunday School class were standing next to me. In the course of conversation, one mentioned

130

a 19-year-old girl who recently committed suicide, saying "I just don't understand why anyone would do that." Then she mentioned another suicide, a 29-year-old. My immediate reaction was that perhaps one or both were gay. That would certainly explain, at least to me, why they had committed suicide! Then one of the ladies said, "They shouldn't be allowed that option in solving their problems."

I so wanted to tell them how much I understood what those girls were bound to have gone through--the terrible loneliness, despair, misery, and eventually a descent into a state of hopelessness. It's the hopelessness that finally makes you take that final step. I supposed neither of these two women next to me had ever experienced such a depression. I yearned to tell them what it was like, how I've lived with it for many years and how at that very moment I wanted so much to die that I was terribly nauseous. How shocked they would have been.

I realized neither of these ladies could possibly understand what my life has been like. Then my mind went toward the Sunday School lesson I plan to teach tomorrow. I might go too far in "stepping on the toes of the 'Religious Right,'" but maybe that's what God wants me to do--to step on their toes. My plan is to share some of the thoughts I gleaned from Philip Yancey's book, *What's So Amazing About Grace.* These thoughts include: "Unfortunately, many people in the world today associate evangelism with a message of hate and associate Christians as having taken on the task of 'moral exterminator' for the evil-infested society around them. Keep in mind that Jesus earned a reputation as a lover of sinners, a reputation that his followers are in danger

131

of losing today. What has happened to the reputation of Christians and of Christ's church when a prostitute would say in response to an invitation to attend church, *Church! Why would I ever go there? I was already feeling terrible about myself. They'd just make me feel worse!* Oh, what a long way so-called Christians have come from Christ's example to love one another."[8]

Sunday, March 26: We had an excellent group of ladies in our Sunday School class this morning. Seven! Large for us. During the lesson I explained that during the Middle Ages, charging interest on a loan was considered a deplorable sin. However, charging interest is now an accepted practice and no one equates it with "sin." When I was a teenager, preachers railed against divorce and drinking. Although we don't "like" divorce, it's no longer preached against and divorced individuals now fill pulpits. Alcoholic drinks are accepted by many Christians. Only "drinking to excess" is now considered sinful (or an illness). The primary sins discussed today are abortion and homosexuality.

The class discussion which followed my lesson centered in on homosexuality. I hadn't planned for this to happen, and I became quite nervous. One of the ladies absolutely stunned me when she said, "I don't believe this is something someone chooses." But not all agreed with her and some adamantly believe it is chosen. This same member criticized those who labeled pro-life people in a negative way. This was probably in response to the example I used of Yancey's concerning Andy Rooney, the newsman, who said, "I've decided I'm against abortion. I think it's murder. But I have a dilemma in that I much prefer the pro-choice to the pro-life people."[9] Yancey was pointing out that "Moralism apart from grace solves little."[10] As the members continued discussing these issues, I was certain none of them (other than Janie) had any idea I was gay.

Wednesday, March 29: This afternoon, I kept an appointment to talk with my pastor, Bob Watson, about my sexual orientation. At the beginning, I found it difficult to know what to say, but his kindness led me to share with him quite a bit about my life and what it has been like to pretend to be heterosexual. One of the reasons I wanted to talk with him was to get his opinion on whether or not I should tell my Sunday School class about my sexual orientation. His advice was not to tell them as a group, but to talk with one or two at a time. "If you talk to them as a group," he said, "you'll experience the very lowest opinions in that group."

He told me that various church members are coming to him to ask if he is aware of my sexual orientation. He assures me they are not upset about it or condemning, but inquisitive as to whether or not he is aware of it. "I think you will be pleasantly surprised by all the support you will find among church members who think very highly of you," he told me.

"Can you tell me who has come to you that already knows about me?"

Looking rather uncomfortable, he replied, "No, I can't do that."

He then warned me, "You need to be prepared for others who will say some unkind things to you. It's important you be prepared for their comments. Decide ahead of time what you will

133

say to them when you are confronted." Yes, several times he urged me to be prepared, to think about this ahead of time.

"It might be a good idea for you to give up teaching your Sunday School class, at least for awhile." That statement took me by surprise. It shouldn't have, but it did.

"How is your mother taking this news?" he asked.

"I haven't told her yet, and I'm not certain I will tell her."

"She needs to be told."

"I feel anger toward her in this regard. She knew when I was in college that I had fallen in love with a girl, but all I felt from her was condemnation. I also felt pressure from her to get married--the same kind of pressure I felt from society. This is what forced me to get married, causing me to live a very unhappy life. I don't know if I will ever discuss this with her."

"How is Jim taking this?"

"His first reaction was sorrow, but I believe anger is beginning to take hold. I think this is to be expected--that he would eventually become angry. This doesn't surprise me."

"Your telling Jim the truth about yourself was an act of grace. You did a wonderful thing by telling him. How are your children taking the news?"

"Anne and J.W. are all right with it. Josh is having trouble accepting it, and I've yet to hear from Michael. I know he is having a very difficult time. He is like his dad. They are both so very prejudiced against gays."

"You've got to give them time."

"Yes, I know. I'm trying to do that. Two couples in the church that I'm certain know about me are the Graysons and the Herringtons but none has said a word to me personally."

"You've got to give people time. This is all new to them. You are probably the only homosexual they have ever known. They don't know what to say to you. Just don't begin a 'crusade.' Whatever you do, share this information on a one-on-one basis. Are you taking care of yourself? Exercising? You've lost a lot of weight, haven't you?"

"Yes, but I'm watching it. I do exercise, and I walk a little."

I continued, "I keep asking myself why I've had to suffer so much, and the only answer that keeps coming to me is that there is something God wants me to do. That's why I've had to come out of hiding. You can't imagine how wonderful it would have been to have had someone to talk with when I was a teenager and was confused about my feelings. There are bound to be other people in this church just like me--each hiding in his or her little cubbyhole of fear and secrecy. I want to do something for them, especially the children who will grow up feeling the same guilt and condemnation I always felt."

"There probably is a reason all of this has happened to you," he said. "Just be patient, and those needing help will eventually find you."

After our conversation, I walked upstairs to the Wednesday night supper, picked up my tray of food, and sat among friends. Nancy Grayson took time to come over and speak to me, even "touching" me on the shoulder. I'm always overjoyed to have someone "touch" me. It's as if they are saying I'm still human, not some monster they don't want to touch.

Late this evening, I wrote to Barbara, sharing with her the conversation between Bob and me. Her reply was encouraging and included the following paragraph: "As I told my Sunday School class recently, my all-time favorite poster shows a pool of light (as if from a flashlight) surrounded by darkness and the words, 'Faith is going to the edge of all the light you have, and taking one more step.' I suspect that may be where you are. But my experience is that if you're walking in the Light, you'll be able to see when you take that step."

Barbara's words of wisdom continued, "I hope you can turn your mind off for awhile tonight, if only so your subconscious can sort through stuff and get through to you. Most stuff really is better in the morning. (And then there's Garrison Keillor, who once said, 'Sometimes you just have to stand up to reality and deny it.')"

Friday, March 31, 2000

Surprise! I seem to be doing much, much better. My fantasies are not so much a part of my life any more. What a relief! And, generally speaking, I'm sleeping a little better and have gained a pound so that I'm back up to 111.5. I will have to admit, though, that one possible reason I had such a good day yesterday is because Janie called me twice--early in the morning and again close to suppertime. We chatted for over an hour each time. Just friendly talk. I finally felt that I was being as good a friend to her in these conversations as she has been to me.

I was delighted to hear from my pastor who wrote: "Dear Cheyne, Thanks for your conversation on Wednesday evening. I had to drive to Dallas yesterday for a series of meetings, and a good portion of the drive was spent thinking about and praying for you. I know this is a difficult time for you. Furthermore, I know that you are trying to do the right thing.

"As to your particular question about Sunday School leadership, my recommendation that you step aside for a while is based on the heart-felt concern for you and the church. Because you have struggled with this issue for so long, it may be hard for you to realize that most people have not struggled with this issue, do not care to struggle with this issue, and simply respond in an emotional manner, particularly when it intersects an area of their lives which is sacred to them (i.e. the church). I have seen this tinderbox ignited a number of times in the past few years (from women in ministry to the Southern Baptist Convention controversy to local church matters), and when the issue becomes a public issue without proper prayer and preparation then it becomes a 'lose-lose' situation, permanently dividing people.

"I am very much afraid that in a public discussion you would be attacked and vilified, and I don't wish to see that happen. For instance, in situations like church business meetings, when a volatile issue is brought up on the floor of the church, more often than not, emotions win out over logic, with people saying harmful and destructive things. And more often than not, I'm afraid, zealots on either side of the issue take over, hampering constructive dialogue.

"On the other hand, as you share with individuals what is going on in your life, they will be able to ask questions, think, and hopefully respond in a Christian manner as they try to process this very difficult revelation.

"I don't want you to retreat from talking about this, but I do want you to be wise in who you talk to and how you communicate. (Jesus' statement about being 'wise as a serpent and innocent as a dove' seems to be appropriate here.) My feeling is that if you deal with this one on one you will be a better resource for people trying to make sense of this; and that your witness for Jesus Christ will be better served as people watch you deal with this in a personal way. One on one people will see the anguish and care with which you are dealing.

"You asked if anyone from your class had come to me with concerns. No one has. You asked about others in the church. And as I mentioned to you, people have called and asked questions about your situation, but they were questions of concern. Yet, even with the questions, there has not been anyone who has even suggested that you leave the church. However, as this becomes more public, I think it would be naive to assume that there won't be a mean statement here or there. That is my rationale for asking you to step aside as a teacher. I don't want you to become a 'lightening rod' for emotional fears and prejudices. I truly think you can best make sense of what is happening to you and with you on an individual basis. Cheyne, lead with your best gifts in this matter, and lead with the Spirit of Christ to guide you.

My sense is that He will grant you wisdom and courage, but most of all the gift of appropriateness, knowing when to speak and when to remain silent.

"Please know that I have attempted to tether my thoughts to God's love and purpose for you. You matter a great deal to God, and to me. Your brother in Christ, Bob"

Upon reading my pastor's letter, a trembling began within my body--throughout my body. Perhaps I was just chilled, but that can't completely explain the phenomenon. I continued to tremble and shake. His letter infused me with both hope and despair simultaneously. Hope in the sense he did not condemn me for being homosexual; despair that I had been asked to give up teaching my class of adult women. I immediately forwarded his letter to both Barbara and Janie, then went for a fast-paced 45-minute walk. During the walk, I prayed for strength for the trials I was facing. I also thanked God for giving me some really good days this week, days with less depression, less tension, less fantasizing. These good days, this uplifting of the spirit, have been needed to prepare me for today.

Barbara immediately replied: "But you didn't say what you think--or are you still thinking? I was struck by his reference to dealing with issues 'without prayer and preparation.' I think he's right about people being better able to deal with your situation one by one, rather than publicly. You gave me that grace, not knowing how I would respond. I know you better than most and I'm not homophobic, so knowing about your sexual orientation wasn't that big a deal for me personally--though you know I grieved to discover the depth of your pain and how long you'd been dealing with it

139

alone. You must consider how you can best give people an opportunity to be (become) the people God created them to be. (Which is, of course, what you're discovering and living out yourself.)

"If one occurred, how would a public discussion affect you? There's a huge difference in wanting people to know and being the subject of a public discussion. Bob's told you how he thinks you can 'be a better resource for people trying to make sense of this.' How do you think you can be the best teacher? You'll always be a teacher, you know. You couldn't help it if you tried. You were born to be an educator, trained to be an educator, gifted to help people learn. There's the writing, of course, and I fully expect your account of your experience to be published, though I hope that's far enough in the future for you to have the perspective to really understand what your experience is. (I suppose a counselor would help here.) But my mind keeps coming back to that *Experiencing God* seminar--look around, pay attention to where you see God working already, and join Him there. I know--terrific principle, but the 'how' ain't so easy.:-)

"And I am very aware that this is your experience, not mine, and that your decisions need to come out of your own heart, not my thoughts. I can't carry your load, but I'm grateful that you allow me to keep you company on the journey. I've learned so much from you already.

"Grace and peace to you, today and all your days, Barbara"

I replied to Barbara: "I'm still thinking. I told Janie yesterday that I feel as if she, you, and Bob make up my 'president's cabinet.' I've now received feedback from all of you as Janie has already

140

told me she will quit the class if I'm no longer the teacher. I talked with her and think I have her calmed down, but this latest message from Bob will bring out her feistiness again.

"In the end, I know it is my decision. Here are some of my thoughts right now (although allow me to change them hourly!)

"1. I really think I can stand up to the ugly comments, so I won't make a decision based on that type of fear.

"2. I have no desire whatsoever to cause conflict and strife within the church. The thought that I could personally control whether or not some kind of division might occur just sends chills down my spine.

"3. But, along that same line, I recently completed teaching a series of lessons where one of the primary themes was that Jesus never backed away from a confrontation. In fact, he seemed to deliberately provoke the 'religious right' of his day. So, do I follow His example and not back away?

"4. A lot hinges on my Sunday School class. Although I will take everyone's advice and not bring this subject up with the group, I think I will begin talking with a few of the individual members and gauge their reactions. This is a precious group of women. However, I may discover they are in total agreement with you and Bob.

"For today, I'm making no decision; but I know I've got to make a decision soon and your input is most welcome.

"Your comment that 'I would always be a teacher' is probably true, but if I resign from this teaching position, I certainly will not be allowed to teach in any other facet of the church. Can you just imagine what might be said if I went back to teaching a 6th grade class of girls like I have done in the past? Gays are all supposed to be child molesters!

"One of my desires (which I hinted at to Bob) is to form a type of support group for those affected by homophobia--to provide a safe place to share. I guess that's asking too much at this time, but there is no doubt in my mind whatsoever that there are many more in our church just like me. I want to fight this prejudice on behalf of all these other people who are hurting or cowering behind their masks. Wouldn't it be wonderful if all of us could be free? And in that freedom be equally accepted as brothers and sisters in Christ? And besides those of us who are gay, just think how many people have children who are gay, brothers and sisters who are gay, aunts, uncles, nieces and nephews who are gay, as well as friends and neighbors who are gay. The silence that prevails on this subject is a cruel silence. It's a silence that literally kills--both physically and emotionally."

About four hours later, I again wrote to Barbara, saying, "I forwarded Dr. Watson's e-mail to Anne, and she called me a little while ago. She, as a 21-year-old, lives in an entirely different world. She simply does not understand the potential problems that can occur in our church. She doesn't understand the attitudes. I tried to explain the situation to her, but made little progress. The prejudice just makes no sense to her."

About an hour and a half later, about 6 p.m., Barbara replied, "I believe Bob's suggestions to you are aimed at taking us all, even the slow ones, where we need to go. Sometimes it's extremely irritating to those of us who are quick, to have to move at the pace of the slower members of our flock, but that's pretty well the speed at which flocks move, isn't it?

"Janie is, of course, exactly right about 'church folks living with their heads buried and their eyes closed.' But I usually hold that you can't make a person with a broken leg walk faster by yelling at her. You just keep company with them by walking more slowly yourself until the healing takes place. As Ernest Hemingway said, 'The world breaks everyone . . . but afterward many are strong at the broken places.' It's true that broken bones are stronger at the formerly-broken spot after they've healed, because the new bone forms a sort of thick callus around the old bone. I think I am getting way too philosophical here, but I find it encouraging to know that brokenness is generally a prerequisite for becoming strong.

"With Janie, I rejoice at the quality of God's creation in you. I would never suggest that you deny who you are but I do believe that giving people some breathing space while they deal with an issue they've ignored heretofore would be the most positive choice for the long haul. You know better than I do that most people's idea of what a homosexual is doesn't include someone like you-- many of them saw Elton John on the *Today Show* this morning.

"I think you stand a far better chance of forming a group of those with different sexual orientations if you allow people to know you as you really are--which hasn't been possible heretofore. How would you form such a group? Wouldn't you have to wait for people to identify with you, reveal themselves to you? Wouldn't they be more apt to do that if you weren't attracting a huge amount of criticism? I'm guessing that if the homosexuals in our church were ready to deal with the stresses of coming out, they'd be out. If they see you come out, acting in love and grace rather than as a focus for controversy, they'll identify with you more readily, won't they?

"I do believe that you and I will live to see the day when gays are accepted as brothers and sisters, equal in Christ. I think that'll happen sooner if you have the patience to be who you are openly, without insisting that people open their own minds immediately. People seldom do what you insist they do. Open the chrysalis with the scissors and the butterfly doesn't fly. But keep shining the light on it, and it will.

"Remember that the ultimate decision is between you and God--not me, not Janie, not Bob."

Saturday, April 1, 2000

Before 6 a.m. the following day, I sent a long e-mail to Carolyn, one of the members of my Sunday School class. I explained how long I had wanted a divorce, shared with her Jim's letter to me and my reply, then concluded by telling her our pastor thinks it best I no longer teach our class. I concluded my letter by saying, "Carolyn, somehow I think it will be easier on you to have an opportunity to read this and take it all in without having me sitting in front of you waiting for your reaction. Now you can better understand my weight loss and inability to sleep which you have been concerned about.

144

"So far, the only person in our class who knows is Janie. I plan to get in touch with Patsy (our class president) today to see if she is available to talk. Word is seeping out about me so that Dr. Watson is now starting to get some calls. I think at this point I will cut and paste his letter to me. That would be easier than my trying to paraphrase it. (and I did just that--sent Carolyn a copy of Dr. Watson's letter) I then concluded by saying, Carolyn, surely you are sitting down by now! This is a lot to absorb on a Saturday morning--and you are more than welcome to share this with your husband. If you want to talk, give me a call. If you need time to mull this over, that's fine. I understand. Cheyne"

Carolyn replied by 8:30 this morning. "Cheyne, you probably thought that I would be knocked out of my chair when I read your e-mail, but I wasn't. Janie and I have discussed this issue in the past. I, like Dr. Watson, think there is too much 'homophobia' and hurt associated with it. I certainly will be discreet with the information. If I were you, I would not make a public statement about it in the class and would be very careful about who I shared it with. I would hate to see you hurt further by all of this. And I hate the thought of losing you for a teacher. You are such a wonderful teacher, but you need to follow God's direction in that one. You have so much to share with others, and I know how much I gain from all of our classes.

"I must admit that I am still very convoluted in my feelings about homosexuality. I have really wrestled with the Baptist Old Testament doctrine about Sodom and Gomorrah and the wickedness there. I also know that Jesus was the last person to condemn anyone and is most loving and understanding. I am so sorry that you have had so many feelings of depression and wishes for death. I KNOW that is not what God wants. I certainly do not think homosexuality is a sin. People can be involved in unhealthy relationships whether heterosexual or homosexual. I still struggle with the idea of same sex relationships. I don't have any idea if you just didn't want to live a lie anymore or would like to have a life partner. That is totally between you and God. I couldn't and wouldn't pretend to give an opinion on that one. Cheyne, be assured that this does not affect my respect for you or our friendship in any way. I don't know many people who would have had the courage to face the situation head on like you have. I admire you for that. I grieve at the pain you have suffered and just wish there was some way I could help make it better. Thank you for trusting me enough as a friend to share this information with me. Like I said earlier, I honor your privacy in this matter. I would be glad to talk with you any time you need to talk. Carolyn"

My reply: "Carolyn, I appreciate your attitude toward my news. I fully sympathize with your feelings about the verses in the Old Testament. I was raised with those same verses and continue to heap guilt on myself because of them. However, as I read more and more in this area, I am learning there are other ways to look at those verses. For example, in the story of Sodom and Gomorrah, when the men appear at Lot's house demanding to have sex with the visitors (angels), we have always been led to focus on the most startling element of the passage, the homosexual element (although I have always wondered about Lot's offering his virgin daughters to the men!) However, homosexuality is not explicitly identified as the Sodomites' damning vice. On the contrary, this

146

passage suggests their indifference to the rules of hospitality by their intent to commit rape is what angers God.

"I know this sounds strange that 'hospitality' could be the primary sin, but we need to study about society in that day to realize that in ancient times a failure of hospitality was considered a serious transgression."

I continued writing about the minuscule number of selected scripture passages used to condemn homosexuality, refuting their condemnation of a loving, committed, homosexual relationship.

"Carolyn, the only reason I am giving you some of these Biblical passages is to help you come to terms with your ambiguity on this subject. However, let me be the first to admit that I continue to have ambiguity. My study of this subject began several months ago. Before then I wouldn't allow myself to read anything at all on this subject. I have always hidden it within myself--I guess I thought if I didn't read about it or study about it, it might go away. So all this researching on the subject is quite new to me. Cheyne"

This evening I wrote Barbara, "I'm leaning pretty heavily now toward resigning. I'm still working through some details in my mind such as when to do it, what I will do during Sunday School, how to explain my resigning to Mother (and whether I can avoid telling her the truth), and how to explain all this to the class without explaining it!"

Sunday, April 2, 2000

A letter awaited me from Barbara this morning. She wrote it in the wee hours. "If you choose to leave your class for the present, I wouldn't use the term 'resigning.' I'd call it a sabbatical, which I believe is entirely truthful. I'm glad the experience with Carolyn went as well as it did, though I think you will have to carry the conversation initially with most people. You have to recognize that it's tough for people to know what questions to ask--you're talking about sexual identity, and few have had much practice on the topic. Never having discussed it before, they have questions but they don't want to get way too personal and offend you, especially when they have affection and respect for you.

"And I'm glad that the tissue consumption is dropping, if only because (I hope) that more controllable emotions reflect a more serene spirit.

"I don't want you to turn down my class until you've tried it a couple of weeks. You know from what I've told you that I could use the help in there, and you can't know whether you belong without giving it a shot. Love, Barbara"

After reading Barbara's letter, I still had plenty of time to get ready for church, despite the fact that this was a time change Sunday--a loss of an hour last night. I had a terrible time getting to sleep last night, then awoke at 4:30 this morning (3:30 if using yesterday's time.) Handbells are to perform at both the 8:30 and 11 a.m. services, and we are to gather for practice at 7:30 this morning. I need to arrive a little earlier to review my part, which continues to give me difficulty. Still, I had time to "talk aloud" my

Sunday School lesson on the Good Samaritan, discovering that tears keep coming when I get to the end of the lesson which reads: "In the story of the Good Samaritan, the man's sacrificial self-giving love is far beyond duty or even human decency. It is much more than that. It is God-like. It is like Jesus himself. It is like Jesus coming to us without us either knowing about him or deserving his love.

"It is as if each of us lies stricken on the road stripped and half-dead. But then an unexpected stranger comes riding up to us. He binds up our wounds and puts us upon his beast while he himself walks. He takes us to a place of safety and rest--and he has paid for it all in full. And his name is Jesus--and into his hands we place ours."

It is always the sentence *He takes us to a place of safety and rest--and he has paid for it all in full,* that always brings on my tears. The tears come even now as I type this sentence. I so long for that place of safety and rest, long for it with all my heart.

Prior to teaching the lesson, I privately handed our class president, Patsy, a sealed envelope containing copies of Jim's and my letters which "outed" me. I told her to wait until she got home to read what was inside.

Today was a long, tiring, emotionally draining day. The handbells played two pieces at each of the services and my part was very difficult. I play eight different bells and need to concentrate entirely and completely on my part in order to have the right bells in the correct hand at the right time as well as remembering to ring them when I'm supposed to. This morning, however, I endured additional stress knowing members of the congregation (I have no idea how many) have just recently learned I'm gay. My imagination took flight as to what they might be thinking about me. I'm well aware that most people, upon learning someone is homosexual, allow their minds to enjoy a flight of imagination as to what that person does "in bed." We don't tend to think things like that about straight people we meet, but for some reason this is "normal" when one learns someone is gay. Sensing I was "on display" I experienced undue stress as I performed with my handbell choir but was able to keep my emotions intact and kept up with all my bell changes.

J.W. is also in the handbell choir with me. He plays the largest bells whereas I play some of the smallest. After the services, we met at Schlotzsky's for sandwiches. J.W. is easy to talk with, and one of the things that really amazes him is that both Janie and Barbara were able to figure out I was gay. He was baffled at their ability to do that. I just looked at him and said, "J.W., parents are supposed to be perfect." -- meaning that he would never have thought that of his mother.

This evening when I ate supper at church and sat next to Barbara, I shared with her J.W.'s comment. "I really didn't know for certain you were gay, Cheyne. I just knew there was something else that was making you so very unhappy. One of the possibilities that had crossed my mind was that perhaps you had been abused. However, I didn't give much credence to that thought because you are too strong a person to have put up with that."

Between lunch and supper, I did a lot of brooding, thinking, and contemplating my life and the decisions facing me. Patsy (to whom I had given the letter this morning) called me about 4 p.m.

150

I was concerned that she might not call. She was very kind and loving--but shocked, of course. She kept saying that all of us have "sin" in our lives. She said this to comfort me. But as she kept reassuring me that we all have "sin," I kept asking myself what made "just being a homosexual" a sin? She had no concept of whether or not I had ever "acted" upon those desires, and yet she still considered me a sinner simply because I was gay. I don't know how many times she made that statement, but I never threw it back at her in any way. I was just thankful she was so loving and understanding.

She mentioned a class member who was concerned that her statements a week ago on homosexuality might have upset me when she stated that sexual orientation is a choice. I assured Patsy that I was not at all upset with what others believe.

She then brought up the incident at the funeral when she and another class member had been discussing the suicides of two girls. Patsy said, "We noticed the look on your face, and discussed it later."

"Patsy," I said, "I realized that neither of you had any concept of what it is like to want to die--no concept of what those girls probably went through."

"You're right. We don't know."

"They are bound to have experienced unbelievable misery and despair. This you can live with. However, when you hit that wall of hopelessness and end up just hanging by your fingernails, you find it impossible to keep going."

She then stated, "We had a neighbor once whose husband was gay. Several times he tried to commit suicide and no one knew why. Finally, they divorced, and he moved to Dallas. It was in Dallas that he was finally successful in his next suicide attempt."

Patsy continued, "Cheyne, all of us in the class have had difficulties of one kind or another." And she mentioned some that I don't want to reveal publicly. Upon hearing of these revelations, I exclaimed, "That's the problem! We don't share our heartaches with each other so that we can support each other!"

My whole conversation with Patsy was emotionally draining, and yet I was delighted she had taken the time to call. Afterward, although I was terribly depressed and teary-eyed, I decided I really needed to get out of the house and eat supper at the church. The simple meal was delicious: chicken spaghetti with toast and a cheesecake dessert. I continued to get teary-eyed off and on during the service and talked with Barbara afterwards. She could see I was just about to fall apart. She reached over and steadied my hand that was shaking as it held my glass of iced tea.

Later that evening, I wrote an e-mail to my pastor, Dr. Watson. On the subject line, I placed the word "Sabbatical" in quotation marks. I stated, "I am ready to step aside as a Sunday School teacher. I have no desire to cause problems within the church. I am grateful for both your and Barbara's wisdom in this matter and realize this is the best decision. I assume I need to talk with Wilson Rhodes (our education director) about this. Is he informed about what is happening? I will try to make an appointment to visit with him either Monday or Tuesday. Your sister in Christ, Cheyne"

As soon as I sent Bob this e-mail, I copied and sent it to both Janie and Barbara. I wanted them to know that I had decided to resign from my teaching position in the church.

Jim called this evening to discuss details of our financial arrangement. During our conversation I shared with him that I was resigning from teaching my class and mentioned that members of the church are starting to contact Dr. Watson about me. Jim said, "Well, surely they aren't coming in support of you!" I found that a strange comment. Did he want to assure himself that I was being condemned by others? Maybe I took it the wrong way, but I think not. I then explained, "Watson says they are contacting him out of a concern for me. Hold on just a minute and I'll read his letter to you." And at that point I read, "As I mentioned to you, people have called and asked questions about your situation, but they were questions of concern. Yet, even with the questions, there has not been anyone who has even suggested that you leave the church. However, as this becomes more public, I think it would be naive to assume that there won't be a mean statement here or there." I don't recall that Jim commented or had much to say after that.

Monday, April 3, 2000

A letter from Barbara awaited me the following morning. "Cheyne, I note the quotation marks around 'sabbatical,' and understand them to communicate your feeling that leaving Sunday School teaching will be more permanent than that word implies. I trust that your sabbatical will be exactly that: a time to rest following accomplishment, time to evaluate the positive possibilities of your current situation, to plan for the future, to just be with God as you allow people to learn to know you, to see and appreciate you as you truly are. When someone quits work on a permanent basis, it's called retirement. Sabbatical, on the other hand, is a holy pause between two periods of God-directed work. The Lord who directed disciples to pick up baskets of leftover food will never allow your gifts and experience and delight in teaching to be wasted. You just don't know yet who you'll be serving next. You still have decisions and uniquely stressful times ahead of you, and I can testify that it takes much longer to truly unwind than most stressed people recognize.

"I know that you are quite strong enough to have kept on teaching, enduring whatever difficulties you encountered. I also know that it takes an entirely different and rare sort of strength to step aside, and wait for what God has planned for you--you have that kind of strength, too. Right now it may be just enduring, but we're promised 'joy in the morning,' a promise strong enough for you to put your full weight on.

"For some reason, I'm remembering a quotation from an old folk song, Scottish, I think, about Sir Andrew Barton, who says to his comrades after being hurt in battle, "I am a little wounded, but I am not slain. I will lie me down to bleed awhile, then I'll rise to fight again." You know my nature, so you know why such a thing would stick with me. :-) You know your own nature, so you know why I'm reminded of those lines now. I believe your sabbatical can be a healing time for you and for others--and that you'll rise to teach or fight or learn or whatever God has for you again. I do

154

think it will be good for you to 'lie down awhile,' at least until you gain weight and resume sleeping."

Having decided to resign from teaching, I began working on my last Sunday School lesson to my class. I also spent time just sitting and reading Psalms--and crying, keeping the tissue box beside my chair. An icy coldness swept over me, so I put my arms through a sweater and wrapped my legs in a throw blanket. I look out my window onto a cold, dreary day. Normal activities like having to go to the dentist to have my teeth cleaned take place despite the ache in my heart, despite my despondency, despite the unrelenting pain that has lodged itself in my heart.

Good news today. The mail brought me a letter from Michael! I had heard nothing from this son concerning my revelation that I am gay. I anxiously opened the envelope and read: "Dear Mother, I am writing you this note not because I can't or don't want to visit with you personally, but because I need the forum of being able to make my point without the distraction of a 'give & take' discussion.

"I love you because you are the reason I'm on this earth, and because I am reasonably happy with the way I've turned out . . . you and Dad deserve the credit for all my good traits . . . (Let's blame television & peer pressure for my bad traits!)

"If you told me you needed me to stand on my head and sing nursery rhymes in a prison visiting room, I would do it for you. Put simply, any decision or action you take in regards to your 'coming out' is O.K. with me. I support you. Your happiness is more important to me than my own happiness.

"Now, sure, that's a nice thing to say, an uninformed observer might say . . . but a person can't say, 'I support you, Carte Blanc,' without knowing what the request for support concerns, right? Well, I would say to the uninformed observer that I can support my mother, Carte Blanc, because I know my mother . . . she is the most honest person of the highest integrity that walks on this earth.

"This lends me to my second point . . . 'the telling everyone about it' issue. From talking to Dad, he feels that you will 'heal' and be happier if people know this secret. That the pain & the suicidal feelings are a result of keeping this bottled up for over 40 years . . . Here's how I see it: I say hogwash. (And I appreciate the fact that I can say this and I know you won't judge me by it, you will [should] take it as advice and then go ahead & do what you feel is the best course of action.) You are who you are based on what you have said & how you have acted over the course of your life. You are defined by the actions of your children whose greatest role model is the person reading this note. I recognize & agree with the statement that sexuality is a major part of the human experience, but I would argue that it is a paltry standard by which the general public could and should evaluate others . . .

"My point is that people should be judged (as Martin Luther King emphasized) by the content of their character. Frankly, I don't understand the 'catharsis' and the positive benefits on you from sharing this with others. If it is what you want, then I support you. If it is not what you want, then I need to have a talk with Dad, because he is under the opposite impression.

"I love Dad, too, but I feel like he may not be totally objective when it comes to sharing his wife's secret. After all, you have just provided him with complete abdication for any role he may have played in his failed marriage.

"He and I have talked about this and we both agree to do what you want.

"In closing, I hope the next time you are feeling depressed you will think about me and how much I love you. Michael."

What a wonderful letter, from a wonderful son. I rejoiced in his words of love and acceptance. However, my elation was short-lived as I then received an e-mail from Gwen Patterson of the Christian Women's Job Corps. Her letter was quite long, four pages of single-spaced typing, and ended with these paragraphs: "Cheyne, I want you to know that I miss you. I love you in the Lord as a sister. I know that you are going through much pain and suffering, and probably have more to come. I hurt for you and cry for your choice. But know this, I still do not reject you, only the choice you are making. I am praying for you . . . I am praying that the Lord will hedge you in and grant you repentance that will lead to a knowledge of the truth, and that you will come to your senses and escape from the trap of the devil, who has taken you captive to do his will (2 Timothy 2:25b-26).

"I would urge you to seek counsel with those who have won the victory over the temptations of homosexuality. When you are ready, there will be help available in caring brothers and sisters in Christ. Yours in Christ Jesus, Gwen Patterson"

I kept seeing her words "escape from the trap of the devil!" Little did she realize that's exactly what I did when I became honest with myself about who and what I am. The devil no longer has a hold on me, infusing me with fear, with shame, with guilt. I'm free-- body and soul--I'm free. Free to be the person God created me to be. Free to live my life in the way He ordains. Free, wonderfully free! Delightfully free!

Tuesday, April 4, 2000

When I awoke this morning about 3:30, I decided to just go ahead and get up. I immediately sat down at my computer and wrote Barbara, updating her with copies of Gwen's letter, Michael's letter, my reply to Dr. Watson, my phone visit with Patsy, my concern about becoming emotional when I teach my "last" lesson on Sunday, and ended by saying, "I would love to be able to give that lesson without all the tenseness and 'being on edge' that has become my trademark lately. Know of anyone who would give me a tranquilizer to use that morning? I'm serious.

"The court hearing for the divorce is scheduled for 8:15 next Tuesday morning, April 11th. Just one more step along this road I'm on."

Before 8 a.m., I wrote to my brother, Tom, (who's almost two years younger than I). Both my brothers are over six feet tall. I'm the shorty in my family. Tom pretty much marches to his own drumbeat and is a professional photographer. I used e-mail to out myself to him and caught him up on my present life.

Not long after hitting the "Send" button on the computer, Janie called! Hallelujah! We talked for over an hour and a half.

As always, she was very supportive and quite upset that I am leaving the class. She said her husband, Charles, just couldn't believe that I would be asked to leave. I think I was able to explain it to her in such a way that she will accept the decision without being outspoken about it. I don't know what I would do without her. She's so good to me. So loving and supportive. So encouraging. She builds me up constantly. "You're the very best Sunday School teacher in the whole world!" kind of building up. I was so "down" yesterday because she had not called me. Then she calls this morning and I'm floating on air!

Barbara wrote to me mid-morning and said, "I am so glad to have your e-mail, though I wish you'd been asleep at 4:25 a.m.! Wondered where you were and what you were doing yesterday, but don't want you to feel that I am dogging your every step. Yesterday was such a gray day--I hoped it wasn't impacting you negatively.

"I am so glad you heard from Michael, and that it was a loving letter. You told me that he'd be okay when he'd had time to think about it, and you were right. He's right about the basis for responding to people, too. In talking about another matter some time ago, my Lewisville sister said, 'I'm totally out of the judgment business. I've learned that I never know enough to be fair.' I decided that she's right. I will say that there are some people I avoid because I've noticed they have a negative effect on me, and it's interesting to try to figure out why that is. Occasionally I conclude it's something about them, more often I discover something still judgmental or just plain ugly about me. I'm working on it.

"Consider whether one thing Bob might have had in mind when he told you to think about what you'd say to people was exactly this--the distinction between who you are and what you do. You'll have to figure that out. Maybe some reference to a 37-year marriage in which you were always faithful, and the absence of any relationship now?

"Obviously, there are things to think about beyond this--but I believe there's a darn good reason God gives us only one day at a time, a concept that moved beyond intellectual for me when Mother was in the hospital. It's marked in my Bible, in fact, including place and date. 'Therefore, do not worry about tomorrow, for tomorrow will worry about itself. Each day has enough trouble of its own.' (Matthew 6:34) Pretty pragmatic, isn't it? Even more so from Eugene Peterson's translation: 'Give your entire attention to what God is doing right now, and don't get worked up about what may or may not happen tomorrow. God will help you deal with whatever hard things come up when the time comes.' The obvious corollary is, 'God doesn't give that much help today for what won't happen until tomorrow.'

"Though I've often noticed that when you get to tomorrow, you notice that he long ago placed resources there to help you, resources you never paid particular attention to before.

"As to Jim, I think he's being pulled between the compassionate side of his nature (which he does have, even though up until now he's limited who he'd feel compassion for) and attitudes he acquired growing up. He's loved you (or who he believed you to be) for decades, cared about what happened to you. It would be tough to quit that. At the same time, what you

160

learn in your early years can be hard to shuck off, and I think Michael has it down pretty well. (I also think it's possible that Jim will ultimately get to the place where he sees this, too.) Meanwhile, maybe discovering how many people do support you may help him see more clearly the extent of God's grace.

"I've talked with my neighbor (and one of your class members), Beth, about you and found her as I knew she would be. You'll not find her to be any different than she's always been, though she grieves to know what you're going through.

"I have talked to Brad and Joan Albritton. I went to visit Joan yesterday subsequent to her mastectomy. She's doing fantastically well, by the way. Sometime Sunday night I began thinking that so far as I knew, they didn't know about your situation, but that Brad is Jim's Sunday school teacher and Joan teaches your mother's class. Also, I know them to be mature believers, and wise. So I went to visit Joan thinking that if the way opened, I'd talk to her and let her tell Brad. It was as if the path were blazed so clearly that I couldn't have missed it, so I did talk to her.

"I had Joan read those first two e-mails you and Jim wrote to each other, since they are so clear and since I knew Jim had given them to the Graysons to read. Tears came to Joan's eyes as she realized your pain, and we talked a long while. Then, as it happened, Brad came home early to check on her, so I had him read the e-mails; and he, too, is as supportive as anyone could be. I told him what Bob had suggested about your stepping away from your class, and he totally agreed with that, saying that 'you just need to let people stew awhile when they're faced with something new, and then most of them will come to understand what's right.'

161

(Brad said he'd thought that perhaps you wanted the divorce because you had things you wanted to accomplish on your own professionally, since you're such a bright, well-educated, hard-working woman. Joan and I laughed, pointing out that you'd always worked and had written two books while you were working and married.) So there's that. I hope you feel better knowing that, as people begin to hear, there are people who care about you and respect you and honor your desire to live your life centered in God's will as he reveals it to you.

"You asked about a tranquilizer for next Sunday. I think you need to call your doctor for an appointment today. Make clear that you need to see him ASAP. Tell him briefly what's happening in your life--the divorce, your revealing your sexual identity to Jim and your children, as well as telling your friends about it, etc. Tell him how much weight you've lost (which, if he's anything like my doctor, he'll already know about, since you have to weigh in if all you want is a splinter removed--only a slight exaggeration!) and how little you're sleeping. Ask him for a mild tranquilizer to get you through the next few weeks--like a month or so. I emphasize calling today because it takes some time for many medications to really work. I suggest 'mild' because I don't think you want anything that will make you groggy--as most antihistamines do me. The only thing I've ever taken is a few Valium from time to time. I've been to the gym this morning, so feel very righteous. Now I am going to eat a boringly healthy breakfast and work on my Sunday School lesson-- so I expect to be home all day. Come by if you want to--and keep those updates coming! Love, Barbara"

162

Janie and I had a good visit today, a very open conversation in which she again shared with me her desire that I find someone special with whom to spend my life--someone to meet not only my emotional needs, but my physical needs as well. She said, "One of the things in Mel White's book, *Stranger at the Gate,* that was a new thought to me was when he explained the need to just have someone to snuggle up next to--that the need for sex is not nearly as overpowering a need as the need to just **be** with someone." Whenever Janie gets on subjects like this, of wanting me to find someone special, I find myself unable to speak. I remain quiet, and just let her talk. Otherwise I might blurt out the truth--that she's the only person I want--and I want her so terribly.

"Cheyne, even though I won't be in town this weekend, I'll drive back on Saturday night so that I can be in Sunday School Sunday. I want to be there to support you when you teach your last lesson to us."

I'm so thankful to know she will be there. The rest of our conversation is described in the following letter which I wrote to Barbara at noon: "I'm glad you talked with Brad and Joan and with your neighbor, Beth. I continue to be amazed at the positive acceptance from people--and very thankful.

"I'm feeling so much better today than I have prior to the weekend events. I've been on the phone with Janie for literally hours this morning. I told her about my conversation with Wilson Rhodes (the church's education director) which I haven't yet related to you.

"He called me as I've been trying to make an appointment with him through his secretary. I immediately asked him, 'Has Bob told you what is going on?'

"Yes, he has spoken with me. He didn't tell me any details of your conversation with him, just the bare essentials. I think you are doing the right thing, Cheyne. It's my personal belief that when a teacher has personal issues that become so great this person needs time to heal and work things out that they should step back from their teaching. I almost called you in when I heard of the divorce. I think getting a divorce is reason enough for you to step out of your teaching position."

"This coming Sunday will be my last Sunday to teach. I've already arranged for a substitute for the following Sunday (April 16th) when I will be taking my Mother to see her friends in Little Rock that weekend."

"I told Wilson that I had not told my departmental directors that I would be leaving and that I rather dreaded doing that. He said I need to tell them, but to just say that because of the stress I am under I need to step away from my teaching job for awhile."

Several hours later, Barbara's reply arrived: "Well good, you've touched base with Wilson. Does it seem just the tiniest bit providential that you'd already made plans to take your mother to Little Rock the next weekend? Sometimes I don't know what is coincidence and what is Providence--but I think I err on the side of coincidence, and I'm trying to quit doing that."

Barbara then took time in her letter to talk about my various choices of classes to attend and some of the members in each class--one whom she feels has a gay son who lives in Dallas.

164

Then she continued, "I did specifically tell Joan Albritton that your mother didn't know, and she instantly said, 'Does she have to know?' I told her that you'd hoped not to have to tell her, but given the way news gets around, you might have to tell her at some point in time. She said what I'd said early on--with the age of that group and your mother's deafness, it's unlikely she'd ever hear a rumor. But who knows. Again, that's your decision. I wouldn't think you'd have to even tell your mother right away that you're not teaching your class, unless you want to. I don't think that comes up in conversation too often, either. Whatever.

"Please read again my emphatic suggestion that you call your doctor. This has little to do with Sunday, so far as I am concerned, and everything to do with your self. You'll make your best decisions when you're less tense--and if you weren't tense, you'd be eating and sleeping. I do not suggest a long-term thing-- but I surely do suggest short-term help. In the same sense that you take aspirin or Tylenol for a headache, though you know you could endure it and outlast the pain, you just function better over a long period when you have help with the tension. The stress is very real, not just 'something in your mind.' It's in your body, too.

"I'm glad you're having a better day. (Sunshine helps, I think.) Barbara"

Less than an hour after receiving Barbara's letter, another letter arrived--from my brother, Tom, who told me, "Your letter made me smile. I didn't even have to be sitting down to read it, because the only part of it that was a big surprise was that you were speaking up and speaking out. Congratulations.

"Mom has never talked to me in any depth about you. Back when you roomed with Karen, she said a couple of things that indicated she was worried, and I know she wanted you and Karen to separate. I acted like it was no big deal even though I secretly thought the two of you were in love. Whatever she thought, she kept between her and Dad.

"I don't have any advice about talking to Mom. Our family (and South Texas culture) was so hung-up about sex, that even though Mom has become more tolerant, she still has a way to go, as far as accepting people without prejudice. Don't let the bottomless pits pull on you. It must be quite a shock to do what you are doing. I don't think I would ever have that kind of nerve.

"Your confidences are safe with me. I wish you the best. As always, Tom"

After reading both Barbara's and Tom's letters, I decided to take Barbara's advice and drove to my doctor's office--to be worked into his schedule. This meant a two-hour wait. I took with me a mystery novel, to help pass the time, but my mind just wouldn't concentrate on the story. Very unusual for me. Books have always been my escape--leaving my life behind in the shadows. Thoughts of Janie kept coming to my mind--the kind of thoughts that I shouldn't have. My imagination took flight as I waited for the doctor.

When Dr. Morris finally entered the examination room, I quickly said, "I know you're running late, so let me make it quick. I'm losing weight and now weigh less than I did when I was in college. I'm not sleeping well and awakening about 3:30 every morning. I think Jim told you we are divorcing, but that's not what

166

is causing the stress. Actually, the divorce is helping me. What is really causing the stress in my life is the fact that I'm gay and am now telling my family and friends about it. Also I have been asked to give up teaching my adult women's Sunday School class." By then, tears were welling up in my eyes, and I was fighting the urge to break down and bawl. I continued, "I just need something to get me through this next Sunday when I will be teaching my last Sunday School lesson." Dr. Morris told me about several available medications, but decided the best one for me at this time would be Xanax because it takes effect quicker than the others. Time was important in my case.

Dr. Morris is a talker. He enjoys visiting, and although it was after 5:30 p.m., he sat down and began visiting with me, telling me about his numerous brothers and sisters and that the problem of being gay is not completely new to his family. "I have a younger sister," he explained, "who adopted two girls. One of these girls decided to be gay." When he said "decided to be gay," my hackles began to rise. No fool would "decide" to be gay! But I kept quiet and listened. Yet what he said next made me even angrier. He said, "She is still welcomed into the family. She was even invited to one of the family weddings." Even invited! The nerve! Why wouldn't she be invited? But I didn't voice these thoughts. Just kept quiet. Over and over he talked about how this girl had *decided* to be gay.

Finally, I could take it no longer and stated, "This is not a decision!"

He took my comment nicely and agreed that it probably wasn't--that it was a bad choice of words. He said the latest research indicates that homosexuality is connected to hormones!

Then as he walked out of the room to write up the prescription, he turned to me and asked, "What church do you attend?"

"First Baptist," I replied. "Thank goodness I don't go to Green Acres Baptist!" (Green Acres is the largest Baptist church in Tyler and is very fundamentalist/conservative.)

He then started laughing, really laughing, then assured me, "I'm not laughing at you. I'm laughing with you."

The nurse phoned in the prescription, I left, and headed straight for the pharmacy.

Wednesday, April 5, 2000

Last night I took my first Xanax. When I awoke in the morning, a little after 3 a.m., I took another pill. It worked. I slept until 7:15! Unbelievable!

Tom, my brother, wrote me an e-mail early this morning. I read, "Dear Cheyne, I think you are right not to talk with Mom. If it becomes a necessity someday, then you can. But it's possible it will never be an issue. Now here are the thoughts I didn't have time to write yesterday. Yesterday I wanted to answer your direct questions and let you know you have my support whatever you choose to do. Today I want to reiterate my support, but also add some cautionary statements.

"Before the cautions, here's a thought: when we were growing up, there was great emphasis in our lives about being reliable, moral, proper, friendly, dutiful, etc., etc. But we were not often urged to HAVE FUN. From the tone of your letter, it sounds like right now you don't have any way to HAVE FUN. That should be your top priority for the next 5 to 10 years. First you have to learn what is fun for you, then learn how to get it or create it or set it up, and then you spend several years actually practicing it until it becomes a natural part of your life.

"I have some concern about your actions that are related to speed--it seems as if you are trying to do too much too fast. Since you've been patient for forty years, why hurry your changes? For health reasons, it is best, according to psychologists, to minimize the impact of life changes. For example, if there is a death in the family, one should probably postpone a planned surgery. If you're getting a divorce, see if there's a way to postpone changing jobs or careers. If you've just gotten married, it's best to delay moving to a new city. Body and psyche can absorb only so much at a time so that even if one plans to do a dozen things, do them one at a time with time-out space in between them.

"One way to look at it is that each big change adds a certain degree of stress to your life. The idea is to make changes without overloading oneself. In the past 12 months or less, I think you have retired from your career of teaching in the alternative high school, filed for divorce, moved to a new place, and come out with a new sexual identity. (Tom then mentioned several other matters involving stressful crusades I became involved in that required appearances in court.) If you feel depressed or stressed, then look twice at all that activity as a huge pile of triggering mechanisms, with no space between them. You asked for a little advice from me, but I'm giving you all I've got. Whoa. Take it easy. Take a vacation. Meet someone you feel like loving. Lighten up. Postpone all crusades and further changes. There'll be time for that later. Now's the time to treat yourself tenderly and lovingly and quietly and gingerly. Be especially easy on yourself, and see if you can discard all thoughts that require anything of yourself beyond just being aware that you exist in a world that is always magically new.

"I can't be clearer: I'm suggesting you don't need to do everything at once. Especially I hope you reconsider your determination to change other people. That's what upsets you and me so much about Mother--she demands that others be what she approves of, and she demands that they accept her opinions. So it seems you may have a hard time keeping yourself from imitating her in that way--not with your own family perhaps, but with the church you attend. You wrote: 'I do plan to stay very active in the church. People there know me and I can't think of a better place to start changing attitudes on this most misunderstood condition.'

"I'm not being flippant when I say forget their attitudes; leave them alone. Instead, go explore the feelings of affection you've kept bottled up for so long. Talk to other women who AGREE with you rather than with those who disagree with you. Find a gay and lesbian support group in Tyler or Longview or Dallas, and attend their meetings for a while. Skip church, and go elsewhere some weeks. Concentrate on developing one or two close personal friendships. It doesn't mean you'll have sex, but it does mean you'll be putting your time and energy into exploring yourself rather than into combating or converting others.

"'So I am already going through some very, very difficult times as I talk with others, and have not even yet faced the prejudicial hatred that will come.' That's something else you wrote, which is your own prediction of what lies ahead for you. Hey, you can very carefully choose who you talk to. If you were shooting rapids down a canyon river (which, incidentally, you are!), and you could see a huge standing hydraulic turbulence, wouldn't you steer around it, rather than into it? And can't you apply that same wisdom socially? The very thought takes me back to hippie days when the question was: Would you rather fight or make love? Which is better for you personally? Which sets a better example for humankind?

"It's not your job to lead others, and it's not their job to help you. It's your job to save yourself. The first step in that direction is to get help. Find women who have already been where you are, and let them guide you. Tell them your story, and then listen to theirs."

Tom then provided numerous web sites and phone numbers for organizations such as PFLAG, SPROUTS, TWIGS, GLAAD, along with Dallas's suicide and crisis center and another Dallas group which promotes the validity of same sex couples. (PFLAG stands for Parents, Families and Friends of Lesbians and Gays. SPROUTS is a group of women who are questioning their sexuality. TWIGS is a group of women in Gay Society. GLAAD is the Gay and Lesbian Alliance Against Defamation.)

"O.K. I've spoken my piece. My hunch is that as soon as you find another woman or two with whom you can openly share, the suicide thoughts and terrible sadness will evaporate, and you will have a chance at the happiness that eluded you while you were trying to live a life molded for you by others.

"My love and best wishes go with you, sister. Tom"

His letter brought the tears. I forwarded his words to Barbara, then cried and cried for hours without stopping. Not only did I experience Tom's love and concern, but his wisdom overwhelmed me. He knew exactly what he was talking about.

During this period of crying, a letter arrived from Barbara informing me about Xanax--what it is, how it should be taken, possible side effects and dangers, recommended dosage, and where to go on the Internet to learn more. Following the Xanax information, she said, "I know you feel warmly hugged after those wonderful letters from your brother. I'm sure it has occurred to you that some of the stories he has shared with you (which I chose not to record in my journal) confirm the theory that a person's sexual identity is genetic, or at least present at birth.

"And I think your brother is exactly right about the pace of what's been happening in your life. Does 'one day at a time' have a familiar ring? :-) And I think he's exactly right about being good to yourself, having fun, taking a vacation.

"In the light of his own advice, I think you need to let some time pass before you even consider 'finding someone to love,' assuming (as I do) that he means a life partner. Just take it easy with yourself. Rest in the company of the family members and friends who accept you for the wonderful person you are. Read

172

stuff for fun, as well as read stuff for information (which I'm pretty certain you're doing). Read your Bible in a new-to-you translation so you can really hear the sense of it, let God's love wash over you and overwhelm you.

"He's exactly right about your ability to choose carefully who you talk to. Of course, you have fewer options now that you've talked to some of your class members, but I'm waiting to see how many (if any) people will bring the subject up to you voluntarily for any reason other than support.

"He's right that there's a ton of stuff on the Internet. I'd already found a lot of it, and assumed that you'd done the same. One site (if memory serves, and it may not) is www.truluck.com which contains his story and a ton of Bible commentary. He's a former Baptist preacher who went to Baptist seminaries, taught in a Baptist college, etc. See you tonight at the prayer service? Barbara"

After agonizing about my reply to Tom, I sent him the following letter at 11 a.m.:

"I know this is a bad time for me to write to you as I have been in the depths of depression for the past 24 hours, . . . part of the sadness comes from the truth that appeared in your kind, insightful letters. Just to know that you perceived the love that Karen and I felt for each other overwhelmed me.

"You are right. I never learned how to have fun. Karen and I had fun. But behind that fun was the ever-present awareness that society and parents prohibited our relationship from being permanent. That knowledge of impending finality propelled us toward savoring every moment we had together as if it were our last--and sure enough that day came sooner than we anticipated.

"After we separated, fun went out of my life, joy went out of my life, friendship went out of my life, and love went out of my life, and, as you so aptly put it, I began to live a life molded for me by others. I became a shell of a person, a person I eventually came to hate. I spent my life distancing myself from ever forming a close friendship with a female for fear of what might happen to me. And I know now that was a most wise decision on my part because I have fallen hopelessly, desperately in love with my friend, Janie, who is heterosexual and has no idea what I feel toward her. It's killing me and I have got to get over this. I am in the depths of an emotional turmoil that I have never before faced in all my life.

"I have contacted a local chapter of PFLAG and have been given their meeting date, time, and location. I plan to go. It's going to be tough, but I have never in my life had an opportunity to talk with someone who has endured the kind of life I have endured. I know I need to do this.

"I appreciate the references you sent. I have spent my whole life in denial, never even reading about homosexuality. Even now I have read only two books on the subject. I believed if I ignored the subject it would go away. Now I know differently.

"Dear, dear brother, thank you so much. Cheyne."

Mid-afternoon, a letter arrived from my daughter, Anne, who wrote, " . . . I think about you all the time and hope you are doing all right. Just remember that there are lots of people who love and care about you (me being #1). You are doing the right thing - which is not always easy. I love you and cannot wait till you come to Lubbock before graduation and we can pack up my belongings together! Anne"

After spending this afternoon at Mother's, I arrived at church in time for the evening meal prior to the service. I sat at a table with Barbara and her husband and two other couples. When I got up to refill my iced tea, Carl Atkins, one of the men seated there who is about my age, asked me, "How are you liking retirement?"

My thoughts the past few days have been on such weightier matters that I actually laughed at him and said, "That's the funniest question I have heard in a long time," and walked away to fill my glass.

I realized later that Barbara tried to cover up for my rudeness by saying, "Cheyne's going through some really tough times right now."

He then commented, "She made her bed, and now she has to lie in it."

During this exchange, the others at our table had already left to work with various children's choirs. Barbara, Jack (her husband), and Carl were the only ones left at the table. Barbara told me later that Carl's comment upset her husband so much that he told Carl what was going on in my life. In other words, he "outed me." As Barbara related this to me, she said, "Actually, Carl seemed to take it quite well and seemed sympathetic. But while we were still at the table, I lit in on my husband for blabbing and told Carl that this information needed to be kept confidential--that Jack shouldn't have said anything about this."

Carl retorted, "I have to tell my wife, of course."

According to Barbara, she must have really climbed all over her husband for talking about me. Strange, it didn't bother me at all that the truth was being told. I told her not to worry about it, and to assure her husband that I was not at all upset with him. After all, I figure it will eventually all come out anyway. What's one more person knowing about it?

When I returned from church, a letter from my brother, Tom, awaited me in which he urged me to get a substitute to teach my Sunday School class: "You don't owe anyone any explanation. And you don't need anyone else's approval for being who you are. But to do this, you have to be beyond the crying state, and you've written that you're still there. Don't fight it, let it last as long as it wants to, for it is a process that releases old blocked emotions. You will eventually get to the point where your tears turn to smiles and laughter.

"Then again, maybe the Xanax will kick the weepiness out of you immediately, and you can handle everything with equilibrium. Personally, I would opt out of Sunday School ahead of time, let someone else take over, go for a walk in the woods on Sunday morning (if it's not STORMY!), and let events take their own course.

"Now I've got to quit offering advice. Once again, I congratulate you for being willing to be in touch with all of yourself. There have been times when I wondered what happened to that tough little sister I used to play with--the one who rode pretend wild horses and shot pretend cowboy villains and who often demonstrated that her biceps were bigger than mine. Now I have every confidence that she has survived and will be part of your life again. More power to you . . . Tom"

Later, Janie called and we talked a full two hours, until after midnight. Talking with her is so refreshing. We talked about her plans to travel to Austin the next day, her experience of falling in love almost instantaneously with her husband, Charles, and her yearnings for time to call her own. After finally hanging up the phone, I called Anne who was still awake.

"What in the world were you doing on the phone all this time?" she asked.

"Talking with Janie," I replied.

"You sound so much better tonight, Mother. I bet it has to do with your talking to Janie."

"Yes, I'm sure that's the reason. I so enjoy talking with her."

Thursday, April 6, 2000

After hanging up the phone, I wrote the following note to Barbara (12:15 a.m.). "I just got off the phone with Anne who leaves early this morning for New York. She told me her dad calls often to tell her 'everything.' One of the things he told her was that Gwen Patterson from the Christian Women's Job Corps called him recently and talked for over an hour. She talked about me and how wrong I was in my choice and how she was praying for me and how she felt I would come to my senses and return to him because the Bible is quite clear that I am doing wrong. Jim finally got fed up with it all and told her that if she believed everything that was in the Bible then she would know that women are never to speak up in church! I can't help but be proud of him for that answer.

"Jim and I are starting to have some disagreements on some of the financial arrangements, but I think we can work through these in an amicable way. At least I hope so. If Jim and I keep finding things about finances that 'bother us,' we may not end up in court on Tuesday to finalize the divorce!

"I'd enjoy a visit tomorrow, but will call first as I have no idea how tomorrow is going to go around here. Cheyne"

Friday, April 7, 2000

I read a note from Carolyn, written at 1 a.m., saying that even though she will be in Waco on Saturday, she planned to make a point of being in Sunday School this Sunday as this would be my last Sunday as their teacher. I learned "after the fact" that she had to make an extremely late drive in order to be here.

My conscience was bothering me about the flippant, rude remark I made to Carl Atkins Wednesday night. At 10:30 a.m., I sent him an e-mail, saying, "I have no problem with what Jack Lawrence told you Wednesday night. I know Barbara jumped down his throat for what he revealed, but I hope he also knows by now that I'm O.K. with this. It's just that when you asked me how retirement was going, that kind of thought had been so far from my mind for such a long time that I reacted in the wrong way. I'm sorry. I shouldn't have been so catty about it. And I apologize."

Sunday, April 9, 2000

I awoke at 5 a.m., earlier than I have been awakening, despite the fact I took a Xanax pill. The early arising gave me ample time for showering, washing my hair, dressing, eating, and going over my Sunday School lesson. I went over and over it aloud until I felt capable of getting through it. However, my emotions were definitely on edge as tears were ready to fall every time I went over the lesson. I knew I was in trouble. I kept reminding myself, "Just 'read' the lesson without trying to ad lib. I'll be a whole lot better off if I read it without really thinking. Just read the words. This will be much safer."

So I practiced this method of reading without thinking, but it didn't work. The tears still came. I was determined, however, to deliver this last lesson. I had worked hard on it, felt it was well prepared, and I wanted to teach it.

I attended the 8:30 a.m. worship service and even then occasionally fought back tears. My emotions were already out of control as I headed for my class. The lesson was from Luke 13:10-17 and was titled, "What's More Important--Rules or People?" Although this was an assigned lesson for me to teach, it was a very fitting lesson for my situation. I explained to the class that Jesus was a great teacher because He forced people to think. This angered others, especially the ruler of the synagogue.

As I spoke, I did just fine with the exposition on the Biblical passage. I then switched gears, and entered into a different phase of the lesson. I said, "I began this lesson talking about Jesus being a great teacher, and one of the attributes of a great teacher is to enable the student to find inner direction. A great teacher helps you find your own goal. Your goals are no longer determined by those around you. You begin to march to a different drummer. You find a whole new direction from God. Many of us are guilty of radar living. Our radar is out picking up moods. We're other-directed. We try to fit in, make it, be right with the crowd."

I don't recall where I gleaned some of these thoughts, but most of my lessons pulled in writings from many different sources. The only original portion of my lessons is the way I "splice together" all I gather. I continued, "Jesus refused to be other-directed. When He is warned that King Herod is out to get Him (this is in Luke chapter 13, verse 31), He replies that that sly fox is not going to set His agenda. He is going to continue to minister for the next three days and beyond, with no change of plan.

"It seems to me there are two ways that those who are other-directed can be trapped. They can be trapped in trying to please others, or they can be trapped by a stubborn determination to rebel against any and all suggestions or directions. To be inner-directed means that our agenda is dictated by the inner voice, the 'still, small voice' of which the Bible speaks in I Kings 19:12.

"Robert Louis Stevenson wrote, 'To know what you prefer instead of humbly saying, *Amen* to what the world tells you you ought to prefer, is to have kept your soul alive.' That's what Jesus demonstrates for us toward the end of this chapter. We have kept our soul alive when we are inner-directed through the voice of the Holy Spirit."

It was somewhere in this part of the lesson that I began to lose control. My voice began to break, and tears sprung to my eyes. I finally just had to stop. At that point I explained to the class, "I really thought I could do this, but I'm not certain I can."

Someone in the class said, "Just give it a few minutes."

I did, but time wasn't helping me gain control. Janie then said, "I'm going to pull my chair over next to Cheyne. Carolyn, you pull your chair up on the other side, and the rest of you pull up close. Let's just surround Cheyne and let her know how much we care for her."

And that's what everyone did as they waited silently until I was able to continue speaking. Even so, as I continued reading, I periodically had to stop to gain control of myself. I said, "I'm not going to sit here in front of you and say that I'm being inner directed by the Holy Spirit to make a change in my life, but I'm also not going to say that this isn't true. Time will tell. But I think I can honestly say that I am taking a route with my life in tune with what Robert Louis Stevenson wrote. In other words, I'm keeping my soul alive by knowing what I prefer in opposition to what the world tells me I ought to prefer.

"I'm making some changes in my life and these changes remind me of a story I recently read which illustrates in a very vivid way what seems to be happening to me. (I adapted the following story from the one told on March 26, 2000, by Mrs. Martha Edwards to her congregation of Park Cities Baptist Church, Dallas, Texas, and shared by its pastor, Dr. James C. Denison in his daily web devotions.) Let's say that the life I thought I was going to lead is similar to planning to take a journey, a journey to--let me just say 'France' because the actual destination is insignificant. I've prepared all my life to go to France. I've packed the right things. I've learned to speak French. I've even learned to cook French food. I've studied French art. I know all about France. And I can't wait to get there. I plan to take France by storm. I'm ready. And I get on the plane, and start for France.

"And right before I land, the pilot says, 'Welcome to Germany.' And I say, 'Oh, my.' And I panic and run up the aisle and I say to the pilot, 'You've made a mistake, I'm not going to Germany, I'm going to France. I'm all ready. I'm packed. It's going to be perfect. Everyone is waiting for me there.'

"And the pilot smiles and says, 'But we are going to Germany. Let's see what you think.' And I reluctantly go back to my seat. And I get my bags, lots of bags that were packed perfectly because I have planned for this all of my life. I have just the right things, and I will look great.

"And the pilot says, 'You don't need all of those bags. I've got other bags for you. I have already packed them. I have prepared them. They are much lighter than those. And they are filled with gifts. And you say, 'Oh, you have presents for me.' And he says, 'These are presents we are going to give away. They are gifts of acceptance and joy and love. The baggage will be very light.'

"I deplane to find a tandem bike waiting for me. And the pilot says, 'You take the front seat, I will just hop on the back.' I get on the front seat and I start to pedal in circles. And I realize all the maps for France are in the bags. I knew all about France. I don't know anything about Germany. And I realize I can't do this. And the pilot smiles and he says, 'Would you like to trade places? I'll lead us.'

"So I get on the back seat. And he begins to show me Germany. And it's beautiful. And I begin to learn the German language, and I begin to meet the German people. I see Bavaria. I realize, 'I never knew all of this was here. This is wonderful.' I start to give the gifts away, and I start to receive many gifts in return. I even teach English to some of the German children there. And quite often I run into people who are busily coming and going from France. And they say, 'It's a wonderful place.' And I say, 'Yes, I know. I was supposed to go there. I had it planned all along. But my pilot had a different journey for me. And my pilot took me to a different place. And it's beautiful, too.'"

The tears came again, and in a few minutes, I finished up the lesson with: "You see, I had planned to teach you ladies for years. I really enjoy teaching this class. I look forward to each and every Sunday. I thought this was what I was supposed to do. But I know now that it isn't what I am supposed to do, and I am being led in a totally different direction. I'm hoping that some time in the future I can 'leave Germany and come back to France,' but I don't know if that will ever be possible. So I will be stepping down as your teacher after today. You will have a substitute next week, and I have pleaded with Wilson Rhodes to find you a permanent teacher very soon. I will keep reminding him of this need, but you need to keep reminding him also.

"I read a 'sermon' this past week delivered by a Canadian pastor that may help explain some of the changes taking place in my life. He described two ways I can talk to you. I can speak to you as a group, laying out concepts drawn from scripture and hope and pray that you latch onto them and apply them in your own situations. But the other way I can talk to you is one on one. I could speak to you individually so that I would not need to talk in generalities as I would to a group. Speaking one on one is much more risky than speaking in great sweeping statements. Speaking one on one involves relationships and trust and honesty. You can't hide in face to face; soul to soul communication.

"I think Jesus knew this all too well. In today's gospel story, Jesus was in the synagogue teaching a bunch of people. Then suddenly there appears a woman, and Jesus stops his sermon teaching and calls this woman over to him. A group message just became personal. That's the way Jesus works best: one on one, face to face, soul to soul. Only then does He have our full attention. And I think the lessons I will be sharing in the future will be one-on-one lessons instead of group lessons. That seems to be where I am being led."

We ended the class in our usual way, by all standing in a circle, joining hands, bowing our heads and reciting together, "May the Lord watch between me and thee while we are absent one from the other." Afterwards, each member hugged me and told me how much they loved and appreciated me. Finally, the only ones left in the room with me were Janie and Carolyn. Then Carolyn's husband walked in and joined us. All three gave me a pep talk, and Carolyn's husband said, "You shouldn't resign, Cheyne. You really shouldn't."

"I must. You know I must," I replied.

"No," he said. "I don't think you should. I don't think you should at all." Janie then joined him by saying, "My husband said he doesn't think she should resign either. He thinks it's just awful she's been asked to quit."

Although their affirmations were kind and encouraging, my nerves were taut. I knew the resignation was necessary, and I felt this was one of those occasions when the longer it is drawn out the more difficult it becomes. Carolyn and her husband asked me to join them for lunch at a Chinese buffet. I dearly love Chinese food, but I had no appetite. I didn't want them to waste money on a buffet meal that I couldn't eat. I therefore declined their kind offer. When I did, Carolyn promised to come by this afternoon to visit with me.

Later in the day, after returning from a walk, my heart leaped joyfully upon hearing Janie's voice on my answering machine: "Hello, Cheyne. It's Janie. I'm just calling to say hello and that I love you and that I have had two calls from Sunday School class members today and one I think had no clue as to why you resigned from the position of teaching and one I think knew exactly. The one who knew exactly said, 'We're going to Germany together.' So anyway I wanted you to know that everybody loves you and are very distressed that you have left. You just wouldn't believe all the positive things class members have said about you. You need to know this. These wonderful and understanding ladies love you. I just wanted to pass that message on to you. I love you, girl. Bye."

Carolyn came over later to visit, and we had a good long, open talk. Afterwards, we went to Paco's for Mexican food. I amazed her with how much I ate! I do enjoy Mexican food! I also enjoyed being with Carolyn.

This evening a letter arrived from Barbara: "Cheyne, I read your report of this morning's class. You did a terrific job. I'm sure you've noticed, as I have over the years, how words and ideas and thoughts and reports of pilgrimage experiences come to you at exactly the time you need them, which seems to be the case here. You took Martha's words of testimony and made them uniquely your own; and I do believe that God will show you Germany, that you'll love being there, and that you'll find others who've been God-directed to Germany. One of my favorite Bible passages is the story of Elijah's running away from Jezebel, and from the desert, and reporting to God that 'I am the only one left who serves you, and now they're trying to kill me, too.' God didn't bother correcting him right away--he just put him back to work anointing new kings, and at the end of telling him what his new assignment was, God said something like, 'Oh, by the way, there are more than 7,000 Israelites who continue to worship me, 7,000 who haven't bowed to Baal.' So I'm sure you won't be the only pilgrim in Germany! And I can appreciate what your use of the idea of talking to people in two ways, as a group or individually, really means to you. I have no idea what opportunities you'll be given to speak, but as sure as God is making you aware of the need, He'll also provide the opportunity and direct you specifically.

"You're terrific, my friend, and I'm so glad I know you. You've handled this with grace and courage and haven't slammed any doors shut. No one could have done it better."

Barbara's letter of affirmation was most welcome. I needed her kind, loving words, and appreciated them, and her, so very much. I'm blessed to have her as my friend.

Monday, April 10, 2000

Carolyn left a message for me on my answering machine: "I think it is evident that the word is out and you are officially 'out of the closet'--be that wanted or not. For the most part, the response has been very caring and concerned. I did not feel that most people were shocked, but truly concerned and had lots of questions. I have tried to be very positive. I have not brought the subject up with anyone, but they all say, 'you do know what is going on, don't you?' I let them tell me. They question whether or not you left Jim for another person, and I assure them that is not so--that you had to find release from an unbearable situation and live a life you felt was honest. Maybe things will not be as bad as feared. I am sure you have had calls and questions also. My prayers are with you in the morning as you go to court to finalize your divorce. I hope all goes well and is amiable. If there is anything that I can do, please let me know.

"You know my thoughts continue to be with you. You are a very special friend, and I am proud to say so. Relax, eat, take a few deep breaths, and I will talk to you soon! Carolyn"

I got quite courageous tonight. After handbell practice I attended for the first time a PFLAG (Parents, Families and Friends of Lesbians and Gays) meeting. I think I counted 27 in attendance, some really nice people. Much of the discussion dealt with Christian beliefs and the treatment gays have received from their churches. It was a good place for me to be tonight.

Driving to the church where PFLAG meets took courage, but not nearly as much courage as it took for me to get out of the car and walk into the meeting. This was my first experience in "outing myself" to total strangers. I had no idea what to expect. I just knew it was important to meet other people like me, people I hoped would understand my embarrassing, shameful secret. The friends and family with whom I have shared my story have been kind and loving, but have absolutely no clue as to what my life has been like. I felt a need to meet others like me.

My knees were knocking as I walked in. Part of me wanted to turn and run, part of me was curious as to what gays and lesbians looked like and acted like, and part of me recognized what a wonderful opportunity this experience could be for me. I walked in and sat down by a woman who seemed to be alone. She was younger than I, attractive, about my height and weight, with brown hair in an equally short haircut. Since no one was sitting with her and there were few empty seats, she seemed the logical person for me to sit beside. The group was about evenly divided between men and women--men sitting with men, women with women, all ages. I later learned they represent a cross-section of our city as far as occupations, talent, and economic status. Partners were happily sitting comfortably beside each other. A man had his arm draped gently around the shoulders of the man next to him, a woman held hands with the woman sitting next to her. Those who belonged together were relaxed and at ease in letting others know they were partners.

I had seen this only once before--when I attended a Metropolitan Community Church in Lubbock several months ago. At that time, my breath was literally taken away when I walked into the church and saw same-sex couples sitting together either holding hands, or with one draping their arm around the other. I sat toward the back of that sanctuary and cried during the whole service. Never before had I been around same-sex couples. It was beautiful. They were beautiful. I envied their happiness, their sense of ease and relaxation, their freedom to worship together as partners, their taking communion together with their arms around each other. The whole scenario was more than my emotions could hold. Oh how I longed to have someone with whom to share my life.

A fellowship was held following that service in Lubbock. I stayed to meet some of the congregation, and was wonderfully ministered to and cared for by these warm, loving people. Now, I was seeing much the same types of individuals and experiencing the same type of atmosphere in this PFLAG meeting, which seemed to me to be very similar to a church service. The speakers confirmed that God truly does love us. Afterwards, we divided into small groups during which time we were invited to tell our own stories. I told mine--mentioning that my divorce was to be finalized in the morning. When I said that I had been married for 37 years, they were amazed I had stayed married that long. I was definitely an oddity in their eyes. Most of them had been married at one time or another and had children from those marriages, but their marriages had ended much, much sooner. The woman I sat next to, Myra, had been married for twenty years and had two grown sons. The stories some of them told were heartbreaking--of having their children taken away from them simply because they were gay. This is what I had feared all of my life so I was thankful my children were now grown. By the time the meeting ended, I had relaxed, made new friends, and looked forward to the next meeting.

Tuesday, April 11, 2000

The divorce is to be finalized today. I'm sure this is why I awakened so early this morning. I updated Barbara about those in my class who "know" about me and also told her about attending the PFLAG meeting. On that subject, I explained, "A great group of people--lots of talk about religion/God. They all feel this ostracism from their churches."

When I arrived at the courthouse this morning, our lawyer was just walking in, so I joined him. Jim was already there. Since we had been able to work everything out amicably, we had used the same lawyer and split the cost between us. We signed the necessary papers and the appearance before the judge was pretty cut and dried. I was asked my name, had I lived in Smith County a set amount of time, same question about the state of Texas, did I feel our differences could not be worked out, do we have any children under the age of 18, any expected, had we agreed on the financial division of property, etc. Jim was asked only three or four questions and was given an opportunity to say whatever he wanted to say or to contest anything. He chose not to speak. So the divorce was finalized in just a few minutes. Barbara had offered to come with me, but afterwards I was glad I had turned her down. Everything went very, very smoothly and very quickly.

When we left the courthouse, I recalled that Jim had told me he had parked in our church's parking lot--which is about three blocks from the courthouse. I therefore asked him, "Would you like a ride to your car?"

He readily accepted, and I drove him to his car. At that point, he took my hand and said, "I wish it had never come to this."

"I wish it hadn't either," I replied.

"I still love you," he said, "but I hope both of us can find someone else we can be happy with."

"I hope so, too," I agreed. "I really appreciate how nice you have been about this. You could have made it quite rough on me."

"I never wanted to do that," he replied as he began to cry and therefore quickly exited my car. I drove away with a heavy, heavy heart. I never wanted to hurt him like that.

Wednesday, April 12, 2000

I awoke feeling terribly sad. I wrote to Barbara, "I'm becoming more and more convinced that instead of gays having to form their own groups, such as PFLAG, churches should provide the comfort, acceptance, and healing gays so desperately need."

A friend I've known for years recently "outed" himself to me. He wrote, "Cheyne, you might be interested to know that there is a gay-oriented church in our community. It is called St. Gabriel's and is located out on Highway 155 South. They have a congregation of about 100 or so members and have an Episcopalian type service. The pastor is a gay woman and the majority of the congregation is female. They are quite warm and friendly and seem to be close knit. You might give them a ring and ask the pastor to call you (and he gave me the phone number). I know this is a difficult area for you, but you could attend once with an open mind and see if it is right for you. Being a Baptist, you might find it difficult to follow the service and it might not be your cup of tea, but you would meet others with whom you could chat about your situation. They do preach love and acceptance. I know the pastor would be happy to discuss her interpretation of the Leviticus issues. If you want to attend the church, I'll make an attempt to leave my church (St. Mattress--grin) and go with you. It has been several years since I've been there so most will not know me."

I replied, "When I read the sentence, 'I'll make an attempt to leave my church (St. Mattress--grin) and go with you.' I laughed out loud. That was a gem! I really needed a laugh today, so thanks!

"My intention, as difficult as it probably will be, is to stick with my church. These are the people that know me. They see me attend regularly. They know what kind of children I have raised. They know me as a Sunday School teacher. They see me play in the handbell choir and they know I've written and self-

192

published books about my parents. I've even given a book review about my dad's story to the seniors' group and wrote the history of the Smith County Baptist Association. They've seen me teach in Vacation Bible School, and serve in other capacities within the church. They see me sit on the third row, center, every Sunday. You understand I won't say this to them, but I'll say it to you! I believe my calling is to be a 'missionary' in this church, forcing them to think about an issue they haven't thought about before and probably don't want to think about now. It won't be easy for me or for them.

"God never promised his children a happy life. In fact, we are warned many times of how difficult life will be for us; but along with that warning is the comforting promise we'll never be alone. God will be with us."

Thursday, April 13, 2000

One of my Sunday School class members, concerned about me, contacted Patsy, our class president. Patsy shared with her what was troubling me as well as our pastor's request that I no longer teach. She then wrote to me, saying: "Patsy and I both agreed you seemed so miserable, and we agreed to pray for you. I know what a difficult time you must be having and I'm so sorry. I won't say I understand because I'm not in your shoes, and I'm sure I don't understand. I do know people can be cruel though, and don't stop to think about taking care of their own business. If

193

people want to discuss your situation with you and invite you over to do so, they should be kind enough to listen.

"Knowing the ladies in our class, I'm sure you have all their sympathy, and sympathy for Jim and your family, too--just working it all out must be very difficult. You are a wonderful teacher, always so well prepared and interesting. Please feel free to talk to me ANY time . . . I would welcome a visit and even if we hold different viewpoints, we can still be friends, and agree to disagree.

"Know that I still love you as a sister in Christ, just as I always did."

This is one of my sad days. I again awoke feeling sad. Perhaps depressed is the correct term. Tears have been ready to fall at the least little thing. Betty, a kind, gentle friend with whom I recently had a long conversation, called me at least five times today. She's worried about me and is fearful (in my opinion) I am going to commit suicide. I shouldn't have seen her the other day when I was as depressed as I was. I absolutely fell apart when I was visiting with her. She is now convinced I need professional help.

I spent time today reading scripture and copied down some verses that were especially meaningful to me. Actually, I cried through most of them. The tears just kept coming today

This afternoon I received a reply from Pastor Watson regarding my Sunday afternoon letter when I sent him a copy of my last Sunday School lesson. I thought he ought to know what I told my Sunday School class when I resigned. His reply included: "Thank you for sending me your lesson thoughts concerning your Sunday School. As to 'putting my mind to rest,' I have to tell you that I have not been anxious about the way you are handling things. You always seem to be appropriate, and even more than caring about communicating in the right way and right spirit. I am grateful for you and your struggle to follow God's call with integrity and care. Please know of my thoughts, prayers, and friendship."

April 14 - April 30, 2000

Friday, April 14: I started my day by writing to Barbara: "I forgot about taking my anti-depressant yesterday. I took a dose at 4:15 a.m. and should have taken another dose at noon, but it just slipped my mind. So I waited and took one at 9:40 last night--and sure enough, I had trouble sleeping this morning. I have to admit that I don't like this at all--to think I can't sleep without medication. Guess I should have taken your advice and called the doctor yesterday for a refill or some other medicine. Since Mother and I are leaving today for Little Rock, I'll be into a big experiment this weekend!

Barbara's reply came at 7:30 a.m. "Please know that I believe you're going to have to deal with 'the more emotional aspects' of your problems, though not necessarily just before you embark on a four-day trip with your mother.

"I think it's time to **make a priority** of finding a counselor, especially a counselor who can prescribe. Such a person would know whether your need is for temporary medication to get through a crisis, or whether you are suffering a chemical imbalance which requires more long-term medication. Just as a diabetic cannot survive by will power alone, but must use the will power to form disciplined eating habits and take insulin, some of us need medication to overcome physical problems. We journalism majors aren't equipped to tell the difference. I don't believe you think less of my husband because he takes medication to lower his cholesterol, after working to do it on his own with diet and exercise and discovering that alone wasn't his answer.

"And I know that because you've always been a strong person, your inclination is to out-muscle the emotion, including sadness; but I believe you're in a place where you need to be strong enough to ask for some help. I ask you to let me know when you get back from Little Rock for many reasons: I care about you and how the trip goes, I want to touch base with you frequently, I'm concerned that you make the trip safely. That last reason gains urgency if you're not sleeping. I figure you can make it, but I wish I thought you'd be getting at least seven hours of sleep each evening.

"Your friend--Barbara"

Sunday, April 16:   Mother and I returned from Little Rock about 5 p.m.   Everything went very smoothly.   We listened to a most enjoyable book on tape during most of the drive--James Herriot's *Every Living Thing*. While in Little Rock, we stayed on the go all the time.   Mother was "pulled" in every direction by friends from church, friends from her former retirement home, and friends from Dad's job.   Since she and Dad moved to Little Rock in 1961, they had spent the better part of their life there.   Everyone wanted to see her, wanted to entertain her, wanted to do something special

196

for her. By Saturday evening Mother, who is 89 years of age, was exhausted--and actually admitted it.

On the drive back, she stated this would be her last trip back to Little Rock. I replied, "Mother, you're just tired. Wait a few weeks or a few months, and then let's plan another trip."

"No," she repeated. "I won't be returning."

Soon after I reached home, I was on the computer telling Barbara of our trip. I said, "Barbara, this is the first trip I can recall when I looked forward to getting home. In the past, it was always Jim 'chomping at the bits' to return home whereas I could have stayed gone forever. I never wanted to return from any place I ever went. But the feeling this time was so different! I literally counted the hours until I could finally get home!"

Barbara replied, "Glad you're here safe and sound. Don't you know why you were so eager to get home? It's your home now, and you have peace there. (Plus, to be truthful, you still need rest, and you had a busy time on your trip.)

"I'd love to have you in my class next week. I had 16 there today, which is more than I've been having, and one was a visitor. I expect a good group next week, given that it's Easter. I'll be surprised if you don't enjoy it more than you think you will. And if you don't, I won't nag you to come again (probably).

"I saw Carolyn after Sunday School this morning and asked how the class went. She said it was okay, then added, 'But we want our teacher back.' They do love you.

"Have a quiet evening, and try to get some sleep. When things occur to you that need doing, just write them down on a list and shepherd your mind back to a peaceful place. Love, bl"

197

Monday, April 17: At noon, I attended the special Holy Week service at the church. As I was walking toward the front steps to enter, I heard the tooting of a car horn. It was Barbara. I waited for her to park so we could walk into the sanctuary together. Not long after locating a place to sit (right in the center of the middle section), I looked up and Janie was coming toward me. Surprised to see her, I felt my body flush all over. I had never imagined she might attend the service. As usual, she was beautiful with that wonderful smile on her face and the lilt to her voice. As the service began, I found myself sitting with Janie on my left and Barbara on my right. "Smelling" Janie beside me was almost more than I could take. I was elated to have her sitting beside me, but at the same time I was fearful I might somehow act in a way to make Barbara think, "It's obvious she's infatuated with Janie." I was practically tongue-tied as I carefully gauged what I said and what I did. I was convinced Barbara was observing me.

Afterwards, Janie and I visited as Barbara moved toward the luncheon area. Standing in the aisle, Janie put her arm around my shoulders and just held me tightly while we continued to visit. Never wanting that moment to end, I listened as she said, "I won't be able to come to the service tomorrow, but I'll try to be here on Wednesday."

"I'll be heading to Austin on Wednesday," I said, realizing we would miss each other.

"Then I'll call you before you leave," she promised.

Tuesday, April 18: Carolyn sent me a note saying, "We still don't know what we are going to do for a teacher this coming Sunday.

198

It was by far the consensus of the class that they would love to have you come to class even if you are taking a break from teaching. Hope you will think about it."

Wednesday, April 19: I drove to Austin to visit with Linda, my cousin from North Carolina, who was in the Austin area visiting her son and his family. She's almost two years older than I, and as children, we spent much time together. As she and I visited this evening, the subject turned to children, their behaviors, and whether their behaviors are learned or something predisposed by birth. Linda, with three children of her own and a lifetime of experience caring for the children of others, stated, "I believe people are just born a certain way and that not all behavior is learned behavior." As she pursued this line of thought, she told me her son-in-law's brother had died of AIDS. "I'm firmly convinced this young man couldn't help the fact that he was gay," she said.

"I totally agree with you," I replied. "I'm the same way."

Without responding verbally to my "confession," she raised an eyebrow with a questioning look on her face as I confirmed, "Yes, I'm gay."

She and I had no opportunity to visit further until the next evening when we went for a walk. Before we reentered the house, I asked, "Would you like to talk about my being gay? If you don't, I certainly understand."

"Yes, I would like to talk about it," she replied, so we remained outside as I proceeded to tell her my story. Although tears came to my eyes a few times, I never did cry, which convinced me I was making progress emotionally! Linda was very kind and receptive, which amazed me because she has been Southern Baptist all of her life. Her parents were very, very strict. Once when we were children and playing a card game in her living room, her mother rushed in saying, "Put those cards away! Hurry, put those cards up! The preacher is walking up the sidewalk. I don't want him to see those cards!"

We quickly did as she asked. I thought the whole incident rather odd. My parents played cards often, especially Canasta, so I had never been taught that playing card games was "of the devil." But Linda was brought up in a much more conservative atmosphere than I.

As she and I later headed to our separate bedrooms, I handed her copies of the three letters: Jim's letter wanting to know why I wanted the divorce, my reply to him in which I "came out of the closet," and my pastor's letter to me. The next morning when she returned them to me, she simply thanked me for sharing with her.

Wednesday, April 26: When I attended the church supper and prayer meeting tonight, I sat at a table that included Carl Atkins, the fellow I had been so catty and rude to three weeks earlier. Thank goodness he was nice to me. He spoke and carried on a short conversation with me. Progress.

Several older women got my attention in order to compliment me on my handbell playing at the service this evening. "How in the world do you play two bells in one hand?" they asked. I just laughed and said something like, "It takes a lot of practice because you have to turn one bell one direction and the other

200

another direction." I'm pleased the members know me and have a good impression of me. This should certainly come in handy in the future in case my church membership is ever discussed/questioned in a business meeting. I keep thinking that the time will eventually come when I will be asked to leave the church because they don't want a member who is homosexual. Consequently, the more positive attitudes I can encourage on my behalf, the better off I will be in the future and the more open the members will be to "my message that we're basically all the same."

Barbara was also sitting at the supper table with me; and in a private moment said, "Mary Lou Reynolds approached Georgia Hunt (two church members about my age) asking if what she had heard about me was true, that I was homosexual. Georgia told her it was true. If Mary Lou has heard about it, then you can assume everyone in that class has probably heard about it or soon will."

This was a class comprised of over 50 women about my age. Their monthly class meeting is tomorrow night, and I'm invited as an "associate" member. Hearing Barbara's news caused me to get cold feet about attending. My courage in facing them was rapidly dissipating!

Upon returning home from church, I wrote: "Barbara , when I invited Nancy Grayson to ride with me to tomorrow night's party, I didn't realize 'everyone' would probably know about me. Do you think that she might prefer not to ride with me? Would you mind checking and seeing because I would certainly understand. I'm reaching the point where I feel I am doing a friend a disservice for just the two of us to be together for fear others might say something about her. Am I making sense to you? In fact, I've thought many times I may be 'soiling' your reputation by sitting beside you as much as I do. I'm starting to feel that old pull toward going back and being the 'loner' that I used to be."

Thursday, April 27: Barbara replied, "Just talked to Nancy. She says you're friends because she thinks you're a terrific person, and she doesn't care how many people 'know.' She just likes you. Both of us are enjoying a new freedom (for lack of a better word) in our friendship with you now that you aren't a committed loner anymore. We'd greatly prefer that you not crawl back in that hole. I can't imagine that being 'seen' with you would damage my reputation in any way. (What does that generally is my shooting off my big mouth!)"

After returning from the party tonight, I wrote a quick note to Barbara saying, "Everything went fine tonight. Nancy was very nice to me, as you might predict, and I had a chance to visit with her privately in the car. No one at the party said or did anything 'out of line.' However, I did get the feeling that several were having trouble with 'the news.' Mary Lou was the most noticeable. Three or four times I glanced at her, found her looking at me, but as soon as she saw me looking at her, she averted her eyes. She never spoke to me the whole evening. Not that it was particularly noticeable as we never ended up in close proximity to each other. Still, it seemed rather strange. I'm sure she's just having trouble thinking through it. Even having lived through it most of my life, there are times I still have trouble 'thinking through it,' so I need to give everyone plenty of time to do the same."

Barbara replied late this evening: "Nancy enjoys your company and values your friendship, which is a step up from 'being nice to you.' (So far as I know, Nancy's nice to everyone!) I think you're right in saying people need some time to deal with it, which I think amounts to finding out that you're exactly the same person now that you've always been, except (seems to me) more real, more able to really be friends. This I enjoy. Talk to you tomorrow."

Saturday, April 29:   Janie came by Saturday to drive me to a wedding shower. Whenever I think I have finally gained control over my emotions, I take one look at her and all those resolutions disappear into thin air. The thoughts, the desires, the nausea take possession of my being. I know that what I feel is totally illogical, but logic continues to get pushed aside in subservience to my rampant emotions. What I feel, what I desire, cannot even be discussed. I just continue to be thankful that she seems to enjoy having me for a friend. I hope I never do anything so foolish that she won't want to be around me any more. That fear of making a fool of myself keeps me alert whenever I am around her.

Sunday, April 30:   Carolyn, who agreed to teach our class this morning, made a point of asking me to join them, so I did. I feel so at ease with that group.

As soon as I returned home, I turned on CNN's live broadcast of the Gay Rights Rally in Washington, D.C. This is the first one I have ever watched, and it impressed me. The speakers were neatly dressed, well groomed, and spoke intelligently. I'm not certain why I was fearful it might be otherwise except that I am as much a victim of misinformation about gays as everyone else.

When the cameras zoomed in on same-sex couples comfortably and openly showing affection for each other (a hand on a shoulder, two partners back-to-back slowly moving rhythmically together to music, some with arms loosely around each other) tears sprang to my eyes. This is a world I was unaware of, and yet it is a world that deep inside I have always yearned for. I envied these couples their openness and freedom to express affection for each other. I spent the afternoon watching the broadcast, and occasionally wrote down statements made by the speakers. I loved what the mother of two gay children said: "Having a gay child is the ultimate test of unconditional love."

About 3:30 p.m., I took a break from the broadcast to write a quick note to Barbara: "I want to let you know why I didn't revisit your class this morning. Carolyn agreed at the last moment to teach our class, and sent me a special 'invitation to visit' late last night. So I did."

After attending church this evening, I went for my daily walk. Returning home, a note from Carolyn awaited me: "Dear Cheyne, I'm so glad that you joined us in class today. It just felt right for you to be there. You were very encouraging to me as I was teaching. I kept getting these little signals to hang in there that I was doing O.K.. Hope I did it justice. I really do appreciate your help. Those were wonderful sources of information. I am always amazed at how much you get from preparing a lesson. If we all would study our lessons that much, wouldn't that be great? Hope you have a wonderful week. Carolyn"

Monday, May 1, 2000

When I awoke at 5 a.m., I entered into my "fantasizing about Janie" mode as I tried to get back to sleep. It drives me nuts!

An e-mail from Joy, another member of the class, arrived this afternoon: "Cheyne, you mentioned in one of your e-mails to me that you started to talk to me about some scriptures dealing with homosexuality. You have always been such an informed and prepared teacher that I would be very interested in your thoughts concerning those scriptures. Sometimes, one gains a different insight or a better understanding of something when sharing views with someone else. If this is too time consuming, don't fret over doing it; otherwise I'd appreciate it. Love, Joy (glad you came to class Sunday)"

After receiving that invitation, I immediately sat down with various reference materials and spent hours putting together my reply to her. Here is most of what I wrote:

"Joy, thanks for asking--and for your willingness to read something different from what both you and I have been taught all of our lives. Although you might not agree with what I am going to write, perhaps it can serve as a starting point for new thought and dialogue. (Little of what I wrote was original, but gleaned from various sources I spread out across my desk and on the floor.)

"As I work through the feelings of guilt that I have lived with all of my life, I'm learning the sad fact that the nation's primary source of anti-gay bigotry and discrimination is Christian churches, especially those associated with the Religious Right. It is a staggering notion, but recent studies illustrate that Americans hate gays and lesbians in direct proportion to the number of times they attend their local church.[11] I find that absolutely amazing! Christ came to teach us to love one another, and yet the churches have become an instrument of hate and discrimination. This in itself indicates something is not right in this area.

"All of my life, being gay has seemed inconsistent with being a Christian because I have always assumed that the Bible condemns homosexuality. The guilt produced by this erroneous teaching tormented me. I wanted to please God, to be His child, to follow His commandments, and yet I was unable to change a basic part of my nature which I believed was 'abominable' in the worst possible sense. I therefore did the only thing I knew to do: I lived my life as a heterosexual, thinking God would be pleased with my decision. But He wasn't. Otherwise, I wouldn't have continually been tormented by death wishes, despite the fact that I was faithful to my husband and refused to even read anything about homosexuality. I did my best to ignore that side of me, all the while begging God to fill me with passion for my husband.

"Now that I have 'come out of the closet' to myself and others, I'm realizing that what the Bible says about homosexuality is not as clear as I had always been led to believe. For example, when the Bible was written, there was not even a word for 'homosexual!' In other words, no writer of the Bible was even aware of 'sexual orientation.' They were ignorant of the fact that two individuals of the same gender could fall in love and commit the rest of their lives to each other. Nothing is said about it in the Ten Commandments. None of the prophets warn us about it.

Jesus doesn't say a word about it! In fact, you have to look rather hard to find the basis churches have used to promote the sufferings and persecutions they have inflicted upon homosexuals.

"So why do some people assert that the Bible condemns homosexuality? Six Biblical passages are normally used. Probably the best known of these is the story of Sodom and Gomorrah where the men of the town attempted to gang rape visitors (angels) who were visiting Lot and his family. However, as you study this story, you'll see that the townspeople's behavior had absolutely nothing to do with same-sex love and commitment. These were heterosexual men (not homosexual) bent upon humiliating strangers by treating them 'like women.' Theirs was a brutal, evil behavior. Jesus himself referred to Sodom several times (Matthew 10:15 and Luke 10:8-12), but in both cases he used those cities as an example of **inhospitality**, not perverted sex.

"In the entire Old Testament, only two passages refer explicitly to homosexual acts, and they are both in Leviticus and included in the list of Holiness Codes:

"(1) Leviticus 18:22: You must not lie with a man as with a woman: that is an abomination.

"(2) Leviticus 20:13: If a man has intercourse with a man as with a woman, both commit an abomination. They must be put to death; their blood be on their own heads!

"The use of these verses to condemn homosexuality is a hypocritical selective use of scriptures. Why do I say this? Because there are many condemnations in Leviticus that we ignore today. Did you know that according to Leviticus anyone who

207

breaks the Sabbath is to be stoned to death? . . . that anyone who curses a parent is to be killed? . . . that rebellious sons, unvirginal brides, adulterers and those guilty of incest are to be killed? . . . that we are forbidden to wear clothing made of different kinds of materials? The term "abomination" is used throughout Leviticus and is even applied to eating what was then considered forbidden food (Leviticus 11:1-47)--rabbits, pigs, and shellfish like oysters, shrimp, lobsters, crabs, clams, and others.

"Sit down some time, read all of Leviticus, and refresh your memory of all the rules (as well as the punishments imposed for rule breakers) that book contains.

"Leviticus contains many laws/rules that seem very strange to us today. For example, a virgin raped by a man must become his wife and stay with him forever. Another rule that sounds unusually cruel to me is that 'bastards' and their descendants, 'even down to the tenth generation,' are denied temple membership.

"So what causes churches to select and elevate certain passages while ignoring others? In the case of homosexuality, it certainly has nothing to do with a desire to follow the teachings of Jesus because this was a subject He never touched upon. In fact, Jesus quoted from Leviticus only once: 'You shall love your neighbor as yourself.' (Leviticus 19:18) Jesus used Leviticus to teach us to love one another, not to condemn one another, not to judge one another, not to ostracize one another. To **love** one another.

"Keep in mind that the apostle Paul, an orthodox Jew who took the message of Jesus Christ to the Gentiles, never required the new Gentile Christians to embrace the Jewish laws. These laws were irrelevant to him. What he preached was purity of heart.

"There is absolutely nothing in the four gospels that talks about homosexuality. There are three passages from Paul's writings that have sometimes been translated in this century in such a way as to suggest that Paul was referring to homosexuality, but again I remind you that the word 'homosexual' is a new word, originating in the late nineteenth century. I Corinthians 6:9 and I Timothy 1:10 are often used to condemn homosexuality, but the truth of the matter is that the Greek words sometimes translated 'homosexual' or 'effeminate' do not mean homosexual or effeminate. We are at the mercy of the translators! And their personal prejudices come forth in this regard. According to Truluck's paper on 'The Six Bible Passages Used to Condemn Homosexuals': The word translated as 'homosexual' or 'sexual pervert' or some other similar term is Greek **arsenokoites,** which was formed from two words meaning 'male' and 'bed.' This word is not found anywhere else in the Bible and has not been found anywhere in the contemporary Greek of Paul's time. We do not know what it means. The word is obscure and uncertain. It probably refers to male prostitutes with female customers, which was a common practice in the Roman world, as revealed in the excavations at Pompeii and other sites.[12]

"Because of the uncertainty of Bible translators over this Greek word, different translators have interpreted this word in very different ways. In some translations, the practice forbidden by these passages is effeminate behavior (which in the ancient world was not associated with homosexuality); in others, masturbation or child molestation or child prostitution. We simply do not know what that word means.

"The most popular New Testament passage used to condemn homosexuality is Romans 1:26-27: 'God has given them (the Romans) up to shameful passions. Among them women have exchanged natural intercourse for unnatural, and men too, giving up natural relations with women, burn with lust for one another; males behave indecently with males, and are paid in their own persons the fitting wage of such perversion.'

"I like what Robert Truluck said: 'Taking anything that Paul said out of its context is like trying to drive a car blindfolded. You don't know where you are, where you have been, where you are going, or who you just ran over and killed!'[13]

"Truluck continues by saying, 'Paul's writings have been taken out of context and twisted to punish and oppress every identifiable minority in the world: Jews, children, women, blacks, slaves, politicians, divorced people, convicts, pro-choice people, lesbians, gays, bisexuals, transsexuals, religious reformers, the mentally ill, and the list could go on and on. Paul is often difficult and confusing to understand. A lot of Paul's writing is very difficult to translate. Since most of his letters were written in response to news from other people, reading Paul can be like listening to one side of a telephone conversation. We know, or think we know, what Paul is saying, but we have to guess what the other side has said. As **2 Peter 3:16-17** pointed out, we have to be on guard against using Paul's writings in unhealthy and destructive ways.'[14]

"When you read Romans 1:26-27 in context, you see 'that Paul's chief concern here is not with sexuality but with theology . .

210

. Paul is saying . . . that as Romans rejected the worship of one God for the worship of many gods, so they rejected opposite-sex for same-sex relations. Paul's concern here is with the *unnaturalness* of this exchange.[15] In other words, Paul was condemning 'straight' people who were behaving in ways that were unnatural to them. Paul believed that everyone was 'straight.' He had no concept of homosexual orientation--because that idea was not available in his world. The whole point of Romans 1, in fact, is 'to stigmatize persons who have rejected their calling, gotten off the true path they were once on.'[16] In the time Paul wrote, his analogy between theology and sexuality worked because only heterosexuality was viewed as 'natural.'[17] He couldn't have known that to homosexuals, engaging in heterosexual sex would be as much a rejection of their true calling, a deviation from the true path, as homosexual sex would be for a heterosexual.[18]

"When one reads the Bible on these matters, it is important to recognize that sexuality is a branch of scientific knowledge like any other. The Bible is a book of spiritual teaching, not of scientific revelation. Just as God did not use the Bible to explain to the ancient Hebrews how to build an airplane or construct a telephone system or manufacture antibiotics, neither did he use it to correct ancient misconceptions about human sexuality.[19]

"The main point in all of this is that the passages that are used to condemn homosexuality cannot be divorced 'from their historical and textual settings . . . Because Biblical scholars differ on the specific interpretations of the passages I've discussed, . . . it would seem obvious that the Christian thing to do is to accept

211

rather than condemn, to love rather than hate. The lesson of Jesus is one of love, not of denunciation of love.'[20]

"I'm heading into another area here for a few minutes realizing your feelings on this subject. I know many believe that homosexuality is a matter of choice. I've always found it so totally illogical to believe this. Why, if you weren't really more attracted to your own sex than to the opposite sex, would you decide that you wanted to spend your life as a homosexual? So that you can live in danger of getting beaten up by gay-bashers, of being called 'faggot' on the street by teenagers, of losing your job because you are gay?[21] It makes no sense, especially when one considers all the fearful consequences this so-called 'choice' brings.

"To describe homosexuality as a matter of choice is not only wrong; it's absurd and obscene. It denies the torment of every teenager who was ever rejected by his/her family for being gay; it denies every gay teenage suicide; it denies the existence of the millions of married men/women who lead lives of quiet desperation, hiding their homosexuality from their wives/husbands and children.[22]

"When I began this 'treatise,' I had no intention of writing so much. But to just make a blatant statement such as 'the Leviticus verses are part of a Holiness Code that we no longer use,' or 'Paul's writings did not refer to a sin of homosexuality,' would not have 'carried any water.' Explanations are necessary. The trouble is, there is even more I could write, but enough is enough. The passage I did not touch upon was Genesis 19:5 where the word sodomy evolved into a synonym for homosexuality when the original word simply meant 'temple prostitute.'

"In summary, three of the passages: Genesis 19:5; I Corinthians 6:9 and I Timothy 1:10 are incorrectly translated. The other three: Leviticus 18:22; 20:13; and Romans 1:26-27 are taken out of their original setting of condemning idolatrous religious practices and wrongly used to judge and condemn people of the same sex who love each other. None of these passages refer to people of the same sex who love each other. None originally were aimed at homosexuals.

"I've heard few if any sermons preached on Luke 12:57 where Jesus says, 'Why don't you judge for yourselves what is right?' As Walter Wink states in *Homosexuality and the Bible*, 'Such sovereign freedom strikes terror in the hearts of many Christians; they would rather be under law and be told what is right. Yet Paul himself echoes Jesus' sentiment when he says, '*do you not know that we are to judge angels? How much more, matters pertaining to this life!*' (I Cor. 6:3 Revised Standard Version). The last thing Paul would want is for people to respond to his ethical advice as a new law engraved on tablets of stone. He is himself trying to 'judge for himself what is right.' If now new evidence is in on the phenomenon of homosexuality, are we not obligated as well as free to reevaluate the whole issue in the light of all the available data and decide what is right, under God, for ourselves? Is this not the radical freedom for obedience in which the gospel establishes us?[23]

"Wink goes ahead and admits that whenever same-sex acts are mentioned in the Bible, they are condemned. But is this Biblical judgment correct? Think about how our argument over slavery has changed even though the Bible clearly sanctions

213

slavery. How did that shift in thinking occur? By studying the whole of scripture--beyond the legal statements into the deeper truth embodied by Jesus' identification with harlots, tax collectors, the diseased and maimed and outcast and poor. God suffers with those who are suffering. Jesus went out of his way to demonstrate love and acceptance toward individuals commonly identified as 'sinners' due to the accidents of birth, or biology, or economic desperation. And Wink goes on to say that 'whatever our position on gays, the gospel's imperative to love, care for, and be identified with their sufferings is unmistakably clear.' Wink urges us not to 'worship the Bible' but to restore it to its proper place as witness to the Word of God. And that word is a person, not a book, and that person taught us to love one another. We in the church need to get our priorities straight, to love everyone including the gay and the straight as well as those who agree with our beliefs and those who disagree.[24]

"Joy, you have forced me to sit down and put these thoughts together. Thank you. I'm sure I will revise these many times. Send me your comments and/or questions. Cheyne"

May 3 - May 6, 2000

Wednesday, May 3: Today was busy with a car repair, preparing Mother's state taxes, and cooking a meal for our class president who is ill with strep. When I attended church this evening, someone who knows me quite well sat at the table next to me. He

214

never acknowledged my presence. I find it strange that he has difficulty speaking to me.

Josh's friend, Charlie, suddenly turned friendly and talkative. He took me completely by surprise. Progress. Maybe he just needed time to realize I really am the same person he always liked.

Thursday, May 4: I slept really good last night. I awakened four or five times this morning, but kept turning over and going back to sleep until I finally awakened a little after 7 a.m. That's a first! The morning was dark and dreary with a bad storm hovering over our area.

About mid-morning, Janie called. "Cheyne," she said, "Wilson Rhodes called me to ask about my substituting as a teacher for our Sunday School class. We ended up having a very long phone conversation; and I told him that it amazed me how you can be respected as an outstanding Christian one hour, then the next hour, after being honest, you are no longer thought of in the same way."

As I listened to her words, I realized she was saying that being honest was my downfall. My mind immediately went to the scripture proclaiming "the truth will set you free," but I knew that the freedom it referred to was an inward feeling, and I **am** truly free in that respect. And, generally speaking, it is a wonderful state to be. But my being truthful about my sexual orientation nevertheless placed me in bondage, enslaved to the prejudices of others.

My mind then returned to Janie's words as she continued to relate all the praise she voiced on my behalf by telling Wilson that I was the very best Sunday School teacher she has ever had, that all the class loves me and wants me to remain as their teacher, and that if I were considered unworthy to teach, then everyone in the church is unworthy to teach because she considers me to be one of the best Christians she has ever known. And on and on along this line. She praised me up one side and down the other. She said Wilson did admit he had heard that I was a good teacher.

She also told Wilson, "Cheyne is such a good person that she even advised me not to sit beside her because people might think things about me that were not true. But I'm going to continue to sit by her because she is my friend. I have a very good marriage, Wilson. I love Charles and I've been married to him for 33 years. You need to know that Cheyne is not hitting on any of the class members."

Her words shocked me. "Did you really say that to him?" I asked.

"Yes, I did. That, and more."

"Did you actually use the term 'hitting?'"

"I did! I thought he ought to know that you aren't doing something like that."

The thought of "hitting" on class members had never occurred to me. This was a completely new concept to me, especially the idea that others might think I was that type of person! I wasn't even certain I knew the meaning of the word "hitting on someone," but I surmised it meant making some type of sexual overture or suggestion.

I have never had any desire to "hit" on anyone! In all those years since Karen and I parted, never have I had any desire toward a particular woman, other than my present infatuation with Janie. I find that amazing in itself, and yet I feel it is the direct consequence of having denied myself any close friendships over the years. Now that I am in the throes of desire, I find that many other emotions which lay dormant over the years are peeking out from their hiding places. My heart is warming up, and I'm learning to care for others in ways new to me. But these new feelings are scary. An unstableness is present, almost a feeling of dizziness in that I'm not certain which way I need to lean. I want to care for others, a characteristic Christian virtue. Caring, however, can also expose the heart to painful experiences such as hurt, heartbreak, anguish and torment. Is it worth it? Wouldn't I be better off not feeling anything at all? Undeniably, YES!

As all these thoughts flooded my mind, Janie repeatedly told me things like, "Cheyne, you are such a good person. I've never heard a bad word come out of your mouth."

Wanting to change the subject, I shared with her the fact that Patsy, our class president was ill, and that I had taken supper to her last night. "See," she said, "that's what I mean! You're such a good person!"

Again, wanting to change the subject I said, "Speaking of our class, I'm having difficulty deciding whether or not to join you on Sundays. If you have a substitute, I'm afraid I might make the substitute feel uncomfortable, and I don't want to do that."

"That's what I mean, Cheyne! You're just too good! You should certainly continue to come to our class. You're not going to make anyone feel uncomfortable."

Janie has me on some kind of pedestal that I don't deserve. When she decided to tell me about Wilson's phone call, she said, "I don't want us to have any secrets from each other." She's so right, and yet I continue to keep secret my feelings toward her. I believe it would be a terrible mistake to tell her how much I'm in love with her; but I suppose in all honesty and fairness to her I should tell her the truth. But just recording these thoughts has my stomach feeling sick for the first time today. All the way up to my throat. A churning nausea. I've got to think of something else and not dwell on this today.

Janie did tell me that she had called our departmental director to see if she had talked with Wilson about me. She had not. "Does she know about me?," I asked Janie.

"Yes, Cheyne, she knows. And she also told me that there are quite a few in our department who would not be at all accepting of you and what you are. She told me she could easily name a few of them."

My immediate inward reaction upon hearing this news was, "All the more reason to remain in that department--to be a piece of grit that will force them to 'think' about their prejudices."

Friday, May 5: After Mother and I ran errands this morning, I took her out for a Mexican food lunch, telling her "This is your Mother's Day meal!" This delighted her as much as anything else I could

218

have done as she loves Mexican food. So do I! Which means I was really treating both of us.

Saturday, May 6: I read William Raspberry's editorial in yesterday's Dallas newspaper titled "Why The Discomfort With Gay 'Marriage'?" I especially liked his ending statement: "But if we believe that sexual orientation is inborn--that some people are as immutably gay or lesbian as the rest of us are straight--and if we know that homosexuals are going to form unions, no matter what we do, shouldn't we encourage those who are so inclined to form monogamous and committed unions? Isn't that the reason we have instituted marriage--civil and sacred--for the rest of us?"

When I returned to my apartment, I sat down at my computer and sent him an e-mail, thanking him for what he had said, and sharing with him a very shortened version of my story.

Sunday, May 7, 2000

When I wrote Barbara the following day about the substitute in our class, she replied, "Glad it went well this morning. Please give consideration to not attending your class for a while, and by 'a while' I mean a minimum of 3-6 months. As you know, not everyone in that class is comfortable with your 'situation,' as you put it. They cannot express themselves freely to other class members so long as you are there, and they need to do so. I believe that the process of discussing it among themselves will work in your favor more strongly than your continued presence in

219

the class/department at this particular time. Because I do care about you (and have since I've known you) and admire the spirit in which you're dealing with this challenge, and because I don't like to say something I'm quite sure you don't want to hear, this is tough for me to write. But, my dear friend, you know better than I that your feelings are involved in a stronger than teacher/class relationship there, and that this emotional pull carries with it a temptation/risk that could harm you permanently, not to mention the danger to your cause and the church body as a whole.

"I believe that if something causes church members to act or speak without thoughtfully processing what they know and learning many things they don't know at all, they take positions that are less than their best selves would take; and, having taken them, many will defend them to the death. If they're not pushed into taking positions right away, but are given time to think and observe and learn and become comfortable with a way of thinking that is brand new to them, they're much more apt to be guided by the Spirit than by old thought patterns. I may be wrong here. It's not my decision. I won't bring it up again, though I'm willing to discuss it if you want to. I don't want to adversely affect my relationship with you, which I value more than you know. But a friend who won't ask hard questions with you isn't much of a friend, and I expect you to yell, "Danger!," to me when you believe that's what I need to hear.

"Maybe stepping away from your class will feel a little like making the transition from mother of a teenager to mother of an adult. You know that all your child's decisions won't be good, but you also know your child needs to learn to deal with the problems that come from not-so-good decisions. And your child really needs to know that he/she can deal with life on his/her own, without your supervision or input. Perhaps your class needs to work this through without your physical presence right now. (I am sure you know I'm not trying to drum up membership for my own class!) I don't know, Cheyne, but I'm convinced that you and the class need some space in your togetherness right now."

In a few minutes, I replied, "What you wrote to me is something I do not want to hear. In fact, I felt physically ill just reading it. I don't think I can think about it right now."

Barbara immediately replied, "You don't have to think about it right now--or, in fact, ever, really. Your call. If you do decide to think about it, you'll have to be quite clear about why the prospect of stepping away from your class makes you physically ill. I can't think of another teacher I know (or have ever known, for that matter) who would experience this kind of pain at the prospect of not teaching for a while. I am so sorry."

Convinced Barbara was misinterpreting what I meant, I replied: "It's not the stepping away from the class that makes me physically ill. It's the hopelessness of the whole situation in which I have found myself! I watched an A & E program last month called *Love Chronicles* which talked about what makes people fall in love, why they fall in love with who they fall in love with, and what happens to them when they fall in love. The description they gave of 'being in love' was described as a 'type of madness,' or 'a clinical insanity.' When I heard that, I knew exactly what they were referring to. It really is a type of insanity.

"I've always been able to be in perfect control of my emotions. Always. (--at least since college.) In fact, I've been in such perfect control that I have essentially been devoid of all emotion. It's been a very safe way to live, and I became an expert at it. This emotion I am now feeling slipped up on my blind side. I don't have any idea where it came from. It completely surprised me, devastated me, and continues to devastate me. I've never truly known what hopelessness really felt like until this happened to me--to be so completely torn between wanting two different things that are completely incompatible. It just keeps me constantly torn up.

"They say that when you are in love you live in a fantasy world where you think of this other person up to 85% of the time. I can also relate to that, although I do feel I am making progress along this line. After all, I've been in love with her for over eight months now. It's time to make a little progress. I relate my situation to that of an alcoholic in taking it just one day at a time. Sometimes I think I have to take it one hour at a time. But I've been able to do so. At times I think I am much improved, and then at other times I feel I am reaching a very dangerous crossroads.

"No, I really don't think I want to be in the class just because of her. But maybe I'm fooling myself there. I've never felt particularly close to other people. Surely you know that. There is no one in our former class that I ever called 'just to talk.' And I didn't miss that. That was my choice. But now I'm in a group (and I'm going to be quite open and honest here) that has put me on a pedestal, and I'm enjoying it. They keep telling me what a great teacher I am, and as awful as it may sound, I like to hear that.

They are a good bit younger than I am, but I fit in because at least three of them have daughters the age of my daughter. I've always been in age groups where grandchildren are discussed instead of college students. I simply feel at home in this group."

Barbara quickly replied: "Go back and read the second paragraph of what you just wrote me. 'Essentially devoid of all emotion'--I believe that, because I don't know how else you'd have managed to stay in your marriage for 37 years. But 'devoid of all emotion' isn't normal, isn't healthy. And now emotion comes at you all at once, in a torrent, like being caught in a flood, I'm guessing. And that isn't normal either, whatever 'normal' is. I just mean that most women your age would have been in a relationship that moved from 'being in love' to 'loving' decades ago. They'd be experiencing a deeply rooted, trusting love, a mutual love. They wouldn't be dealing with what is, essentially, first love. (They say that if a certain number of years separates children in a family, a younger one might not function as a younger child, but as a first child. Perhaps that's true for love, also. Heaven knows it's been 'a certain number of years' since you really loved someone in a non-blood-kin way.)

"Your situation isn't like that of anyone else I know. The gay people I've known and been friends with before were not, when I knew them, coming out, especially not coming out after decades in the closet. They'd become comfortable with who they were, they had non-turbulent relationships with people who knew them as they were.

"And I know you're working at 'making progress' toward not having your focus on the other person all the time. I'm afraid that what that means is a step back in the direction of 'devoid of all emotion.' And this is why I long for you to find a counselor who can help you understand what's happening to you, help you deal with it in a way that will allow you really to grow instead of moving back toward a denial, stunting of emotion.

"I also know that in 'our' class you never called anyone just to talk. I seldom (if ever) do that myself. And I know that makes me a definite minority. I can be perfectly satisfied doing a lot of things by myself because that means I do it when and if I want to. And I have family in town or nearby, and that fills most of my need for other people.

"I don't believe that you want to stay in your class just because of her, but I think that proximity is far more important to you than you realize. And far more dangerous. You must know how the other members of that class would feel should they become aware of your emotion, and deeply-felt emotion is mighty tough to totally conceal. Some people are sensitive to that sort of thing, as if they had antennae. And I know how much it must have meant to the class members to have a great teacher--which you are, both in the teaching part and in the caring for members part. I've always known that. And I understand how wonderful it feels to have that love and approval, commodities that I think were in short supply in your marriage. But there's no shortage of women with daughters the age of Anne. (Even in my class, there are several.) And while I don't think you'd have new friendships as deep as those you have now immediately, I do think you'd have less problem forming them now than you used to. You're much more free now, much better able to give the time to friendships. And, as

224

I keep reminding you, I think it's entirely possible that you'd return to that class at some point. But, for now, I believe the class needs the absolute freedom to find out who they are, and to know that your personal presence isn't the only reason for the class to exist. They need to discover their relationships with each other are as strong as their relationship to you, and they (and you) need to give God time to show them what He has in mind. They won't do any of that work so long as they're depending entirely on you.

"It's been a long time since I watched Casablanca--but didn't Humphrey Bogart separate himself from Ingrid Bergman for reasons that he deemed more important than what he wanted for himself? (And shouldn't I be thinking of scripture instead of old movies?)

"I still care about you enormously."

My reply went out about 8:30 p.m. "Of course you are right about the abnormality of both being devoid of all emotion as well as this torrent of agonizing emotion. I realize neither of these extremes is normal. And, of course, you are also correct in that I am pushing myself back into an emotionless state. That's the only way I think I can survive. I don't need a counselor to explain to me what is happening. I know what is happening. I live with it hourly. I fight it constantly. I wake up with it. I go to bed with it. I awaken during the night with it. I force myself during the long walks (sometimes over an hour in length) to quote memorized passages or poems. This keeps my mind focused. The reason I play the piano is to keep my mind focused. I wish reading would do that for me, but I still can't read. Of all the books you loaned to me, I have read only 155 pages in the first book! That's not me. I used to sit and read a whole book in a day or two. I'm absolutely amazed I am unable to read. Just lately I've gotten to the place where I can sit and watch a little TV.

"I find it impossible to comprehend what anyone can do to help me. It's all with ME. It's like a demon has a grasp on my very soul and yet how can that be if I'm a child of God? Where does love come from if it doesn't come from God? And if love has to come from God, then why has this happened to me?

"I'm also aware of the dangers of others sensing how I feel. It scares me half to death, keeps me in knots when I am around her. Several times I have come close to doing something that would have been so normal for me to do but which would have been quite unacceptable. At the last minute, my brain kicked in and logic took over. But it scared me so much that I was almost shaking when I realized what a close call I had experienced."

Past our normal bedtime, we were still writing back and forth. Barbara replied at 10:30 p.m., "You said you find it impossible to comprehend what anyone can do to help you. I'm thinking maybe an analogy might be being lost in the woods surrounded by tall trees. There's a path, but you can't see how to get to it from where you are. But a pilot, flying overhead, could see that path clearly and use a radio to communicate to you which way to go to get out of the forest. You're too surrounded by it, too immersed in it, to see the way to a better place. But someone trained to listen, someone who can hear you, someone with experience might help you find the way out. I can't do that--no training, no experience, no objectivity where you're concerned.

226

"And of course I know when I speak to you about potential problems that you're aware of them. (Have you ever thought that perhaps life is simpler for stupid people? I read about a recent study where people were given a test and then asked to evaluate their own performance on it. Those who'd done well believed they'd done much less well than they actually had; those who'd done poorly believed they'd succeeded. In other words, incompetent people think they're doing just fine, thank you.) I cannot tell you how risky I think your current situation is. One slip, and things change permanently--too much like walking the high wire without a net. What is it they say about risk? 'There are the chances you needn't take, the ones you have to take, and the ones you choose to take.' From my perspective, this is one you're choosing to take. You certainly don't have to, and you don't need to. And the risk is so enormous when laid beside the chances of anything good coming from it.

"I believe there's a future for you that's much brighter than just survival, though, obviously, that's the first priority. :-) Maybe you should add to your journal a list of what's better about your life now than last year. I'd probably start with the freedom to live it your way, then move on to privacy when you want it, and the challenge of setting your own goals. Those are all good things, but sometimes a bit lonely. And there's a lot more good stuff ahead, including the possibility of a real relationship between equals. At the very least, you have a lot of friends now that you weren't aware of before.

"It's late, and I'm headed for bed. Good night. I hope you sleep."

227

I started to reply, and actually wrote several paragraphs, but concluded I was too tired and too emotional to think clearly about what I really wanted to say. Barbara's comment that my "feelings are involved in a stronger than teacher/class relationship there, and that this emotional pull carries with it a temptation/risk that could harm you permanently, not to mention the danger to your cause and the church body as a whole" was really a scary thought. She was right. I could ruin myself, my reputation, be useless in the cause I am determined to support, and bring harm to my church. These dangers I must keep uppermost in my mind at all times.

Monday, May 8, 2000

Tonight I attended my second PFLAG (Parents, Families and Friends of Lesbians and Gays) meeting. I thoroughly enjoyed it. I like the people. I applaud their openness in talking about their "partners," or their "loves." I enjoy their laughter, their humor, their friendliness toward each other, their openness, their Christianity. Tonight all those who attended the Millennium March in Washington, D.C. "reported" on their experiences. Many positives were shared, such as the fact that the people who attended looked so "normal." Very few "far-out" looking people were there, and yet the group of "queens" were the ones who were interviewed and video-taped by CNN. According to the reports we heard, the participants were friendly, kind, thoughtful, and considerate toward each other. They made a good impression on the citizenry who came into contact with them.

Some of the signs carried by our local participants included: "G O P (Guilty of Prejudice)"; "I Love My Gay Son Unconditionally"; "Focus on Your Own Family." One of the members who carried two of these signs, said that many, many people came up to her to ask if their picture could be taken beside her sign (which was "G O P" on one side and "Unconditionally" on the other). One fellow wanted his picture taken by the "Unconditionally" sign so he could send it to his mother for a Mother's Day gift. She has not contacted him for 7 years. Obviously, she doesn't love him unconditionally, and he is devastated by her rejection.

Tuesday, May 9, 2000

I included Mother in my "errand running" the next day as I'll be out of town for about a week attending Anne's graduation ceremony from Texas Tech, then helping her move from Lubbock to Austin. One of the purchases I made was a blue ceramic cross (6" x 7") overlaid with numerous small pieces of broken ceramic. The explanation on the back of the cross says, "The Lord Takes Broken Pieces and By His Love Makes Us Whole." God knows how broken I am yet I believe He will eventually make me whole and usable by Him.

During the afternoon I visited with Barbara for two hours. When I left she gave me a loaf of homemade bread. How I love homemade bread, especially with lots of butter! Yum, yum! I ended up eating three huge slices topped with fig preserves for supper. Delicious.

During our visit this afternoon, Barbara alluded to a conversation she had about me with a male friend who thought I should talk to a psychologist to determine if I really was gay. "What did you say to him?" I asked.

I asked him, "You mean just like you did when you were a teenager and realized you liked girls?"

May 10 - May 20, 2000

Thursday, May 11: After arriving in Lubbock, I found myself able, for the first time in months, to concentrate on reading and actually completed The Reverend Troy D. Perry's book titled *The Lord is My Shepherd, And He Knows I'm Gay.* Troy Perry is the founder of an open and accepting congregation known as the Universal Fellowship of Metropolitan Christian Churches. After reading both his book and Mel White's *Stranger at the Gate*, I yearn to locate some biographies of lesbians to determine if "sleeping around" is just a male thing. I refuse to believe this is common among all homosexuals.

I have thought about Janie so much today that tears keep coming. I'm now fully cognizant of the important battle in which I am engaged. I am being hit with more temptation than I think most people could stand. I must make up my mind that I will not give in despite the pain. I must be determined, stand firm, and never let Janie know how I feel about her.

Saturday, May 13: Anne graduated Summa Cum Laude with Honors from Texas Tech. I'm so proud of her!

Saturday, May 20: After returning to Tyler yesterday, one of the first things I did this morning was to call Janie, offering to drive her to the wedding of a mutual friend of ours. She seemed delighted to know I was back in town, and then explained that her husband, Charles, would be accompanying her to the wedding. "Be sure to look for me at the wedding, Cheyne. We can sit together."

I had no intention of either looking for her, or sitting with her at the wedding, but when Anne and I walked into the sanctuary, Janie had already spotted us and was waving and signaling to us to come sit with them. I couldn't very well ignore her. So we joined them. Later, she informed me she will be out of town for the next ten days. Barbara is also going to be gone for quite a while with part of her absence overlapping Janie's absence. Anne will also be "out of pocket" so I'm bracing myself to be without my "support group."

Sunday, May 21, 2000

I decided weeks ago to no longer attend "my" Sunday School class but to go to Barbara's class. Nevertheless, as I began driving to church, my stomach began churning. "Fear" came upon me, a nameless fear because I'm not certain what it is I am fearful of. But fear, nevertheless. The old nausea, the nervousness of wondering what to expect. When will I get over this? The feeling certainly wasn't connected to seeing Janie, because I knew she was out of town.

A visiting pastor spoke today on the declining enrollment and participation in local churches. In elaborating on possible causes, he mentioned the way many churches treat divorced individuals by turning their backs on these wounded people. I found the sermon quite moving because I could feel its application in my life. Mother was sitting beside me, and she was bored to death! She kept looking at her watch, then afterwards said to me, "Aren't you glad the handbells don't have to play today or you would have to sit through the sermon twice!"

Feeling out of place in the new Sunday School department, I skipped the opening exercises and headed for the classroom where Barbara was making some preparations. I admitted to her that I wasn't having a very good day. Just admitting that brought tears to my eyes.

"You need to expect to have these kind of days occasionally," she replied.

Barbara taught a good lesson and alluded to the fact that Christians have eventually begun to pray for the "innocent" victims of AIDS, but have yet to pray for all AIDS victims--that we still tend to judge others. Good for her.

Afterward, walking to my car, I spoke for a few minutes with Barbara who told me she and our associate pastor, Evelyn Carpenter, had recently had a conversation about me. But Barbara, who was in a hurry, did not elaborate. She simply said, "You need to visit with Evelyn."

This reminded me of a conversation I had last night with my son, J.W. He had visited with one of the members of my class, Connie. He and Connie have a great relationship because J.W. and Connie's daughter used to date. In fact, Connie's daughter was in on this conversation and J.W. just wanted me to know that both of them are aware of my sexual orientation. (Connie is the one who sent word to me that if I was "going to Germany" then she was going with me!)

According to J.W., Connie kept telling him what a good teacher I am and how upset the class is that I am no longer teaching and that there is a staff member who is on their side in getting me back as a teacher. Consequently, when Barbara spoke to me this morning about Evelyn Carpenter, it dawned upon me that she is most likely that staff member. I do know that Connie and Evelyn are good friends, or perhaps I should reword that to say that Connie is quite an admirer of Evelyn and speaks with her frequently. So I think it is a logical conclusion that the "supporting staff member" is probably Evelyn.

J.W. tickles me sometimes by his openness about my sexual orientation. He told a fellow teacher about me, then stated, "But I don't feel any different about her." The teacher retorted, "Well, I should hope not!"

Barbara, in answering a note I had sent to her, said: "Susanne Miles, a member of my class, came by to visit. She's my good friend from way before I began teaching that class--by which I don't mean we hang out together, but we sometimes get together for long talks. I told her about your 'situation,' since I know her well enough to know she'd be supportive. As she was--and then asked

233

me if I knew that her uncle had died of AIDS. Which I didn't know; but she said, 'We always knew he was gay.' She helped care for him during his final illness, and was holding his hand when he died. Susanne's spiritual gift is, I think, compassion--at least, that's the way she helps me most. She said that when I spoke of praying for people with AIDS this morning, she wondered if I knew or remembered about her uncle. Susanne will be a blessing in your life as you get to know her."

May 23 - May 30, 2000

Tuesday, May 23: The May, 2000, issue of *Texas Baptists Committed* (the magazine of a much more liberal group of Texas Baptists who are committed to block our Baptist General Convention of Texas from being "taken over" by the Southern Baptist organization) contained quotes by well-known Texas Baptists, all of whom agreed in one way or another on the sinfulness of being homosexual. I know what I feel, what I desire, what I need, and wonder why God would cause me to have these feelings just to live a life of misery. When I contemplate my aloneness, I hurt and feel such a deep, deep longing throughout my entire physical body and soul that cries out for a partner. In her open but non-direct way, Barbara periodically reminds me of the fact that those who now "accept" me will not be so accepting if I were to have a partner. That hurts.

I know I can leave the church and find acceptance among a group of worshiping gays, but that seems cowardly. If all of us leave the churches to worship with our own kind, how do we show heterosexual Christians that we are no different than they? That we love God just like they love God? That we're called of God for special purposes just as they are called by God? That we are all part of the same Body of Christ? It's only by mingling together, listening, and sharing, that understanding will take place and truth be observable. This, I believe, is the key to changing opinions and bringing about acceptance. I'm pulled to do my part in this battle for approval, for acceptance, despite the fact this fight will undoubtedly be one of the most difficult to win. Prejudice is an insidious evil. People don't understand homosexuality, and they don't want to understand it. Actually, they've never been given an opportunity to understand it because homosexuality is never openly discussed. The silence is deafening.

Barbara continues to urge me to find a counselor. I guess I really ought to do that. I'm definitely on the mend, but I continue to have great emotional upheavals.

Myra Hudson, the woman I met at the PFLAG (Parents, Families and Friends of Lesbians and Gays) meeting last month, sent me an e-mail late tonight hoping I had a nice visit with Anne and telling me she had just returned from a camping/canoeing trip to the Buffalo National River in Arkansas.

I replied, "I envy you your trip! Sounds wonderful.

"I've been wanting to ask you a little more about what you do. One of my friends from church has been 'almost demanding' that I find a counselor. I am really doing much, much better than I was several months ago, but still fight some heavy emotional battles. I feel that is to be expected considering the drastic turn my life has taken. But maybe we could get together and talk some day. I am finally getting to the point where I think I can talk without a box of tissues close at hand."

Wednesday, May 24: A message arrived late this evening from Myra: "The 'counseling' I do these days is more of a ministry, not an occupation. I am trained in psychology (masters level) and biblical counseling and certified as a pastoral counselor. I simply sit with folks, listen, and share whatever the Spirit lays on my heart. I would be happy to sit with you some time, if you want. Tissues are not an issue. I have gone through cases of them myself! Take care, Myra"

Thursday, May 25: Early this morning I wrote to Myra: "I really would like an opportunity to visit with you. To be quite frank, I have never before had an opportunity to share what has gone on in my life with another gay person"–and then I proceeded to tell her a little of my story before copying and pasting the two letters Jim and I sent to each other.

Along with writing to Myra, I carried on quite a correspondence today with Barbara, and included mention of Myra and her experience as a counselor.

As I wrote to Barbara, I reminded myself she leaves for Italy tomorrow afternoon and will be gone for three weeks! Janie is due back in Tyler in two days, will be here for only a week, then will leave on a ten-day trip to the northeast. Just knowing they won't be available has me already feeling nervous and lonely.

236

Monday, May 29:   This afternoon, when I went over to Mother's to balance her checkbook and go over her finances, she shared with me the news of the death of one of her Little Rock friends who had been living with another woman after the death of her husband. Mother disapproved of their living arrangement, and today her criticism became harsher as she declared, "They are lesbians."

My heart lurched when she used the term "lesbians," and in almost a combative tone I asked, "Why would you say that?"

"People have actually seen them kiss each other on the lips," she replied.

Not knowing how to reply and not wanting to extend this conversation, I made no comment. An uneasy quiet prevailed, and the subject was dropped.

When I returned home, after fighting off an urge to call Myra in order to have someone to talk with, I allowed my feelings of despondency to take over.   I'm uncertain about God's acceptance of me. My Baptist background hammers away at my unworthiness and the abomination of who I am.

Tuesday, May 30:   This evening, after walking for an hour, I decided about 8:30 to cool off in the pool. This was my first time to use the apartment pool, and I thoroughly enjoyed it. However, I was alone, and I know that can be dangerous. But I enjoyed the aloneness--until I developed a terrible cramp in my right leg. I was in the deep end of the pool at the time and knew immediately I was in danger of drowning if I didn't keep my wits about me.

The pain was excruciating, and moving the leg seemed impossible. Any movement of any kind was terribly painful--but I had to move! Sheer determination made me slowly move to the side of the pool. As I hung onto the side with one hand, I massaged the knot in my leg with the other hand. Climbing out of the pool at that point was impossible. Finally, the knot went down and the pain lessened and I was able to painfully climb out of the pool.

Wednesday, May 31, 2000

This morning I was greeted by an e-mail sent by someone who never sends me e-mails, but just calls instead. Janie!

"Dear friend, I arrived back on Sunday evening, very tired, both physically and emotionally. I've been very down today. The convention went well. The attendance was fair . . . lots of conflicts this time of year . . . weddings, graduations, etc. I enjoyed seeing friends from all over Texas and catching up on everyone's families.

"I had the wonderful opportunity at convention to hear Rabbi Harold Kushner speak. I thought of you and wished you could have heard his inspiring talk. He really was outstanding. I bought his book, *How Good Do We Have To Be?* You will love this book, and I will share it with you. I do hope all is going well. Miss you and love you, Janie"

I called Janie about 8 a.m., and we visited for well over an hour prior to my attending my weekly Bible study.

This afternoon, I called Janie and told her I wanted to bring some papers over for her to read. I promised not to stay.

However, I ended up staying for a long time. The visit was going along just fine until I somehow found myself in the position of having to admit I was still experiencing a lot of pain and that the idea of climbing back into my hole was looking very inviting. Janie then asked, "Cheyne, what is the source of your pain?"

"I can't talk about it, Janie."

"Talk about it. Tell me the source of your pain."

I became very quiet, and then said, "I just can't talk to you about it."

"Cheyne, I know the source of your pain. I've known about it for a long time, and it's time we talked about it."

At that point, I started to stand up, grabbed my purse, and said, "I need to go. I can't stay any longer. I don't want to talk about this."

"Cheyne, you've got to stay. It's time we talked about this. We've got to get this out in the open because, you see, I know what it is. I know what your pain is. You're in love with me, aren't you?"

By then I had sat back down on the sofa. At her revelation I bent over, touching my head to my knees and began to wail, "Don't, don't, don't, please don't."

Janie reached over and began to rub my back. My mind was shutting everything out so that I'm not even certain what she said. Something like, "Oh, Cheyne, I've known about this for a long, long time. You know I'm just not inclined that way. I just can't be in love with you like that."

"I know. I know. I've always known that."

"I feel honored that you feel this way about me. You're such a wonderful person, so brilliant. Look at who you have fallen in love with (and then she made some derogatory statements about herself and her abilities). You're seeing me through rose-colored glasses."

"Janie, I have never seen you through rose-colored glasses. But you see me that way. I'm not brilliant."

"Cheyne, what are we going to do about this? We've got to talk and decide what we are going to do about this."

"I thought you'd never want to see me again once you found out how I feel about you."

"Oh, that's not true. You're my friend. I enjoy talking with you and sharing with you. I talk with you about things I don't talk with anyone else about. But if being with me brings you pain, then we shouldn't be together any more."

At that point, I stood up and paced the room, first toward the door, then over to a front window where I leaned my head against the glass. Then as I turned around to walk back to the sofa, I gave a little laugh and said, "I'll have to admit there is a certain amount of relief in getting this out in the open."

"I know how painful love is, Cheyne. I've been in love before where it was quite painful. I'm well aware of how painful love can be. If being around me is going to cause you pain, then we need to decide now what steps we are going to take."

"Janie, the despair is not as great when I'm with you. I want to continue our friendship, but I just can't believe you would want to be around me."

"Cheyne, you must realize how long I have been aware of your feelings for me, and yet all of that time we've continued to be friends."

"But I don't want anyone to link your name to mine. I don't want you to be hurt by being friends with me. Everyone is soon going to know about me and then if you are still my friend, they will start assuming things about you, too."

"Oh, they already are!"

"What do you mean?"

"Don't kid yourself. People are already thinking things like that, but it doesn't bother me. If someone were to come up to me and say something, I would just quit going to church!"

"But, Janie, that's the wrong thing to do! Then you would convince them that what they said was true!"

"I hadn't thought about that, but I can see you are right. You have such courage to face them all the time. I just don't have that kind of courage, but you do. Who else knows about this?"

"Barbara is the only one. She guessed it that first time I sat down and visited with her. At one point in our conversation Barbara said, 'Cheyne, are you in love with anyone now?' and I just turned away from her with tears in my eyes. She then said, 'You don't want to talk about it, do you?' and I nodded. Then ten to fifteen minutes later, she caught me by surprise and asked, 'You're in love with Janie Robbins, aren't you?'"

"Anne knows, doesn't she?"

"Oh, no!"

"Oh, Cheyne, Anne is bound to know!"

"Oh I hope not. I certainly hope not."

241

"Why? Why does that bother you?"

"Well it does. I don't want her to know. Let me tell you what else Barbara said to me. She said, 'If I were you, I'd be in love with Janie, too.'"

At that point I was afraid to look at Janie, but I could sense that tears were springing to her eyes.

"Barbara was trying to get me to quit teaching the class long before Dr. Watson suggested it."

"You mean she was telling you to quit teaching at the same time I was telling you to hang in there and stick with it?"

"Yes. She didn't think I should continue to be around you. She was afraid that certain people just have antenna that can pick up on the fact that I'm in love with you.

"Janie, do you know how long I've been in love with you? Do you recall that Sunday just you and I were in the class together, and visited about our families?"

"That was a long time ago!"

"Yes, in August! That's when I fell in love with you." And I shared with her the emotional roller coaster I went through that afternoon.

"I did everything right. I stayed away from girls. I never had a close friend. I never touched women. I didn't put my arms around them or anything. I followed all the rules, and (by then I was bawling) still it happened to me. I didn't want it to happen. And we weren't even friends at the time! We were just acquaintances! I don't know why this had to happen to me."

She reached over and gently rubbed my forearm with a couple of her fingers and said, "Your skin is as soft as a ten-year-old's skin. Cheyne, I just don't know what to say. Tell me what to do. Did I cause this? Was there something I did that caused this to happen?"

"No, you had nothing to do with this."

"I want to help, but I feel so helpless, as if I'm the cause of this."

"But you're not. You're not the cause of it. It just happened. We hardly even knew each other."

"This happened a long time ago, didn't it?"

"In August! Yes, a long time ago. How long have you been aware of it?"

"It was in October when you came back from your trip to Singapore. That's when I knew."

"Over seven months ago! Janie, you've known for seven months that I'm in love with you?"

"Yes."

"I'm too old for this, Janie. I'm feeling things that teenagers feel."

"It's because you weren't given the opportunity to date normally as you should have been."

"You're right. I'm totally inexperienced in what is happening to me. I don't want this to bring harm to you if we remain friends, and I'm afraid it will. I don't want you to have your name connected to mine."

At this point in our conversation, Janie named several female couples, heterosexuals, who made trips together every summer. This was news to me. "No one thinks anything about it," she said. "And my good friend, Lisa, who now has Alzheimer's, she and I used to walk down the street together and into stores together hand-in-hand. People aren't going to think things about us."

"Oh, but they will! They will because I will be labeled gay and whoever I am with will have that label also placed on them."

"Well, it just doesn't bother me. Cheyne, you've got to make me a promise. Promise me you will contact the woman from PFLAG and talk with her. Don't you really want to talk with her?"

"Yes, there is a part of me that does want to talk with her."

"I think she is just reaching out to you in kindness, and I think you need to be willing to talk with her. If something develops between the two of you, then that would be great; but you've got to open yourself up to new relationships. You really need to find someone to be with. You've got a lot of years left and you don't want to spend them all alone."

I promised. As she walked me out to my car, I could tell she was undecided about giving me the usual hug when we departed. By keeping a lot of distance between us, I let her know it wasn't at all necessary, and she almost took me up on it. But at the last minute, she said, "Give me a hug, Cheyne." And I did.

As we said goodbye, Janie said, "Call me, Cheyne. I want you to call me."

"Janie, you just don't know what a game I play with myself as to how long I can go without calling you."

"You can call me every day if you like. That would be just fine. If you don't call me, I'll be calling you! I love you!"

"I love you." And I drove away marveling at what a turn my life had taken. I was amazed that my most private secret was now out in the open to Janie. I felt overwhelmed this had happened. And then I realized how foolish I was to assume she was unaware of my feelings for her. How dumb I was! And now I wonder how many others could see the truth. I hate to even think about it.

Thursday, June 1, 2000

When the phone rang about 7 a.m. (I awoke about 5 this morning after getting to bed about midnight), I knew it had to be Janie. No one else calls me this early in the morning. She explained she had written two long e-mails to me, but her computer didn't send them and they were lost. She was thoroughly disgusted and rather angry about it as writing doesn't come easily to her. I'm certain she spent a lot of time working on what she wrote.

"Cheyne, I didn't want you to think I was ignoring your question concerning how I knew you were in love with me. This is something I felt long before we ever talked about your being gay. There was a restlessness in you, Cheyne. Every time we talked, there was always one more thing you wanted to say, but never could. You were never able to tell me everything. But I never went there with you as I thought that would be very assuming on my part. If I were wrong about what I thought, I would have looked very foolish. I just want you to know that I am not uncomfortable with our friendship, and I'm glad the barrier is now gone. We can at last be completely honest with each other. Cheyne, I love you to death. I think you are outstanding. You are the finest person I have every known. You have inspired me so many times, given me a sounding board. I don't know what I would have done without you. You just represent what I consider to be a good human being. You are so good at helping me put things into perspective. I really need you in my life. I want to continue to go down this little journey of life with you."

After a few minutes of conversation, I said, "Janie, I sent you an e-mail this morning. You mentioned yesterday the question I raised at an earlier time as to whether or not love has to come from God, and I can't recall why you mentioned that yesterday."

"Well, I don't remember saying it, but I do believe that love comes from God. Love can't come from the devil. I don't even believe lust comes from the devil. If it weren't for lust, we wouldn't have procreation!"

"Janie, you are different!" and we both laughed.

"Yes, I am, Precious!"

"I just wish I could get over this, that it wouldn't last much longer."

"Well, I know it can take a long, long time."

"That doesn't give me much hope!"

"Cheyne, you need to meet someone that you can have for a partner, to share life with. I really want that to happen to you. Right now, it's as if you are in some kind of adolescent stage, going through things that you should have gone through a long time ago. I'm worried about your eating. You need to put some flesh on those bones. You are getting too thin."

Wanting to change the subject I said, "Janie, I know that you and Charles tell each other everything, but I would feel very uncomfortable for him to know about this, to know that I've fallen in love with you."

"I haven't told him, Precious. This is something that is just between the two of us and no one else."

Toward the end of our conversation, Janie said, "You have to promise me that if our friendship brings you too much pain, you will tell me. I don't want to ever be the cause of pain for you."

"I promise to tell you."

After we hung up, I began thinking about a meditation written by Ted Loder that included the words: "Expose my shame where it shivers, crouched behind the curtains of propriety, until I can laugh at last through my common frailties and failures, laugh my way toward becoming whole."

I'm almost in a state of shock as to what has happened to me. My appetite has again left me. I didn't sleep much last night thinking, thinking, thinking of Janie's knowing I'm in love with her. I feel shattered at my inability to keep my feelings to myself and devastated she has known for such a long, long time. What a fool I have probably made of myself. And yet there's that part of me that is overwhelmingly grateful to her for her friendship and her willingness to continue to be friends with me. That truly amazes me, and makes me feel quite humble.

Can I continue to look her in the eye? The things I have thought about us make me ashamed. Over and over I hear Janie say, "I know the source of your pain, Cheyne. I've known it for a long, long time."

I began thinking of the devastation I have brought down upon myself, upon my life. Many people experience life-changing tragedies such as death of their spouse or child, or loss of a job, or the destruction of their home, or bleakness from some tragic illness, but these are brought about by some outward cause. What has happened to me is an inwardly-based misery; one I should have been able to control, but I couldn't.

My well-ordered, well-structured life has crumbled. It is no more. And what I am left with is the shell of a person I don't even think I know. There's been a death in my family, and it's been me. I'm gone.

Why did I fall in love with Janie? How many times I have asked myself that question, over and over and over? Why?

I had buried my emotions deep within me for many, many years. They were buried and safely contained. I picture a brick cylinder inside of me, similar to a deep well, but completely enclosed, sealed. This cylinder safely contained all those emotions I ignored for over forty years. I picture the cylinder so full it was bulging at the seams.

That Sunday in August when Janie and I talked about our families, for the first time in all those years, a crack appeared in the cylinder. Emotion seeped out. That first emotion was sorrow for Janie and some of the sadness in her life. This new emotion, sadness and empathy, pushed its way out of my hidden recesses.

This little bit of sympathy that seeped out created a crack in that cylinder causing tears to trickle down my cheeks while my whole being began aching with sorrow for Janie. I was amazed to feel such sorrow for anyone, but especially for someone I didn't know very well. The key, I believe, was Janie's acceptance of homosexuality as something natural for certain individuals. We had broached a subject I had always refused to talk about, actually refused to even think about. And yet, the two of us that morning discussed that subject. Never before had I heard anyone say that homosexuality was just the way God made some people--that it was not a choice. Surely it was that discussion that brought the crack in my well-constructed wall (cylinder)!

During that afternoon, after first shedding tears for Janie, I began to feel a sense of hope, a sense of joy within my heart that there was someone who, if she knew about my homosexuality, would respect me anyway. I began imagining opportunities of talking with her about it, of at last being able to reveal my true self to someone who might actually like me anyway. Hope! Hope permeated my total being. Now more emotions were seeping out. First sorrow, now hope! The crack was widening, but I still was unaware of it. If I had given thought to what was happening, perhaps I could have stepped in and shoved those emotions back into "the container" and sealed up the crack. But I was almost in an euphoric state by then. Hope. I hadn't felt hope for so many, many years. The feeling was so new, so strange, that I relished every little bit of it. Joy flooded me. A friend. Someone to talk with. Even then there was no "little voice" within me warning me of the "mine field" I was stepping into. Too many years had passed since I had thought of another woman that my barriers had crumbled from age and from neglect. Blindly and ignorantly I allowed my new emotions full range.

Suddenly, the hope vanished when a terrible despair set upon me. The crack had widened even further and various emotions were pouring out. Despair. Why was I feeling despair?

I recall standing by the stove with tears running down my cheeks and realizing I had no clue as to why I was feeling so miserable.

Then, as I contemplated the cause of this acute pain and anguish, a new emotion flooded through me. The crumbling cylinder's wall allowed emotions I thought had disappeared to pour through me. Can I even use the word "love" when I remember those feelings? It was more like lust. I was shocked. Totally shocked. I don't recall ever in my life having feelings similar to these. They crept up on me, surprised me, and yes, shocked me. Devastated by what was happening to me, I experienced a pain totally new to me, a desire that mortified me, a sickening feeling in my stomach, an awakening of a need within my body I thought disappeared a long, long time ago. What was happening to me? At the time, I didn't understand it, and despite the numerous attempts to analyze the emotions that flooded through me that afternoon, I have never really been able to put it all together. This is my best attempt so far. Once that crack came in my "wall" that Sunday, it just kept widening and widening so that more and more emotions seeped out until the wall just tumbled into ruins and that primary emotion I had buried so long ago, that need to hold a woman, to love her, rushed out and centered on Janie Robbins.

Why Janie? Who else? I had no friends, just acquaintances. That's all Janie was. Just an acquaintance. A member of the Sunday School class I taught. But I saw in her something special, something different. She was kind, loving and tender-hearted toward all people, even those who are different. I fell in love with Janie because she is a good person, someone I enjoyed being around, someone with whom I could talk. That's the

250

way it was with Karen. We loved to talk and share thoughts and feelings. And speaking of Karen, my feelings for her have practically disappeared. I suppose they really have disappeared. There's still a curiosity in connection with her, a curiosity of wondering what I would feel toward her today if we were to see each other. But when I think of who I would most prefer to be with, there is no doubt whatsoever in my mind. Janie.

When I allow my mind the freedom to dream, to fantasize about her, I feel bodily reactions--a hollowness within me followed by a type of constriction in my chest, then this pain. I've got to get over this. I can't continue to live with these desires. They are so wrong, so sinful. I don't allow myself to fantasize nearly as much as I used to. This is a good sign, I think.

This new setback, Janie's knowing that I am in love with her, has really thrown me. Am I that transparent? I'm having trouble sleeping again, and my appetite is not what it should be. I'm amazed that the thoughts of suicide haven't started entering my mind on a regular basis. Really amazed. Can I continue to keep those thoughts at bay?

Soon after lunch today, I sent the following e-mail: "Janie, I know you are concerned as to whether or not there was something you did that caused this problem I'm experiencing. I feel I need to assure you that you are totally innocent. You did absolutely nothing you shouldn't have done. Actually, I don't think I did anything I shouldn't have done. That's one reason I feel so devastated by it all. I keep hearing you say, 'I know the source of your pain, Cheyne. I've known it for a long, long time.'

"Janie, I can't believe this is happening to me. Just this morning I began thinking of the difficulties I have brought down upon myself, my life." And then I continued with what I have just recorded in my journal of my analysis of what happened to me on that Sunday in August. I then wrote: "This new setback, your knowing that I am in love with you, has really thrown me. I tried so hard to keep it a secret, and to be told that you've been aware of it for such a long time fills me with such shame, such a feeling of embarrassment that it's difficult to even put into words. I am humiliated. I ponder continually what is really happening to me, whether all I am going through is truly a part of God's plan for my life or if the devil is having a field day tormenting me. I'll admit that I'm drawn more to that second thought.

"Just when I think that things can't get any worse, they do. I yearn to hide, but refuse to do that. I promise you I'll never step out of line with you. Never."

Just before supper this evening, an e-mail arrived from my brother, Tom, who said, "Mom called last week and, among many other things, asked a couple of questions about you: (1) if I had heard from you, and (2) if I knew what was going on. I take back my recommendation that you not tell her what's up with you.

"I'm sure you and I have both been influenced by her statements in the past about Warren (one of our relatives who is gay). She specifically apologized for being so critical of my friendliness toward Warren throughout the years. She surprised me by saying I was right, and she was wrong. I wondered if her reconsideration had come from something you said to her, because it's been years since I've said anything to her. I simply avoid talking to her about Warren.

"And there are other considerations: if you are politically and publicly active in Tyler, she will eventually hear something, and she would be more upset about being excluded than anything else. And mad at all of us who didn't clue her in. And there's the opposite: if keeping her uninformed causes you to pass up living the way you want to live, then you both lose out.

"So even though I take back my previous recommendation, I sure don't have a new one. I guess you just have to weigh pros and cons of either action. If you do talk to her, I suggest you arrange for her to think all of us are being informed at the same time. Love and best wishes, Tom"

I immediately replied, "My suspicions are definitely aroused by what you said about Mother. Especially the apology concerning your friendship with Warren. Amazing! I have no idea what brought it on, but it certainly wasn't anything I said.

"A little over a week ago Mother and I had what I would term an 'interesting' conversation. She is feeling as if (in her words) she is a 'millstone' around my neck. I assured her she wasn't. That led us to her previous belief that there was a man in my life and the 'guesses' of who it was. She deeply apologized for doing me that way. I have finally succeeded in assuring her there is no man in my life.

"Then she brought up the fact that she regrets not having supported me back in the '80's when Jim and I had decided to divorce. She and Dad talked us into 'not giving up.' She now realizes that was a mistake, and that I would have been much better off if they had simply supported our decision.

"I have a feeling Mother is doing a lot more thinking about the divorce than she has yet put into words. Although I have tried to be 'up-beat' when I'm around her, she is probably seeing through me. I've suffered more lately than ever before and just don't feel like sitting down and visiting with her about anything. I am probably fearful of her bringing up subjects I don't want to talk about.

"Tonight I'm stepping out into something new for me. I have attended two PFLAG meetings and met a woman who is a pastoral counselor. We are going to meet in less than an hour to talk. I definitely need some counseling, but I'm uncertain this is the route I should go. However, this new step I am taking is the opportunity to actually talk to another gay. I've never done that before."

I then drove to Myra Hudson's small home about 10 minutes away. I sat on her sofa while off to the side she sat in a stuffed chair. We visited from 6:30 until almost 9 p.m. Although I didn't bawl like I have in the past, I used up a bunch of tissues as I told her everything. When I described my 'brick cylinder' that developed the crack and allowed my emotions to begin to escape, she liked that analogy. She said that she had always used the idea of a bucket that finally becomes so full of emotion that it begins to spill over--based on the theory that we are able to contain only so much emotion before it has to escape.

When I had completed my story, Myra asked, "Are you wanting advice?"

254

"Yes, please."

"First, I would advise against your telling your mother about your sexual orientation. She may not want to know. Tell her only if she asks."

Then she asked, "Do you realize there is no future for you and Janie?"

"Yes, I know that. I've always known that."

"You know that you and Janie can never have a physical relationship?"

"Yes, I know that. I know I've got to get over my feelings for her."

"Then whenever you begin fantasizing about Janie, picture yourself walking along a beach with Jesus by your side. Every time the thought of Janie pops into your mind, force yourself to picture the beach scene."

"One of the things you told me tonight is that you cry and feel sad and are not certain what it is that is making you cry and feel sad. It's important that you focus in on what it is that makes you cry. Identify the cause. Grieve over that particular thing. You'll never be able to fill up what you call 'your empty shell' until you have grieved through all the issues that are causing the tears. And you can't do that until you identify those issues--which can be very difficult to do."

When I left, she suggested that sometime we ought to go out for pizza together or something like that. Myra is about eleven years younger than I am. Her former husband does not know she is gay, but her sons and her mother know.

June 4 - June 17, 2000

Sunday, June 4: Dr. Watson preached an interesting sermon. For the first time, I heard him use the term "sexual orientation" in his talk about the eunuch that Phillip met in the desert (Acts 8: 26-40). I thought that rather brave of him to head that direction. Then later in the sermon, which was about witnessing, he stressed the need to include everyone in the church, explaining that the church is to be all-inclusive, not geared to just one or two particular groups of people. Personally, I felt he might be opening the door to eventually discuss the inclusion of gays, but I may be reading more into the sermon than he intended. It's always nice to hope.

Tuesday, June 6: Days have passed and no word from Janie. I have fallen into the depths of despair and keep telling myself to "just survive." That's my only goal today, to just stay alive. I want so badly to die. I finally left the apartment and rented four videos. I've got to just stay alive today. That's all. No other goal. Just live. It's been almost six full days since Janie told me she knew the source of my pain.

Wednesday, June 7: 7:30 a.m. Janie called. I can't believe it! And she sounded like her old self as she shared with me all the "house" problems she has been going through. When she heard my voice and the hesitation in it when I said hello to her, she asked, "Cheyne, is anything wrong?"

"I just thought you didn't want to talk with me anymore."
"Oh, no, no! Not at all."

And off our conversation went. My heart is so much lighter.

Friday, June 16: I'm not writing as much as I used to, probably because both Barbara and Janie are out of town. Hence, no communication with them. But I've started communicating on a fairly regular basis with Myra. My guard stays up concerning my feelings toward her. I am determined to feel nothing personal toward her or anyone else. Love is too painful.

Saturday, June 17: Myra, in replying to questions I posed yesterday, replied, "I, like you, have lived most of my life 'in the box' of safety and meeting others' expectations. Only in the last three years or so have I begun to truly know and live from my adventurous spirit." After sharing information about some trips she had taken, she answered my question as to which church she attended. "Right now I worship on Sunday mornings at St. Gabriel's Community Church. It is a small evangelical, non-denominational gay-friendly church here in Tyler. Since my summer in Wyoming I view 'church' in a different way than I once did. I'll share with you sometime. Hope you have a good day! Myra"

Saturday. Barbara is home. I assume Janie is home, but she hasn't contacted me.

257

Wednesday, June 21, 2000

Days pass and I'm not in the mood to write or to do anything. What a struggle life is! Janie hasn't called or written. Nothing. I realize she could be ill, or there could have been a family emergency, or something could have happened to her parents, but still I picture her here in Tyler choosing not to contact me. How am I going to stand it? Not ever visiting with her again. Not ever seeing her again. I am in abject misery.

Knowing Barbara had returned, I shared with her all that has been going on, especially the conversation Janie and I had in which she admitted she has known the "source of my pain" for many months. Several days ago, I also informed Barbara of my contacts with Myra and the advice she gave me. I ended this letter to Barbara by saying "One of my constant prayers is a thankfulness for you, for your friendship and your willingness to put up with me. You're one in a million, and I know it. I just don't say it often enough."

To which Barbara replied, "Myra's advice sounds terrific to me--grounded in faith, pragmatic (I hate pie-in-the-sky advice), and positive. Next time you see her, tell her about your sleeping problem (if you haven't) and see what she thinks you ought to do about that. That concerns me, especially right now when I am sleep-deprived myself and know how it feels.

"I suspect that your mother may already know as much as she wants to know. The mental image to substitute for thoughts of Janie (walking along a beach with Jesus by my side) is a positive thing, it seems to me. I know this is a foolish question to ask of

258

someone as analytical as you are, but have you tried to identify specific things that draw you to Janie? Obviously, primarily physical, but I always think there's something beyond that when the attraction is so strong, and maybe part of it is Janie's openness about her emotions, which is something you've not allowed yourself to experience. Perhaps when you recognize what that part of the attraction is, you'll be better able to recognize those qualities in someone else. (Remember, I'm a journalism major, not a therapist, so give any suggestion I make all the attention it deserves!) I think you'll be able to identify the cause(s) for the tears as time goes on, too.

"Raining, and I want to turn the computer off.

"Don't talk too nice to me. Makes me think you've heard that I have a terminal illness."

In replying to Barbara's question as to why I'm drawn to Janie, I wrote: "I have tried many times to analyze my attraction to Janie. I'm convinced it is not physical. Not at all. I think if it had been physical I would have been attracted to her when I first got to know her. But we were acquaintances for a year prior to my falling in love with her.

"Pure meanness on the part of God? Oh I've thought that many times. I don't think I deserved this at all. And I feel anger and sometimes hate and sometimes just sorrow. If I had done something I shouldn't have done I could say I deserved what I got. But I played the game by the only rules I knew; and even though they hurt all the time, I stuck with them. I denied myself a chance to be happy, and you'd think I'd be rewarded for that with something positive instead of this agony I'm experiencing. It's as

259

if the world has turned upside down and I'm powerless to make it right.

"But I'm digressing from the question. What attracted me to Janie? All I can think of is what I wrote in that letter to her-- probably learning of her openness and acceptance of homosexuals. What a bombshell to have someone sit and talk with me about a subject I had always refused to bring into my consciousness and to have that person verbally demonstrate love, kindness, and acceptance toward people I had always been taught were abominable. My guard was always up but never toward this danger. Who would have thought a Christian existed who displayed a loving acceptance toward homosexuals?

"When I watched a television special called *Love Chronicles*, one of the premises was that a certain chemistry is built into us so that when we meet an individual under intense conditions, we are drawn to them: hence my attraction to Janie."

There was more in the letter to Barbara, especially additional information I had gleaned from the television special. I copied that letter and forwarded it on to Myra. She replied, "From my experience, both in what I have learned professionally and through personal experience, all of your 'reasons' for attraction to Janie are certainly reasonable, if anything in the realm of love can be reasonable.

"We are attracted to individuals who manifest those qualities which we have not recognized or nurtured within ourselves. The scent is possibly the greatest source of arousal. For women, physical attraction is usually not the primary force behind attraction. The emotional attraction is far greater. The circumstance of the meeting is certainly a factor. The more intense the situation, the greater the emotional bonding that occurs.

"I am looking forward to my 'adventure' this weekend in attending the Gay Pride Parade in Houston. In my 3+ years of being 'out' in the gay community of Tyler I have been blessed to meet and become friends with some really neat women, and I will be sharing the weekend adventure with several of them. They are all younger (some much younger) than I am and with partners. In all honesty I must admit that at times I miss the company and friendship of someone nearer my age (and not in a relationship) who can identify with my experiences of long term marriage and children. Let's face it. There are not many single, 50+ year-old-lesbians freely walking around in Tyler, Texas.

"I say all that to say this. Cheyne, as you express your appreciation for my staying in touch and offering friendship, in all honesty, there is mutual appreciation from my end. May you have a peaceful night's rest! Psalm 4:8 Myra"

About 3 p.m. I replied to Myra, "Today was my regular 'checkup' day; and I confessed to my doctor the stress I've been under, my inability to sleep, and my loss of appetite. My weight continues to drop, but very slowly. I tried on some of my daughter's discarded jeans. If I had looked at the size, I would never have attempted to try them on, but they fit! . . . and I decided to just keep them. Then I noticed they were Size 5! I was amazed as I always shop for Size 12, sometimes Size 10.

"Anyway, what I started out to say is that the doctor is putting me on Prozac. I can't comprehend how a medicine can help a depressed person when the depression is not chemical but due

261

to an emotional cause. Goodness knows it would be wonderful to get some help. This has been a horrible week as far as emotions are concerned, but I know exactly why it is horrible. Janie was supposed to return home four days ago, and I haven't heard a word from her. I don't know if she is ill, has a family emergency, or has just chosen to end the friendship. I so hate to push myself onto her if she is wanting to back away. I'm just having a tough time coping.

"You mentioned there not being many women in our age group who are 'out' who have been married and have children. The only gay women I know are the few I've met at the PFLAG meetings! There's not another gay woman in Tyler that I know!

"I can't help but be somewhat envious of young gay women. To have the courage to come 'out' when you are young would be wonderful. I never felt that option was even available to me. After this awful experience I am going through with Janie, and the painful emotions that keep me tied up in knots, I'm determined to never again fall in love. It's pure misery.

"I think the time has come for you to tell me a little more about yourself. So far, our friendship has centered on my problems. Rather a selfish situation on my part. So tell me something I don't know about you, maybe how you met your husband, why you married him, or something. Were you ever in love with him?"

To my inquiry, Myra responded: "Shame on your doctor for prescribing the Prozac and not explaining how a chemical can be helpful in alleviating what would appear to be an emotional problem. For him to prescribe this you would probably be diagnosed as having a clinical depression.' Your sleep

262

disturbance, appetite loss, weight loss, and emotional roller coastering which have continued for longer than a two to three week period are all symptoms of 'clinical depression.'

"When we have emotional stress and upset in our lives we feel sad, down, fatigued, depressed. We have the 'blues.' Over a period of time, this emotional 'slow down' actually slows down the chemical processes in our brain. Our brain becomes like a 4-cylinder engine hitting on only 2 or 3 cylinders. As the chemical processes in our brain actually slow down, a chemical change occurs. This chemical change then perpetuates the 'slow down' and you now have a clinical/chemical depression as opposed to the simple 'blues.'

"The anti-depressant acts as a 'jump start' for the brain, a little extra boost to get the production of those serotonins back up to par. Now, you know more about depression and anti-depressants than you ever really wanted to know! Sorry, I got a little carried away. But it is really one of my pet peeves when doctors prescribe medications, particularly neurologic or psychotropic medications without explaining why and how they work!!

"I started dating my ex-husband between my junior and senior year in high school. He was six years older. I was the intelligent, competent, 'most likely to succeed' valedictorian of a small high school. I went to a fairly large university right out of high school only to discover that I was shy, insecure, lonely, and had no sense of my own identity outside the roles I maintained in small-town USA. Of course, this is all from a backward glance.

"Wow, it is 10 p.m. and I am pooped! More of the saga later! Would you enjoy meeting somewhere for a light dinner Friday evening? We could continue swapping stories.

"Hope you have a better day tomorrow! Myra"

Thursday, June 22, 2000

What an absolutely horrible day. Terribly, terribly depressed today. Down in that very deep hole. All I've done is lie around, cry, and do lots of nothing. This is my second day on the Prozac and it certainly hasn't shown any signs of helping me.

Friday, June 23, 2000

I took two sleeping pills last night about 10 p.m. and slept good until about 4 a.m. After that I kept awakening, then going back to sleep and finally got up about 6:30. This gave me a good night's sleep. I don't think I feel quite as far down in the pit this morning, but I'm still down pretty deep.

Barbara wrote early this morning and asked, "How are you feeling today, my friend?"

I immediately replied and told her I slept little, but that I planned to meet Myra tonight for supper. "I won't be very good company and have absolutely no appetite."

Before 10 a.m., Barbara replied to my confession of thinking Janie might be wanting to end our friendship: "Everything you've ever told me about Janie indicates that if she thought it was best not to maintain your friendship, she'd be the first to let you know. Therefore, I assume she's out of town or otherwise out of pocket. I can't imagine that she'd just ignore a call. If you'll focus on logic and prior experience, you'll recognize that, too. Remember, this is the woman who was perceptive enough to ask if you're gay. This is not a person who hides what she's thinking or feeling. Please, if you go into a funk, let it be one that you enter on a somewhat realistic basis, and not one you slide into on the basis of imagination alone. Work on imagining something wonderful you'd have to cope with!

"When discussing spiritual matters, I've often said that we need to make our decisions based on what we know, not based on how we feel. Emotions are notoriously unreliable indicators of truth.

"Have you been able to exercise any? Body motion sometimes helps produce a tranquil mind.

"Surely something would taste good to you! In my family, ice cream was always the specific for illness, so I suggest a Dairy Queen Blizzard. (I'd choose Butterfinger!)

"You're going to be well, and you're going to truly enjoy your life again before this year is over--and, quite possibly, before this month is over. I'm glad you're going to see Myra, and I'm glad it'll be in a restaurant! Love, Barbara"

My reply went out about 11 a.m.: "Thanks for the encouraging words about Janie. I'm completely aware of how absolutely imbecilic I am being, how irrational--but it's as if another person has taken over my body. I've always been able to be 'in control' and now my emotions are completely beyond me. I'm aware of how I surely look to you and would look to others if they knew about this! Beyond comprehension! Goodness knows that I myself have trouble comprehending it. I tell myself old women are not supposed to have feelings like this. I know that just accepting the fact that I am gay is a big enough jump for you, but to even begin to fathom my being in love with another woman must stretch anyone's limits of understanding! Thanks for not preaching to me about it, just guiding me. I need that.

"Eating Blizzards is a good idea. That always sounds good. Heath Bar is my favorite.

"I skipped my exercising yesterday, but I usually walk for 45 minutes to 70 minutes! Usually about an hour. Normally I perform various exercises for about 12 minutes each morning, but that has been going by the wayside. When I walk, I usually keep a little notebook with me that contains all the poems and Biblical chapters that I have memorized. I mentally recite them as I walk. But I've had to give up on that lately. My mind just won't focus for long stretches of time."

Barbara's reply: "Having accepted that you're gay (which took about 35 seconds, since it explained quite a few things), I have no difficulty accepting your being in love. I do have a problem (as I'm sure you've noticed) understanding why it makes you a touch irrational from time to time. Please feel free to call me on my own periodic fits of irrationality!

"Memorizing is terrific, isn't it? I need to work more on that. When you get ready for a new passage, consider II Corinthians 1:3-5. That's so short you can do it in a flash! I'll never believe that God is the source of affliction, but this passage assures us that He's the source of the comfort/strength which enables the affliction to (ultimately) be the source of blessing. Which is tough to believe some days, but still I do believe that, mostly on the basis of past experience and the truth that 'faith is substance of what I hope for, the evidence of what I don't yet see.'"

June 26 - July 5, 2000

Monday, June 26: Barbara wrote: "I haven't heard a word from you for several days. Are you okay? You know you don't have to tell me anything you want to keep to yourself, but I'm not sure you know how much you're in my thoughts.

"Talk to me about something!"

I quickly replied, "Janie wasn't in Sunday School yesterday nor at the wedding in the afternoon. One of my class members asked me where she was. Then another asked the same question at church yesterday. I don't know where she is. I haven't heard a word from her for 19 days. My emotions are on a regular roller coaster, up one day, down the next. Thank goodness I don't stay down for three or four days in a row. If I did, I wouldn't still be around! It's such a battle.

"Several of my class members approached me Sunday and told me they had discussed me in Sunday School and they all thought I needed to return to the class as a member. It's nice to be wanted. Carolyn is teaching and they made a point of telling me that she would enjoy having me there, too. Since I like being with them so much, it's quite a temptation.

"Myra and I had a good visit at Jason's Deli. We have much in common. She was married for twenty years and has two sons. She understands the pain I am going through with Janie because she has experienced something similar. She advocates complete separation from Janie, a suggestion you would heartily endorse.

"By the way, I thought your lesson Sunday was extra good. You really are a wonderful teacher, but I've always known that."

Barbara wrote a long reply which included this question: "Do you think I could meet Myra sometime, or would that disturb a sorted-out arrangement in your life? Church friends here, PFLAG friends there, I mean. I feel no need to discuss 'what you should do' with her whether it relates to Janie or anything else. I just think she sounds like a person who is actively involved in figuring out life and helping others do the same, and I value folks like that. Think about it, please.

"I suspect you know how I feel about your return to the class you were teaching. I doubt it's possible for you to be there without teaching. I know how it was for me the year I took off and went back to 'our' class. And I don't think you've been apart from it long enough to make a truly balanced judgment about that. I hope you'll give the standing aside (from the class, not just the teaching) at least six months, until you feel better both physically and emotionally. I'm convinced you'll feel hugely better both those ways by the first of the year. Pray about it, please; and make a conscious effort to know the members of my class better. I know you're not there to stay, but I think that knowing those women can enrich your life as it has mine. It's certainly not an exact parallel, but getting to know these people better has something in common with Acts 8. Think about it as you read your lesson for next week.

"I wouldn't wish what you're going through right now on my worst enemy, but one positive thing about it for me is that I'm learning to know you so much better. And I like that, as I always believed I would. You have so many strengths, and right now you're feeling so weak. I wonder if realizing how little control any of us really has on our lives is a prerequisite to experiencing the reality of God in a new and powerful way? Love, Barbara"

Tuesday, June 27: 8:09 p.m., I wrote to Barbara: "I swallowed my pride and called Janie. Her husband, Charles, answered and explained that Janie is touring Texas with a friend who is visiting our state for the first time. She'll be back tomorrow night. He sounded very friendly toward me which relieved my mind considerably as I was fearful Charles might know of my feelings toward Janie!"

Barbara answered: "I read this two or three times and considered not saying, 'Told you so!' (about Janie and about Charles). But I am weak. So . . . told you so!"

Wednesday, June 28: I awoke feeling better. Usually I can tell within a few minutes of when I get up what kind of day I will probably have. I find that rather amazing. No tears at all today!!!

And no effort to keep them away. I'm at last starting to hear the bugles of the cavalry coming to my rescue.

Thursday, June 29: Janie called today and we had a nice long conversation about what was going on in both our lives.

Saturday, July 1: This is Day 11 of taking the Prozac, I have had no tears for 3 or 4 days. Amazing. What a change!

I spent all of yesterday afternoon chauffeuring Greg, a wheelchair-bound friend whose wife is in my former Sunday School class. I assumed he knew I was gay, but I was wrong. That's when I discovered how much more difficult it is for me to "out myself" to a male. His reactions were so different!

"I'll take you to a gay bar," he said, "so you can have a good time. I'll even pretend to be gay myself which shouldn't be too hard to do since I'll be sitting in this wheelchair." His comments could all be summed up in what he eventually said: "All you need is to have a good romp in bed. That would get you over your depression."

Greg isn't very knowledgeable about homosexuality and thinks I am just mixed up. Our conversation covered various topics--my divorce, for example. He was surprised to learn I had asked for the divorce. He was unaware, almost shocked, that Dr. Watson had asked me to "take a sabbatical" from teaching my Sunday School class. I think what really surprised him was that after I had confided in Dr. Watson he had asked me to no longer teach. This floored him.

Sunday, July 2: The Prozac has me feeling differently. It's really hard to explain. No tears, but more than that I'm feeling no emotion of any kind. Sterile might be a descriptive word for it.

When I attended Sunday School, I spotted Janie in my former Sunday School department directly across a wide hallway. My heart start racing. I hadn't seen her for 3 1/2 weeks. I immediately turned and went into my new department to avoid her seeing me as I didn't think I could properly handle our greeting each other.

When our classes were over, I spotted her again as she visited with friends in the other department. Still wanting to avoid her, I headed straight for the staircase despite my yearning to speak with her. She looked gorgeous! I had to garner all my will power to head down the stairs. However, when I reached my car, I decided to sit in it and wait for her to reach the parking lot. After a short wait, I spotted her coming my direction. At that point, I exited my car and called to her when she was only a few cars away. Excited to see me, she hurried over and greeted me with a hug and said, "How are you doing, Precious? It's been ages since I've seen you."

We stood beside my car and visited for about ten minutes. Janie was as friendly as ever. "Give me a call and let's meet for lunch some day this week," she said.

That evening at the church service, Barbara and her husband, Jack, sat beside me. I really appreciated that. At one point in the service, as members of the congregation were "passing the peace," she gave me a hug and even drew my cheek up next to hers. That surprised me, and felt so good. She has no idea

271

how much I appreciated that. Not only did it "feel good," but it was a brave act on her part to hug a lesbian in front of the whole church. I wonder if she thought through what she did? Later, I wrote to her to express my appreciation for her action, calling her "courageous."

She replied, "Oh my, I'm about to erase a momentary and quite undeserved perception of myself as courageous. I never gave it a thought, then or now. When I'm near someone I care about and we're passing the peace, I very often hug that person afterward. I figure Bob (Dr. Watson) can have us pass the peace his way, and I'll do it my way. I hug men, I hug women, I touch people I love--what can I say? I hugged you because it was a moment for expressing joy and togetherness and claiming our mutual identity as God's dearly loved children. I'd worshiped, and affirming that calls for affirming each other, doesn't it? I've called you friend since I first met you, you know, and nothing has happened to change that. I don't expect it will.

"No guts, no courage. Hate to disillusion you! I do have a few good qualities that I will trust you to recognize accurately as we go along."

Tuesday, July 4:   Myra and I attended the July 4 outdoor band concert in the park. We sat in our lawn chairs at the side of the outdoor amphitheater and had a perfect view of both the band and the audience. Just prior to the start of the concert, I spied a couple walking toward some seats. I thought, "That surely does look like Janie and Charles, but she looks so young!" I kept debating in my mind if it really was them or wondering if I was just "wanting" it to be Janie. But as I kept watching, and having a very difficult time paying attention to Myra's conversation, I became more and more convinced it really was Janie and Charles. By then my heart was pounding like a triphammer, my stomach was in knots, and I got that hollow feeling in my chest. She was absolutely beautiful. I just kept staring, hoping she would look my way, but she didn't. Everything about her was beautiful. Her long, blonde hair hung down straight instead of all frizzy. The summery red and white dress she wore made her look like a teenager. She and Charles were probably the nicest dressed people there. He was wearing slacks with a red knit shirt. They both looked fashionable while most of us were wearing shorts or jeans. When they sat down, I looked back and caught Charles' attention, but never did see Janie look at me. She eventually shifted her position to where I couldn't even see her.

After the concert, when I noticed them walking in the other direction, I turned that way as I asked Myra, "Would you like to meet Janie?"

"Not particularly," Myra replied.

At that, I knew I would be making a mistake to pursue the meeting, so, with a sick feeling in the pit of my stomach, I went with Myra toward her home. I so wanted to say "Hi" to Janie.

When Barbara and I corresponded this evening, I told her that Myra agreed to the three of us having lunch on Saturday.

Monday, July 10, 2000

The two-hour lunch yesterday with Barbara and Myra was very pleasant. Because they were both from Kilgore (about 30 miles southeast) they had much in common to talk about. Later, Barbara wrote, "I enjoyed visiting with Myra a lot, and would have liked her if I'd just met her somewhere without your involvement at all. Remember I'd suggested the possibility of an emotional involvement with her, and you said she was way too young? Well, it crossed my mind that there's about the same difference in your ages that there is in my sister and her husband. Myra's not that young, especially considering her maturity. You may never have an emotional attachment to her, but if not it would be because the chemistry wasn't there, it wouldn't be because of her age. I'd really like to know her better. Maybe it'll happen, but I've no plans to wedge myself into your friendship."

Tonight at PFLAG, the president of the Dallas chapter spoke to us. When his son told him and his wife that he was gay, they were stunned. They had no inkling their son had a different sexual orientation. After the initial shock wore off, they accepted their son as he is and have since become strong supporters and advocates of gay rights. His talk was most interesting. Myra had been unable to attend the meeting, so called afterward to ask about it. I am aware that a bonding, a closeness, is developing between Myra and me, and yet I feel no emotional pull toward her at all. I wish I did. There are times, however, when I yearn for a closeness with someone.

Monday, August 7, 2000

Monday, I received a letter from Corinna, my former Austin neighbor with whom I recently visited–and took time to "out" myself to her. Her boys are the same ages as Michael and Josh and even though she is 10 years younger than I, she has a grandson the same age as Anne. Our children moved freely between our homes and yards, and I so enjoyed having her family live next door to us. Corinna wrote, "I'm so glad you told me (and others) your story because that is the way, one by one, our society may come to accept homosexuality as just another way to be. I've told a couple of my friends, without mentioning names, and it caused them to think about the subject in a different way--as if it were someone close to them. Little by little, these conversations will make a difference."

There are times when I feel as if I am just "twiddling my thumbs" and not accomplishing anything, so Corinna's letter was a bright spot for me, which I shared with Barbara. My life has really been hectic lately. Perhaps that's good. Six days in Houston caring for my newborn grandson and six days in Austin helping my daughter settle into her new apartment. Then "company" here in my apartment for two days. Add to that my mother's health problems. My, My, My!

275

Tuesday, August 8, 2000

Barbara wrote, "I was reading this book this morning which I've read before and for some reason found myself in the chapter called, 'Testimony.' I hadn't planned to be there, but it's where I was sent, so to speak.

"'Christian testimony has two dimensions. One is testimony to the church and the world, where witnesses tell others about the action of God. The other is testimony to God, where witnesses tell God the truth about themselves and others . . .

"'These testimonies are directed to God as offerings of honor and praise. And they are also directed to other people, telling them the effects of God's power so that they, too, might know God's power in their lives. *I was on a downward road, no hat on my head, no shoes on my feet, no God on my side, no heaven in my view*, the narrative of one former slave began. *Too mean to live and not fit to die. The handcuffs of hell on my hands, the shackles of damnation on my feet. But the Lord spoke peace to my dying soul, turned me around, cut loose my stammering tongue, sent me on my way. And ever since that day, I'm sometimes rising and sometimes falling but I made my vow to the Lord and I'll never turn back no more. I'm going to run on and see what the end's gonna be.*

"'The power of testimony is to give voice to the faith that lets people run on to see what the end's gonna be. Stories like these, told in the context of oppression, are what the theologian Leonardo Boff calls testimonies charged with hope. They keep alive the truth--a truth that society often does not honor. Life is stronger than death. People can change with God's help. God is worthy of our thanks and praise . . .

"'The practice of testimony is an important part of the healing that is taking place all over the world through Alcoholics Anonymous as people stand up to tell painful truths about themselves to God and other people. The practice has also shaped the renewal of a church of the people in Latin America, where Archbishop Oscar Romero of El Salvador and thousands of other Christians have proclaimed the Gospel, urged the poor to speak of their lives in relation to its stories, and paid the martyr's price for doing so.

"'**The practice of testimony requires a person to commit voice and body to the telling of the truth. It guards the integrity of personal and communal life, as much on the grand stage of history as in the small exchanges of home. Today, living in a world where falsehood is strong, we need to support one another as we rise to bear witness, speaking the truth about what we have seen and heard. When we do, we are also supported by another community, one that has inspired Christians since the earliest days: the great cloud of witnesses who have gone before us (Hebrews 12:1).'**[25]

"This struck me in the context of your friend's comment about conversations. Testimony comes in all forms, of course-- public, from pulpit and platform; written; how life is lived. The testimony which has been most effective in my own life has been that which is shared in the context of living that life, the testimony given in order to maintain a relationship, the testimony that's required in the context of community. Which is why I (and your friend, I assume) are much more moved/changed by your kind of testimony than we are by the testimony of others--though I do understand why that very public testimony is necessary to provide encouragement and assurance of acceptance. I don't think I said that very well earlier, and maybe not this time, either."

I thanked Barbara for sharing the "Testimony" excerpt from the book she was reading and confessed that what holds me back from speaking to more people than I have is not a fear of their reaction toward me but a knowledge that the subject might upset them, cause them discomfort and embarrassment.

Barbara replied, "When the time comes to speak to individuals, I think you'll know.

"You may never lose that urge to tears, and I'm not sure that's a bad thing though it does cause us to make adjustments in our perception of who we are. I never cried in public until Daddy died, and then I began crying at telephone commercials and often in church and other times--and I still do. Go figure. I'm not sure self-control is all it's cracked up to be. Maybe we need to know we're vulnerable and human, and maybe other people need to know that about us, too."

August 25 - Monday, September 10, 2000

Monday, August 25:   I attended a Sunday School departmental party this evening. At least 50 people were present and we had a great time eating, visiting, and playing games. I'm glad I went. I know I am "out" to many in this group but have no idea how many!

Consequently, I felt rather nervous walking in, and I immediately looked around for Barbara but didn't see her. She was eating in another room. When we began gathering for fellowship and games, Barbara spotted me, came over and gave me a hug. Upon returning home, I wrote to her: "Perhaps you did not notice it, but when you greeted me tonight and began visiting with me, more than one pair of eyes kept watching us. And this is not my imagination working overtime! As much as I enjoy being with you, sitting and visiting with you and having you for a friend, you are hurting your own reputation by being so nice and friendly to me. You need to give this some serious consideration. Perhaps we shouldn't sit together when around others. There's no sense in raising eyebrows and instigating questions that should never be raised."

When she didn't respond to this e-mail, I eventually cornered her about it. She said, "I asked my husband if he noticed anything, and he said he didn't. I then asked Georgia Hunt if she noticed anything and she was amazed such a question was even asked. After that, I decided not to poll the whole department!"

Sunday, August 27: I wrote Barbara: "Myra came over last night. This was the first time she's been in my apartment, yet we met four and a half months ago. She picked up supper for us and brought a video from the library for us to watch. I felt quite odd about the evening, asking myself if this is what others would term a date? And yet we never touched each other. If a man had been visiting instead of a woman, he would probably have made a move of some kind. And I'll have to admit that the idea of sitting close to her, just enjoying the physical nearness of another person, was very appealing to me; but we kept our distance. Later, after she left, I asked myself why homosexuals are perceived to be promiscuous?"

Barbara's reply: "Glad you and Myra had the quiet, pleasant evening. I think you were due one. As to your question about why people tend to think gays are promiscuous, I think part of it is the behavior of those who are in the public eye--most recently Anne Heche and Ellen what's her name, not to mention the divorce of the two who were married by the Methodist minister who pretty much gave up his career path to perform their ceremony. And part of it is the number of intimate sexual relationships so many gays seem to have before finding a partner to commit to. It's certainly true that tons of heterosexuals also have a number of sexually intimate relationships before marriage. My own question would be whether or not the expectations of society, the public commitment, cause the breakup of those relationships or not. But then, I don't even know why I do a lot of things I do myself, so will probably not understand this. Sounds to me as if you and Myra are friends right now, which is different from dating. I think most young people occasionally do what you all did with people of the opposite sex, but consider it a friendship thing rather than a date. Depends on the emotions involved, doesn't it? And I'm not surprised that you experienced a longing for emotional closeness and the comfort (?) of touch. You've had a rough few weeks (months, actually) without much of that, and we all need it in some form or other. Please notice that heterosexual women often hug each other, hold each other, in times of emotional stress. You never have--but most of us do.

"From the little I know of her, I think Myra is a neat person, a 'grown-up,' so to speak. Maybe you should just enjoy her company and not kill yourself analyzing stuff. If something develops between you, time enough then to analyze.

"Hope you can sleep tonight. I may go to bed early again, though it's unlikely I could sleep that long two nights in a row. (But I'd like to!) "

Monday, August 28: I received this message today from Barbara: "I've reread what I said about gays being viewed as promiscuous; and I didn't do too well there, either. What I was thinking is that the people who identify themselves publicly as gay don't have a great track record for commitment; and since they're just about the only gays people (think they) know, that's the assumption that's made. It's also true that the commitment level of most people who seek public attention (actors, sports figures, whoever) isn't that dependable whether they're gay or not, but we know so many heterosexual people in our everyday lives who are faithful that we don't make that same assumption to the same degree.

Thanks for being patient with me when my mouth outruns my brain. (After all, I'm only 64!)"

Janie and I hardly ever talk any more, but today we spent over an hour on the phone "catching up." I continue to miss her constantly.

Sunday, September 3: As I noticed next week's Sunday School lesson, I wrote to Barbara: "I think it might be easier on you to teach next week's lesson without my sitting there. Good old Romans 1:26-27. As I read in one commentary 'If Paul had intended to condemn homosexuals as the worst of all sinners, he certainly had the language skills to do a clearer job of it than emerges from Romans 1:26-27.' But I feel certain there are many who see the condemnation very clearly in those verses. Anyway, if it would help for me not to be there, let me know. You know I'd do most anything for you."

Late afternoon Myra and I joined a group of about twenty from St. Gabriel's for a Labor Day pool party held at the home of a female couple. Relaxing among this friendly group was just what I needed. Most of us stayed in the pool to find respite from the blazing sun! This was my first gay/lesbian party, and I felt as if I had entered a different world. Actually, I <u>had</u> entered a different world.

Most in attendance were couples who enjoyed the freedom to show affection toward their partners. Some held hands, some draped an arm around the other. Numerous times I caught myself staring at some of them because their tender, loving behavior was something I had never seen between two women. Alcohol was available, and I'm not accustomed to parties with alcohol. I have led a very sheltered life, and I stuck to my soft drinks. However, toward evening, some of the women began to lose some of their inhibitions--due to the alcohol, I assume. One couple, with arms around each other, shared a hammock. Feeling a touch of envy, I kept letting my eyes stray in their direction. Other couples in the

282

pool occasionally kissed. The backyard was fenced, providing privacy, and these couples who normally had to hide their fondness for each other in public places were free in this setting to express their affection openly. Yes, it was a different world I had entered this afternoon and evening--and I liked it.

Sunday, September 10: However, that change was short-lived as the Sunday School lesson this morning dealt with perhaps the most famous of the infamous "6 Biblical passages" condemning homosexuality which was included in the broader lesson of Romans 1:18-32. Barbara did an excellent job of never touching on the subject of homosexuality until her concluding statement when she explained there was no time to discuss that part of the passage. She then handed out her "Lesson Leftovers" that she regularly shares at the end of each lesson--information she didn't have time to discuss with the class. Her "leftovers" included, among other things, *Views of Some Texas Baptist Leaders on Homosexuality.*[26]

Russell H. Dilday, Jr., president, BGCT (Baptist General Convention of Texas):
According to the Bible, God's ideal for sex in marriage is one man, one woman in a monogamous relationship for life. Any divergence from ideal is contrary to God's will and therefore sinful. Homosexual practice is a perversion of God's plan and is described in the Bible as an abominable sin. Of course, there are other perversions, such as adultery and premarital sex, which the Bible also condemns as sexual sins.

David Currie, director, Texas Baptists Committed:
Homosexual activity is sinful as I understand the written word of God. Practicing homosexuals should not be elected leaders nor should persons practicing greed, hatred, anger and prejudice (as a lifestyle) be church leaders. The church must balance Christ's call and example of treating sinners with grace and love while affirming biblical morality and the truth that things are clearly right and wrong.

Phil Lineberger, president BGCT 1990-91:
I do not believe homosexual activity is natural or biblically acceptable, but I do believe people who have these tendencies need to be treated with respect as human beings created in the image of God.

Phil Strickland, director, Texas Baptist Christian Life Commission:
I believe that the Bible teaches that homosexual practice is inconsistent with Christian living. The Bible teaches the same about adultery, vengefulness, greed, self-righteousness and an unforgiving spirit. This is to say that while homosexual practice is sin, it is not the only sin, but one sin among many which estrange us from God. We follow Jesus as we welcome all sinners to repent, to receive the forgiveness of God and to enter into the fellowship of God's people.

Barbara noted (and later told me) she chose these "less condemning" statements from among nine listed in the report.

I haven't talked with Janie in a very long time. Despite the anguish our separation brings to my heart, I remind myself that this is the only life I can ever have in regard to her. I no longer allow myself to live in the unrealistic fantasy world I created.

Wednesday, September 13, 2000

Barbara and I began discussing the phrase, "hate the sin, love the sinner" after I had indicated how much I hated that phrase. She replied, "I'm not crazy about the phrase and can easily see how you might hate it. I see no sin in being born with a specific sexual identity, as I've told you--but as I've also told you, I can't find any part of the Bible which condones any sexual relationship other than a faithful heterosexual marriage. That would include premarital sex and adultery, obviously. I imagine few people in any Sunday School class are free from all sexual sin, but I'm doubting many will be honest with each other about that fact since they don't HAVE to be.

"It is also true that I cannot imagine interrupting a friendship because of any judgment I might make as to sin in someone else's life. This would leave me with zero friends--and no one who'd be willing to be MY friend, since my sinful characteristics are painfully obvious to anyone who's spent much time with me.

"I also do not say that I've thought my last thought about this matter. I continue to read about it, both the things you give me and things I find elsewhere, and I do not know where God will lead. I only know where I am now."

Barbara's letter was a long one that ended with, "You're a terrific person. I thoroughly enjoy your company and talking with you about real stuff (as opposed to who won which game or who wore what where). And I need who you are in my life."

I tried to analyze Barbara's opinion about homosexuality; and I believe she has reached the point of accepting the fact that homosexuality is not chosen, but she feels quite strongly that relationships between homosexuals are sinful.

I read somewhere that once an individual decides to "come out of the closet," it's a never-ending process. That's true. Every once in a while I feel a nudge to tell a certain individual. I'll think about it for awhile, then usually decide this is a step I need to take, and then I'll do it. For the most part, the responses have been positive, and I am developing closer friendships with more and more people.

Barbara and I wrote several letters back and forth tonight as did Carolyn and I. Here's a little of what Barbara wrote: "I remember how unclear I was as to who I am as a person when I was in high school and at Baylor University, and I try to imagine what it must have been like for you in much more difficult circumstances. I know I can't really do a good job of that, but I have no problem staying aware of the pain you endured for so many years, never knowing if anyone cared about you for yourself or just who they thought you were. One good thing about pain, it certainly makes a person compassionate--and we all need a certain amount of compassion!"

I replied, "I focused in on your statement 'never knowing if anyone cared about you for yourself or just who they thought you were.' You're right. I played a role all of my life. I always tried to be 'good' and follow all the rules. I wanted to be accepted, and I especially wanted my parents to be proud of me. I knew they suspected I was homosexual. I also knew they believed homosexuality was wrong and totally unacceptable for their only daughter. This was a tightrope I walked all of my life--pretending to be someone I wasn't in order to please my parents and society in general.

"There was never anyone with whom I could let down my guard, a guard that was always up. Even when Karen and I continued to correspond, I was cautious and circumspect knowing her husband also read my letters.

"I think it was the loneliness that hurt the most. The challenge of succeeding at whatever I attempted was always just that, a challenge. This constant striving 'to be best' became a way of life. Actually, I think I was trying to prove my worth more to myself than to anyone else. And I'm still caught up in that. I guess when you do something all of your life it is difficult to change. The primary change I am making that truly amazes me is my willingness to share my 'secret.' So many have told me how courageous I am but I don't feel courageous at all--just free. Unshackled. Out of bondage."

September 19- October 8, 2000

Tuesday, September 19: I received an e-mail from a friend who works with Vicki, one of the women I sent my "out of the closet" letters to but haven't heard from. My friend wrote: "I had the most amazing and refreshing conversation today with Vicki. I didn't bring the subject up; she did. She asked me if I'd received the e-mail from you about your news. I said that I had and had known for quite some time. She stated that she still loved you as a friend and would never shun you but she did disagree with your 'choice' and its effect on Jim. I made the comment that it wasn't a choice but that God made you that way. She said that she just couldn't believe that God made homosexuals but that they chose to be that way. She also said that she didn't know very much about homosexuality and really couldn't make that judgment. I very politely said that 'we would have to agree to disagree on the subject.' I explained to her why I did not believe that it was a choice. She said that she was very proud of the comments that your pastor made to you and acknowledged that he was a very compassionate man.

"She also said that she wanted to respond to your e-mail to let you know that she still cares about you as a friend but wasn't exactly sure what to say. She and her husband had lengthy discussions on the subject and she indicated she would send a message to you as soon as she had her thoughts collected.

"I feel you have a friend in Vicki . . . I think that she is trying to keep an open mind. It was a very positive conversation. Good for you girl!!!!"

Thursday, September 21: I dreamed about Karen last night. We were visiting the Smithsonian although it didn't look at all like the Smithsonian. But that's where we were. I can still see her sitting in a chair facing me. As I looked at her, I thought, "She is really quite attractive." Her makeup, as usual, was flawless; her blonde hair perfectly coiffured; and, of course, she was still quite young. In my mind she will always be 19.

The two of us experienced an all-encompassing feeling of comfortableness with each other. At one point we became separated when one of us left a rest room ahead of the other, but in a very short period of time we were effortlessly drawn together again. I don't recall our ever touching each other and yet I felt enveloped by contentment.

Saturday, September 23: I was both surprised as well as elated to have a phone message from Janie. She explained that she had been in Austin all this time because her aunt had fallen and broken her hip!

I had already convinced myself (how many times have I done this?) that Janie no longer wanted to have anything to do with me. I'm always surprised (and relieved) to learn I'm wrong.

Friday, September 29: Myra invited me to her home where nine of us gathered for good food and games such as Scattergories and Trivial Pursuit. It was a good time, and I really enjoyed the evening.

Saturday, September 30: I've received two written requests from Carolyn to come back and visit our Sunday School class. I plan to go in the morning. She thinks I haven't returned because I feel uncomfortable in the group. She's right in a way. But the feeling of being uncomfortable has nothing to do with everyone's knowing I'm gay. It has everything to do with sitting in a room with Janie and being fearful that I'll look, act, or speak to her in some way that will let others know I'm in love with her. I don't want that to happen. And I also don't want to inflict pain upon myself by being in such close proximity to her. I'm hoping that won't happen, but I'm ready to give it a try--to experiment.

Sunday, October 1: I headed to church for the early service and then decided to attend Carolyn's class. I felt right at home with this group. Everyone kept asking where Janie was and no one seemed to know.

Sunday, October 8: A week later, as I took my seat in my Sunday School department, Carolyn walked over and sat beside me. "Do you know anything about Janie?" she asked. "I haven't talked with her for a long time," I admitted, "but I do know that her aunt fell and broke her hip."

Then in a surprised voice Carolyn said, "Well, there is Janie now!"

I didn't look. I hadn't seen her in such a long time I wasn't certain how I would respond. Carolyn then commented, "She's heading our way now."

I finally turned around. No pain when I saw her. I was so relieved. I felt no pain at all. She looked as wonderful as she always does, and we greeted each other as she sat down beside me. Still no pain. When we entered our classroom, I debated the wisdom of sitting beside her, but decided that everyone would expect us to sit together and my not sitting next to her would raise unnecessary questions. So I did what was expected of me and sat down beside her, all the time feeling comfortable in her presence. I was excited to realize I could look at her, sit next to her, talk to her and still feel no pain. Relief flooded through me along with a hope that the worst was over. I was healing.

I called Janie that afternoon because she asked for details about an upcoming appearance by Rabbi Kushner. We talked for a long time. So enjoyable. But again, no pain. I'm thrilled and relieved. How wonderful it would be to feel nothing but friendship toward Janie.

Monday, October 9, 2000

Greg, the friend I occasionally chauffeur around, sent me an e-mail explaining that he had contacted a counselor friend of his about me. Greg has had difficulty understanding my claim to be lesbian. He thinks I have "jumped the gun" and that I can't be a lesbian if I'm not having an affair with a woman. This has been a very difficult issue for him.

He shared with me the letter his counselor friend sent to him: "Got your e-mail. Yes, I do know something about lesbians. As with any sexual orientation issues, this one has more to do with how a person experiences intimacy with other people, and not just sexual intimacy (that's actually the easy part). So the fact that she has not actually had genital sexual contact with another woman would not mean that she is premature in claiming that she is a lesbian. She would know that pretty well before she ever has a girlfriend.

"Think back to being a teenager. You were pretty sure whom you wanted long before you found a way to actually score with a woman. Although you had not had any heterosexual genital sexual intimacy, you were quite correct to assume you were heterosexual. In much the same way, the 60-year-old woman can say that she is a lesbian. Sexual activity is not determinative of sexual orientation. Sexual orientation is determinative of sexual activity. You can have the orientation without ever having the activity.

"Sexual orientation is so much more than a preference or a choice. It is not a matter of 'liking' something the way we like (or dislike) cherry cokes, for instance. It is a whole way of experiencing the world.

"In our world, it is not at all unusual for someone 60 years old to finally get around to recognizing that their true orientation is as a lesbian. Many, many, many lesbians marry and have children (sometimes finding no other options in their world at the time) and eventually recognize and find the courage to act upon their true orientation. It does not invalidate the good times and the good feelings that almost certainly were present in the marriage. It does not mean the marriage was a lie.

"I think we are moving into a world that will not FORCE young people to marry. Lesbians will not be forced into heterosexual marriages. Society will not push as hard for conformity. We will celebrate diversity and welcome it even in our own families. ('I have a dream . . . ')

"We will not be so quick to demonize the adult actions of people different from us. We will decriminalize consenting intimate actions between consenting adults. We will let people love whom they will.

"The Church will have to quit loading the rifles of people they are setting up to persecute those whom the church regards as sinners. We will have to learn to let God be God and not get ourselves mixed up on this point and start acting like 'vengeance is mine,' because the Lord said, 'Vengeance is MINE, I will repay.' We can get comfortable knowing that all these years, God has run the Universe without needing me to stick MY nose in and punish sinners. My job is to confess MY sins, not others' sins. Oh, yes, I have a dream today.

"And if we can make some of those 'dreams' come true, we will have worked to make our prayer come true ('Thy Kingdom come, on earth . . . '), at least on our little corner of the earth, and in our hearts.

"Tell your friend that you know she did not come to her decision easily, and that you know it took lots of courage to say and do what she did. Tell her that you will be praying that she will find new strength with each day to be the person God created her to be.

"Greg, nobody can CHOOSE to become a lesbian. That is a matter of creation. (For that matter, nobody can CHOOSE to be straight; that, too, is a gift of the Creator.)

"We are what we are. It is what we CHOOSE to do about it that separates the women from the girls, in the case of this 60-year-old lesbian.

"Of course, when anybody asks me, I tell them don't wait till you are 60 to get real with yourself and your family. Get with it, time's a-wasting! Be who you ARE. Let the chips fall. Let other people figure it out, you are responsible for yourself. Don't be captive of other people's ignorance and prejudice.

"Move on. And anyone who refuses to bless you, move away from that person--no one needs their condemnation.

"And I rant and rave some more, because I think it is criminal what happens to lesbians and gay men in our society. But sometimes it is with their own consent and cooperation that they are persecuted.

"I think your 60-year-old might merit a medal for valor."

What a letter! I was ecstatic upon reading it and shared it with Barbara, Myra, and Janie.

October 11 - November 8, 2000

Wednesday, October 11: Myra wrote to me this morning: "Happy Coming Out Day! How does it feel? I think we should celebrate."

I replied: "Happy Coming Out Day to you, too! I've had an emotional morning, so when you asked, 'How does it feel?' I'm not certain how to answer. But generally speaking, I wouldn't trade it for anything. I'm doing another Beth Moore study and this one has to do with bondage and setting ourselves free. It's a hard study for me and this past week was especially difficult. However, the video lesson today (about 16 women were there) focused in on one type of bondage that is handed down from one generation to another-- prejudice. The only prejudice mentioned was racial prejudice, but that certainly isn't the prejudice I've had to live with which impacted my life decisions. I used up a bunch of tissues, but I don't think anyone noticed. Some in the group know about me, but it's a small minority. I feel emotionally drained right now. About celebrating--that's fine with me."

Thursday, October 12: "Myra, there's to be a concert in Bergfeld Park at 7:30 this Saturday evening featuring the East Texas Symphony Orchestra. They will play Tchaikovsky, Gershwin, Debussy, Grieg, Strauss, Berlioz and Bizet. Can't beat that! (Except no Schubert or Mozart.) Anyway, are you interested in going? Many of the selections were listed in yesterday's newspaper and they sound wonderful."

Myra replied: "Well, I guess you might say 'you beat me to the draw.' I did read about the concert and was thinking along the same lines. Sounds like a great lesson in the classics! What are our plan options? You can come over to my house, and we could walk to the park. What about dinner? You could come over earlier, and I could fix something . . . Or we might split a Bruno's half lasagna or one of their large salads. Be in touch. Myra"

As I drove Greg around today, I mentioned the upcoming concert, indicating my plans to attend.

"Alone?" he asked.

"No, I'll go with a friend."

"A man?" he asked.

"Now, Greg, why would I go with a man?"

"Well, what's her name?"

"Myra."

Then later in the afternoon I told him about a movie I had seen that I thought he would enjoy called "Saving Grace." Again

295

he put me through the usual quiz as to whether I went alone or with whom. I again had to tell him "Myra."

He then jumped to all kinds of wrong conclusions despite my protests to the contrary. He then asked, "Where did you meet her?"

"At a PFLAG meeting." And then I explained the group to him.

Monday, October 16: Last night at church, while our pastor was leading a discussion in our fellowship hall, Barbara moved her chair so she could sit close to her husband. That display of "harmony" caused my heart to ache. I actually experienced a feeling of resentment as they enjoyed each other's company and companionship. Their affection for each other was publicly acceptable whereas Barbara's interpretation of scripture prohibits me from experiencing anything similar.

I'm afraid Myra may become personally interested in me. I don't want her to be hurt, and I don't want to lead her on. We've never touched each other, but our friendship is deepening.

Wednesday, October 25: I attended for the second time St. Gabriel's, the little gay/lesbian church. About sixteen had gathered for a two-hour praise and worship service—a service I find one of the most worshipful I have ever participated in. I always leave feeling as if I have truly worshiped.

Thursday, November 9, 2000

Looking back on this past year of turmoil I realize God sent special people into my life to help me over the really rough spots. This past May, an e-mail friend sent me the following paper titled PEOPLE. It hit home when I read it, so I filed it away for future reference. Now as I look at it again, it seems to be even more apropos to the past year of my life.

'"People come into your life for a reason, a season, or a lifetime. When you figure out which it is, you know exactly what to do. When someone is in your life for a REASON, it is usually to meet a need you have expressed outwardly or inwardly.

'"They have come to assist you through a difficulty, to provide you with guidance and support, to aid you physically, emotionally, or spiritually. They may seem like a godsend, and they are. They are there for the reason you need them to be. Then, without any wrong doing on your part or at any inconvenient time, this person will say or do something to bring the relationship to an end.

'"Sometimes they die. Sometimes they walk away. Sometimes they act up or out and force you to take a stand. What we must realize is that our need has been met, our desire fulfilled; their work is done. The prayer you sent up has been answered and it is now time to move on. When people come into your life for a SEASON, it is because your turn has come to share, grow, or learn.

'"They may bring you an experience of peace or make you laugh. They may teach you something you have never done.

297

They usually give you an unbelievable amount of joy. Believe it! It is real! But, only for a season. LIFETIME relationships teach you lifetime lessons; those things you must build upon in order to have a solid emotional foundation.

"'Your job is to accept the lesson, love the person/people (any way); and put what you have learned to use in all other relationships and areas of your life. It is said that love is blind but friendship is clairvoyant.'

Thank goodness for all the friends who have stood by me.

November 17 - November 19, 2000

Friday, November 17: The thought crossed my mind several times today that only a year ago I was living in (surviving) abject misery and despair. How much better I am now! I occasionally sing to myself as I take my walks. Such a change!

Myra called to invite me to her house tomorrow afternoon to watch a video and eat soup and cornbread for supper. She's also invited a male friend who doesn't cook for himself. I'm looking forward to it. As I was watching some TV show tonight, a scene of a couple gently kissing for the first time awoke a feeling in me that I thought had disappeared. And I thought about Myra, and the possibility of kissing her.

Sunday, November 19: I've promised myself to mention some dreams I had this past week. The one I had last night was almost a nightmare. I can't recall the exact reason, but in the dream I returned to the house to live with Jim. It seemed as if it were against my will, an unwelcome change in my life. A cousin whom I haven't seen in over forty years was in the dream. She was still a beautiful young 20-year-old, but blind! It seems as if I had returned to the house to care for her. I recall the feelings I was having in dreading the bedtime, worried that I would be expected to sleep again with Jim and not wanting to. Part of me kept saying, "This can't happen to me because I'm now divorced," and yet I was so afraid it really was going to happen and I dreaded it.

Dreams are so strange. Where do they come from?

About three nights ago Karen's mother and father were in my dream. They didn't look at all like they should, but I knew who they were. In the dream, her dad was a large, handsome, well-built man with light-brown hair, and was probably in his late 30's or early 40's. In reality he was a short, stooped, bearded intellectual. In the dream he put his arm around me, handed me a check for $1,000, and apologized for the problems he and his wife had caused Karen and me, apologized for making our lives so miserable by not accepting us as partners. I wanted to tear up the check and throw it at him. But I took the check telling myself it was a pittance compared to the years of suffering caused by our parents' lack of acceptance of Karen's and my love for each other.

Thursday, November 23, 2000

Thanksgiving! A wonderful day! Everything about it turned out practically perfect. I walked this morning, despite the mist and sprinkles.

I accompanied Myra to the service at St. Dismas, a small open and affirming church. I thoroughly enjoyed the mass and being with the approximately twenty people who gathered for the service. Everyone present has had to combat some problem-- death of a child, alcoholism, drug addictions, homosexuality, etc. In other words, we were all broken, mending people coming together to support each other. It felt good being there. The meal was absolutely delicious! Afterwards, Myra and I went to my apartment to watch another video that I had on hand (*Angela's Ashes*). As usual, we sat on the floor with our backs against the sofa. A large vicuna rug provided a soft seat for us and pillows at our backs made this a comfortable viewing position.

After the movie, we watched some TV, the last part of *Who Wants to Be a Millionaire*, then the beginning of some news show. As we watched the TV together, our hands would occasionally touch, then we'd pull away. Neither one of us wanted to be the one to make the first move to hold hands, and yet I felt we were both wanting the same thing. Finally, Myra took my hand and asked, "Do you mind holding hands?"

"No, not at all," I replied. A little later Myra suggested we turn off the TV and just talk, which suited me fine. At one point, I turned toward her and said, "I realize the Prozac hasn't completely taken away all my feelings." At this comment she gently kissed me. My response was so positive that we were quickly in each other's arms.

There is no way to describe the wonderful feeling--as if I had "come home" to what I have always wanted--to hold and kiss a woman. It was absolutely fantastic. I kept thinking, "It's been over forty years since I've felt like this, forty years since I have held and kissed a woman." Kissing Myra was so natural for me, so desirable. I thought the Prozac had numbed all my sexual feelings, but I discovered tonight that this was not true. Despite our passionate feelings, we both held back. I have a lot of thinking to do on that subject. She felt wonderful. At one point she called me "Sweet," and my heart just pounded. She was worried about me, afraid I was being overwhelmed with guilt and asked during one of our "cooling off periods," "Are you crying?" I assured her I was all right. I was not crying. I kept telling her how good she felt to me.

What worries me the most about all of this is that I know I still have feelings for Janie. The pain still comes whenever I allow myself to think about her. I feel very unfair to Myra to be kissing her when I know I still have feelings for Janie. But it isn't as if I am deceiving Myra. She knows about Janie. I just don't want to ever hurt Myra. I don't want to use her. And this worries me.

November 24 - November 29, 2000

Friday, November 24:   I left for Austin this morning. Since Mother broke her hip during the early morning hours of August 11, I have been caring for her every day, many times 24 hours a day.

Now that she is able to get up and around on her own, I felt a need to get away for awhile. Anne is visiting a friend in New York City and invited me to stay in her apartment. I accepted her offer and enjoyed a few days of freedom from all responsibilities.

I thought about Myra a lot, wishing she were there with me. I thought often of calling her, but had no idea what I would say except that I was missing her. I've always been better at talking with someone in person than over a phone.

Monday, November 27: I picked up Anne at the airport at noon, drove her back to her apartment, then drove directly from Austin to Tyler (224 miles) in order to be at handbell practice by 5:30 p.m.. I was only five minutes late! It's good to be home.

Tuesday, November 28: I took Mother to the beauty shop this morning. When I returned to the apartment, Janie called! I couldn't believe it, but I was absolutely delighted. She indicated it had been at least three weeks since we had seen each other. We chatted for an hour and a half. She wanted to know what was going on in my life, so I told her about kissing Myra.

"What was it like?" she asked.

"Wonderful," I replied.

"Oh, I'm SO glad!"

And I knew she was. She has been wanting me to find someone for such a long time. She asked me if Myra liked me. "I think so," I said.

"Well, she'd have to be nuts not to be absolutely crazy about you," Janie insisted.

"Oh, Janie!" I said.

"No, that's right," she replied. "You're such a precious person."

We then discussed some problems she was experiencing. My heart aches for her. She grieves so deeply and has been grieving for a long time.

Last night I sent Myra an e-mail telling her I was home and inviting her to come over for supper tonight. Five days have passed since we last saw each other and kissed for the first time. An e-mail awaited me this morning saying she had just received the invitation and wanted to know if I meant Tuesday night or Wednesday night? I replied "Tonight," explaining it would be a simple meal. Later, Myra told me she was so delighted to know I wanted to see her again that she shouted in joy. Because I had not called her, she was fearful I might not want to see her again.

I prepared a quiche and a pistachio ambrosia salad. After the meal, we enjoyed hugging and kissing. My feelings for Myra are growing daily. This pleases me very much.

Wednesday, November 29: Myra came tonight to use my computer. We again ended up being affectionate. I can't believe all this is happening to me. I'm so happy. And I feel absolutely no guilt, no shame.

Friday, December 1, 2000

A long letter from Myra arrived this afternoon, a letter she wrote upon returning home Wednesday night: "Dear Cheyne, I came home, put myself in a tub of hot water, bathed in candlelight, and soothed by the music of Yanni, I began to weep. Yanni's melodies are so passionate and soulful they often pluck chords of emotion in me.

"When I first met you, there was some interest/attraction. I saw you not only as a courageous woman but also as someone who had some common experiences, someone who could be a friend, someone who was 'single' and could be a partner in just 'doing' things. And I will also confess there was probably a bit of physical attraction--I've always thought you were/are 'cute as a bug!'

"As we visited and I got to 'see' you more, I liked what I saw. You are an amazing woman--courageous, caring, desiring truth, determined to live in truth, having the fortitude to keep moving, growing, and being who you are and becoming. Your sensitivity, humor, intelligence, and playfulness are equally admirable.

"I just wanted to be available for friendship, encouragement, and support for you--even knowing at the same time my own neediness for friendship, encouragement, and support. Yes, just a friend as you dealt with your 'full plate'--coming out of the marriage, 'coming out,' struggles and disappointments with church and friends, your 'getting through' your feelings about Janie, and then your mother's illness. And, I thought I was pretty successful

304

in cutting off any physical/romantic attractions I might have had. Had a lot of practice in that, you know!

"I remember the trip to Dallas at the end of October. I had so much fun--great conversation over dinner, poking around and being just a little silly in the bookstore, your gracious indulgence with the shock of my son's bleached hair, your sharing your poetry and spiritual experience on the trip home. I was overwhelmed and delighted with the sense of friendship I felt.

"These last few weeks as we have spent more time together, conversing and sharing, I've had to be honest with myself about the growing 'attraction'--my desire to hold you, touch you tenderly, and kiss you passionately. After Wednesday night (before Thanksgiving) with, I believe, both of us wanting the same thing--to hold hands, touch, and be close--and my leaving with a far too familiar ache in my heart, I simply decided that I could not do this again. One, I could not stay away from you and let the feelings die a painful natural death over time, nor two, could I be around you and continue to ache inside.

"So Thanksgiving evening--Oh I want you to know I was so proud and pleased to have you with me at St. Dismas--I mustered every ounce of courage I might have and said 'Let's turn the TV off and talk.' I held your hand and when you turned to me and said that the Prozac hadn't killed everything--you were feeling something, I kissed you.

"I will admit that I was a bit surprised but very pleased with your response--warm and tender--like you might like me!

"I don't know about you, Cheyne, but I am definitely in 'uncharted' territory here. I feel happy and excited, and I feel a little (a lot of) uncertainty as well. I was thinking as I wept in the bathtub--What do I want? This is my answer:

"I want you and me to listen to Yanni's music together. I want you to hear the song 'Desperado'--then you'll know my greatest fear and pain. I want to dance with you while Kenny Gee plays the music.

"Yes, I want to dance with you literally. I also want us to keep dancing--figuratively, as well. I want to keep doing the steps as whatever it is--be it friendship, relationship--between us develops into whatever it is supposed to be. I don't have a clue! I just know I'm tired of running from myself and others. I want to do it differently this time.

"Well, Cheyne, I hope some of this makes a little sense. I just want to be honest. I've said a lot about me and what I want-- aren't I self-centered! I will close with as much honesty and lack of self-centeredness that my humanity can muster by saying--I love you. I truly want for you what is best and good for you in your life. I love you, Myra"

What a thrill! I'm flattered she likes me enough to write a long letter--and to be so open and honest about her feelings.

I replied to Myra: "I don't intend to do much commenting over the Internet about the wonderful letter I just received. I'm counting the hours until I see you tonight."

Myra invited me to eat spaghetti with her tonight, then afterwards to help her decorate her Christmas tree. She now holds and kisses me the minute one of us steps inside the other's dwelling. We just hold, and kiss.

306

Supper was very good. It's nice being with her. I'm learning to appreciate her more and more. She's intelligent, kind, giving, respected, and most honorable and truthful. In other words, she's one-in-a-million. I'm very fortunate that she cares for me so much.

Putting lights on her tree didn't take long, so we had hours to enjoy holding and kissing. Despite the Prozac's dulling of my emotions, I am experiencing a passion that I haven't felt in over forty years. I find it unbelievable that I'm now finding life so enjoyable; and that I look forward to the next day, the next week, the next year. Unbelievable!

December 3 - December 11, 2000

Sunday, December 3: When I awoke Sunday morning, I wished Myra were there with me. Not Janie, but Myra! Now that's a welcome change!

I was already seated in Sunday School when Janie walked across the room to sit beside me. Seeing her walk toward me brought no sensation of longing, no pain. A calmness permeated my being, and I realized my intense feelings toward her were gone. What a relief!

I didn't call Myra today. Many times I wanted to do so, but just didn't. I don't know why. I just didn't. At both the morning and evening church services I wished she were sitting beside me. But if she had been there it would have been very, very difficult not to hold her hand, and I don't think my church is ready for that. But even now, at almost 10 p.m., I'm thinking of her, wishing she were here.

Prior to the evening church service, Anne called. The subject turned to politics and she said she really is ready to get this disputed election over. She's in the minority at her office. Her boss, a Baptist, said to her the other day that "We Christians know that Bush is the better man."

Anne then stated, "I'm not going to tell you what I said back to him."

"Go ahead and tell me," I ordered.

Anne then replied, "I said, 'Bullshit!' Don't include ME in your WE comment as if all Christians are Republican!"

Her boss then apologized to her for making the comment.

I sent an e-mail to Myra telling her of the incident and added, "Don't ask me where she got her nerve!"

Myra replied, "Oh, I KNOW where she got her nerve!! I look forward to meeting Anne." After writing a little about one of her sons, she added, "There are no words to describe Saturday!!"

Monday, December 4: I called my doctor to ask the schedule to get off the Prozac. I really want to get off it. I have practically no emotions so I don't want to stay on this drug much longer.

Saturday, December 9: Last night (Friday, December 8) was exquisitely marvelous as Myra spent the night with me. Feeling a woman's body next to mine for the first time in over forty years was a heavenly sensation! I felt as if I had "come home," as if I were where I was supposed to be. I felt calm, happy, and contented with no feelings of guilt or shame. To be truthful, I visualized Jesus standing beside the bed, smiling down upon us with the most glorious, approving smile. The feeling of his blessed Presence delighting in our happiness was more meaningful to me than any marriage ceremony. During my 37 years of marriage I never pictured Jesus being anywhere near our marriage bed or in any way approving of our physical relationship. And yet I was now feeling His approval throughout my whole being. I knew that in God's eyes Myra and I married each other last night. The happiness I felt was so overwhelming I seemed to be constantly reminding myself it was real--that holding Myra in my arms was no dream. I savored every minute, aware that I was feeling a physical closeness I had longed for for many, many years.

Sunday, December 10: Last night we attended an all-lesbian party which was a "first" for me! Invitations went out to 117 lesbians, and I'd estimate at least 80 people were there (including five males). We ate lots of fantastic food, were entertained by an all-girls' band, and played some crazy games that had me "in stitches" as I realized I had led a very sheltered life.

Even though we left the party at midnight while it was still in full swing, it nevertheless was very difficult to get up this morning in order to be at church before 7:45 a.m.! Our handbell choir played in both morning worship services.

Monday, December 11, 2000

I mailed about 80 Christmas letters which said: *Two years have passed since my last Christmas letter, so here's a quick update on what has been going on in my life. After 37 years of marriage, Jim and I separated at the beginning of this year and our divorce was final toward the first of April. Both of us, I believe, are finding life a more positive experience now. Jim still lives at our old address, and our son, Michael, has moved in with him. I have a little apartment, where I enjoy my own space and very few responsibilities.*

The usual question I hear is "What are you doing with your time?" This always amazes me as I seem to stay quite busy; and yet my "busyness" is of my own making, doing things I enjoy doing. I'm active in a Bible Study, do a lot of walking, worship with several new congregations while retaining close ties to my home church, play handbells, do a lot of writing, and occasionally find time to read.

I have a new grandson, Jared, born July 6, 2000 to Josh and Sandy. He's a precious, precious child! . . . Anne graduated from Texas Tech in May--Summa Cum Laude with Honors. She has a job in Austin and is delighted to be back "home." J.W. is into his 12th year of teaching. Hard to believe, isn't it?

My mother broke her right hip in August, but is up and about with the aid of a walker. I predict a cane will soon replace the walker. She is doing great and will turn 90 years of age on December 28.

Despite the valleys I have gone through this year, I am much happier than I have been in a long, long time. I recently read the following: "By the grace of God, our suffering can be transformed into something that brings life and light to this world." I believe that is what is happening in my life, and I praise the Lord for his tender care and guidance.

May knowing that you are in the hands of an all-powerful, all-loving God bring you peace. Cheyne

Wednesday, December 13, 2000

Cold, cold weather. It's beautiful outside with all the ice, but tree limbs are breaking off, power is out in many parts of town, traffic signals don't all work, and water pressure is going down. (Later note: This turned out to be a terrible ice storm that wreaked havoc all over East Texas. Some homes were without electricity for a month or more.)

I was quite surprised today to receive a letter from a fellow Jim and I knew in the early 60's. Actually, he was a friend of Jim's prior to our marriage, and we occasionally visited in his home. He had received my Christmas card (with letter) and replied: "I truly appreciated receiving your card; I've thought of you so frequently this year. I had a note from Jim via e-mail . . . he and I go a 'long ways back,' and he shared the info about the divorce. Bless his heart, he's still hurting from it, but I fully understand and appreciate YOUR feelings, too. I probably understand your vantage point more than I do his. As I explained to him, I've known that I'm gay for many years now. I had to reconcile that fact with my wife and our son many years ago. I enjoyed your quote about transforming our suffering into something bringing life and light into the world. Very true, indeed. My wife remarked over and over again about how the 'Holy Spirit marches through our lives wearing combat boots.' Also a very apt expression! I've still got a few cleat-marks to show for that presence!!

"I hope we can stay in touch. I hope your life is proceeding happily in the direction you wish it to take. I wish for you only the best. Know that our friendship remains solidly intact! Best always . . ."

I immediately responded: "What a most welcome letter! You are a gem to take time to write, and yet I have found so many others reaching out to me who 'understand.' It's as if we are all members of the same club--put on earth to support each other. I've been amazed at how many of my friends are affected by either being gay or having a gay child. If everyone 'came out of the closet' at once, the nation would be flabbergasted!

I then took time to tell him "my story" as to why I married and what my life has been like. I concluded with "Thanks for being so open and honest with me. I really appreciate it. And I'm so glad you have a partner. I have just recently become involved with a woman, and I feel as if 'I have come home.' It's been so long since I have felt that kind of peace and contentment. Wonderful.

"Again, you are wonderful to have taken time to write to me. Thanks so very much. Cheyne"

He answered right away thanking me for my prompt reply and explained that he had confronted his being gay many years

312

ago and came out to both his wife and his son. "She had a pretty tough time with it at first," he said, "but later on she came to grips with the reality of the situation and became my most staunch advocate. She'd remark, 'Honey, you didn't ask to be gay any more than I asked to have MS!' Very tolerant, very understanding . . . I was blessed to have that sweet thing in my life those 30 years--even if I WAS hiding the truth from her and me both."

Then he admitted when he came out to Jim not long ago, he obviously hit him "too close to home" because he never received a reply to his letter.

Thursday, December 14: I shared with Barbara the letter I had written yesterday to my Dallas friend. She replied today: "Interesting reply--especially the line that says you've recently become involved with a woman and feel as if you've come home. You haven't confirmed that to me previously, although (of course) I have suspected as much--and I also suspect that YOU suspected I suspected as much! (Diagram THAT sentence.)

"You mention no names, but I assume (given the lack of other evidence) that you mean Myra. If that's the case, it's a bit odd that I foresaw that possibility long before you did. I like her very much (not that it matters to you, but it does matter to me, since I plan on being friends with you forever), and think she seemed a bit more at ease with me last Tuesday than the one other time we met. Hard to be comfortable with someone you don't know at all, whatever the circumstances are--but I'm hoping we'll get to know each other better and trust each other.

"Because I've been your friend longer than I've been hers, let me say to you the same thing I've said to you about Jim. When you're coming off a painful, emotion-fraught time in your life, you need to take it slow and easy in any new relationship. I don't think you're a person who'll ever be comfortable with a series of relationships, so be very sure before you commit to another. On the other hand, you 'feel like you're coming home.' Is that the person, or is it the acceptance? You're one to think things through, so I imagine you've already dealt with these things. Still, I need to remind you whether or not you need reminding! Thank heaven you're evidently comfortable with MY foibles! bl"

When I answered Barbara later that day I admitted I had decided to let "the cat out of the bag" because I figured she knew anyway. Myra and I met on April 10 and we went until Thanksgiving before ever holding hands. Then I wrote, "Myra is a good person, an honorable person, and one who has suffered quite a bit in this life. I find pleasure in just being with her, and we have every intention of growing old together. Since I'm not far from the 'old' category, we laughingly talk about the future when she will use a walker to push my wheelchair.

"Thanks for sticking by me even though I know I'm following a course you disapprove of."

Barbara replied, "'Thanks for sticking by me even though I know I'm following a course you disapprove of.' Not exactly the right phrase. 'Don't understand,' maybe, or 'disagree with,' or 'worry about.' But I've got no right to disapprove of anything you do, and I honestly don't feel disapproving. I still value people by

314

the fruit of their lives—which is different somehow. At least to me. I wish you all the best, as you know. bl"

Monday, December 18, 2000

Janie and I met at McAllister's and visited about an hour and a half. Afterward, I wrote Myra about the meeting to tell her how delighted I was to realize the painful feelings toward Janie are gone! Hallelujah!

What a blessed relief to be able to sit and visit with her and not experience that old painful yearning for something I could never have. Janie is also delighted my pain is gone.

I shared the good news not only with Myra, but also with Barbara who quickly replied, "I'm so glad that the pain of unrequited (In kind) feeling for Janie is gone. Now THERE'S a Christmas gift! How are you doing without Prozac? How are preparations coming for your mother's 90th birthday party? In other words, are you doing okay? Is life becoming more joyful for you more of the time? Can you sit down and read a book?

"Your nosy but caring friend, Barbara"

To which I replied: "This Christmas in comparison to last year's, will be much different for me. It's as if I have to pinch myself constantly to be assured my feelings of happiness and contentedness are real. Just unbelievable. I'm doing great. I've just completed my two-week withdrawal period for the Prozac. I took my last pill yesterday morning. This week, and possibly the next, will 'tell the tale.'

"I think I am capable of sitting down and reading a book, but I've been so busy lately that I haven't given it a try. My choices of books have definitely changed. I find that interesting. I used to read 'trash.' Nothing undesirable, just quick-reading novels and mysteries. This past year I have read more non-fiction then fiction, especially religious books. This is new for me. Sometimes as I struggle through a book that I have to 'think about,' I ask myself why I don't find some quick-reading novel to enjoy.

"Progress is being made with plans for Mother's 90th birthday celebration. When I first envisioned this event, I saw it as a very simple 'cake and punch' affair for her fellow Atria (retirement home) residents. Then someone suggested I should invite members of Mother's Sunday School class. So I'm including them along with you, Myra, and Janie, but Janie will be out of town.

"Today I purchased a tri-fold board to display pictures of Mother and her family. I need to get that ready. Tomorrow I take Mother to the beauty shop and hope to complete all my Christmas gift buying and wrapping. By my taking everything one day at a time, things seem to be falling into place.

"One of my New Year's resolutions this year is to start my 'praise book,' listing all those things to be thankful for. Such a thought would have never crossed my mind in the past. That's how far I've come. Thanks, friend."

316

Friday, December 22, 2000

As I continued to prepare for Mother's 90th Birthday Celebration, I wrote a "coming out" letter to Marta, a friend from the 60's. Her reply not only pleased me but brought back memories of the past. She stated, "First, let me assure you that I'm not 'on the floor' although the possibility that you were so unhappy never consciously surfaced either. At this moment, I get a sense of your face and being that overcomes me with sadness . . . but that is retrospective and, of course, I had no idea in point of fact. Societal and parental expectations are truly crushing and you persevered so valiantly, so sacrificially, all those years, Cheyne. In the 1966-68 scheme of things, I saw only a dedicated, wonderful, beautiful wife and mother, somewhat reserved but always giving unstintingly of herself. (You were the pie crust wizard who showed me that working in the least amount of water equaled flakier; you shared recipes I still have; you and Jim were always available for forays to the Night Hawk or such for food and fun.) You were the one with a burning desire to write. You were the one who stretched herself to meet a most interesting variety of jobs over the years. Your Christmas letters always brought news of some additional mastery . . . always humble, always capable and skilled. I admired you enormously then, and I admire and respect you enormously now. Your letter gives me a broader perspective, and I understand a pervasive pain of forty year's endurance that can only be relieved in your courageous stand. I applaud you and am thankful for the support of your children. Forty years in the wilderness! May you surely know the presence of the Lord as He holds you in the palm of His hand!

"It seems the older I get, the more flimsy and useless our facades are and the only true dialogue is soul to soul. I sense that is what you have shared with me here, and I am deeply touched. Love, Marta"

Our letters brought back reminders that my homosexuality was never spoken about openly by my parents. However, one afternoon after I had been married almost twenty years and already had my fourth child, my dad privately said to me, "I want to apologize to you for what I used to think about you." His statement, which came completely out of the blue, needed no explanation. I knew exactly what was on his mind although this was a subject he and I had never broached. Actually it was a subject Mother brought up only the one time when I was seventeen. No other words were ever spoken by them to me on this subject. Nevertheless, my being homosexual was like the proverbial "elephant in the living room" that everyone pretended was not there.

Consequently, when Dad voiced remorse for "what he used to think," I knew instantly he was referring to his belief that I was homosexual. I didn't ask, "To what are you referring, Dad?" I knew to what he referred.

At that time, I felt I had two choices: (1) I could simply accept his apology and thereby let him believe he had made a terrible mistake when he convinced Mother I was a homosexual, or (2) I could be honest and confess that he owed me no apology because he had been correct--I am homosexual.

318

Confessing to the truth, however, would deeply hurt him, hurt him more than having judged me unfairly. At least that's what I concluded. I therefore replied, "That's all right, Dad. No problem." And that's all that was ever said between us on this subject. Dad passed away in 1996.

Sunday, January 21, 2001

The contentment Myra and I feel when we are together is based upon the assurance that in God's sight we belong to each other as permanently as a heterosexual married couple. We know this to be true because when we are together, we are enveloped in a sense of peace and serenity, invariably aware of Christ's presence as well as of His fantastic gift in bringing us together.

I once heard it explained that because we were taught that homosexuals are bad people, and because we don't see ourselves as bad people, we therefore have to conclude that we must not be homosexual. But Myra and I had reached the point of acknowledging that we really were homosexual. In doing that, we braced ourselves to be overwhelmed with a feeling that we must be "bad." When this never happened, another terribly heavy burden was lifted from our shoulders.

Our relationship with Jesus Christ, through the Holy Spirit, began growing. Many nights as we lay in each other's arms, we would discuss scriptural passages that we were studying in various study groups or verses we had recently read. Myra has a beautiful singing voice, and sometimes as we lay in bed, she sang praise songs to me or voiced a prayer. I think of her as our "spiritual leader."

I eventually concluded that in denying who and what I was for most of my life, I had been cut off from having a close relationship with God because I was denying who He had created me to be. Now that I am "out of the closet," I am more open to God's leadership and direction, realizing He is now able to use me in ways He never could before. Hallelujah!

Sunday, February 11, 2001

When I arose this morning about 6:30, I turned on the TV to have a little entertainment while I exercised. I ended up watching the final minutes of a sermon by a preacher in Marshall, a town about 55 miles east of Tyler. This preacher was condemning homosexuality. I jotted down his name and address thinking, "I need to contact him." (Days later I did write to him, sharing my personal story of what a sad life I led trying to abide by teachings such as his. He never wrote back.)

Sunday, February 18, 2001

I again turned on the TV and caught the same Marshall preacher, and he was again ranting and raving against homosexuality! I couldn't believe it! He really was stirring up the hatred toward us.

But on the bright side, one of my friends at church, Georgia Hunt, asked me last Wednesday, "Who is that 'cute girl' that sits with you in church?" At first I was baffled by her question, then I realized she had been viewing Myra and me from the choir loft! I proudly shared with her Myra's name and explained that she was my friend.

Friday - Sunday, March 9 - 11, 2001

Myra and I attended the Southern Regional PFLAG Conference in Dallas. We had a wonderful time being seen as "a couple." We felt free to publicly hold hands and even to put an arm around the other. Never before had we experienced such freedom to state before others that we were "together." It felt so good, so free, so right.

I discovered during the meetings that my emotions were constantly bubbling near the surface. I kept hearing statements I had never heard before, some I had never really thought about and yet they applied directly to me. For example, in discussing gender, the speaker pointed out that despite the wide range of gender identification, a person's gender identification has nothing to do with sexual orientation. In other words, in my case, it is all right to be feminine (which I consider myself to be) and yet to have a sexual orientation making me desire a woman for a partner. Another way to put it: A woman doesn't have to look or act "butch" to be a lesbian.

Other comments that hit home included: (1) The more painful the outing, the more potential for happiness. (2) When you first hear something affirming about homosexuality, you decide to come out. (3) Negative comments about homosexuality from family causes an individual to stay in the closet. All of these comments were true for me.

End of July, 2002

Mother passed away November 14, 2001. We never discussed my sexual orientation.

As the months pass, I am becoming bolder and bolder. In the summer of 2002, I joined Soulforce in its silent vigil at the Southern Baptist Convention in St. Louis. Soulforce, founded by Mel White, the author of *Stranger at the Gate*, offers a spirit-based activism aimed at reconciliation with those who oppress the gay community. Participating in this vigil, I stood on a sidewalk along with many others, wore a shirt that said "Stop Spiritual Violence" and held a sign that said the same. Churches that preach homosexuality is sinful and that homosexuals will go to hell are committing "spiritual violence" against gays, lesbians, transgendered and bisexual individuals. Soulforce fights religion-based oppression, and their message is dear to my heart.

Myra and I, as an openly gay couple, are now working closely with a group of leaders inside another large Baptist organization in which she and I participate in dialogues on the subject of homosexuality and the possibility of Baptist churches becoming more open and accepting (or perhaps I should say "less condemning and rejecting").

As Janie and I were visiting in July, 2002, reviewing all the changes which had taken place in my life, she said, "If it weren't for me, you wouldn't have ruined your life."

I assured her that what she said was ridiculous, but I knew from her statement she had assumed a burden of guilt regarding my divorce. Wanting to allay those feelings, I sat down the following day (July 23, 2002) and wrote:

"Janie, I keep thinking about what you said yesterday indicating that if it weren't for you, I'd still be married. You regretted that you had in some way upset my life. Those weren't the exact words but this is a subject I have thought about many, many times. You are right. If it had not been for you, I would still be married. But please be assured that I wouldn't trade my life now for what I had then for all the money, power, and fame the world might offer. No way.

"Yes, you changed my life. You changed it by your words of love and acceptance of homosexuals. Your words amazed me. Never in all my life had the thought even occurred to me that a gay person could be loved and accepted. I was stunned. And as I've written to you before, that's what started a whole series of emotions.

"I truly believe God sent you into my life in order to set my feet onto this new pathway of activism for homosexuals. I won't downplay the pain I suffered for at least a year; but even so, I can now look back on those events and those emotions and see God's hand at work in my life.

"Each time I feel a little bit of success in my efforts to enlighten others, the thought comes to me that 'Janie needs to realize that if it weren't for her, for her kind, loving, and sensitive heart, I wouldn't be here. She is behind every bit of success I experience. One of these days I hope she will be aware of the part she has played in my demonstrating with Soulforce at the Southern Baptist Convention, in the letters I have written to the *Baptist Standard*, in my participation in the meeting of The Ten at the Cooperative Baptist Fellowship, and whatever else I do in this regard.'

"Janie, my life now is unbelievably good. I never envisioned in all my wildest dreams I could be happy like I am now. Myra is truly a gift from God. I am continually thankful for her, for her love, and for our relationship. But even more than this, I am free of the fear I lived with all of my life--a fear that someone would discover my 'shameful secret.' There is no way to explain to someone who has not lived with that burden of fear how liberating it is to be unshackled from that bondage. It's absolutely wonderful.

"And surely you know I was not happy in my marriage. Why should you have any kind of regret that I'm now divorced?

"So promise me to never again feel that you are somehow to blame for 'ruining my life.' That is an absolutely ridiculous thought for you to have. Much love, Cheyne"

Less than two hours later, this reply arrived: "Dear Cheyne, Thank you for the wonderful letter you wrote to me. Please know that there are VERY FEW people in my life who have given me the heart-felt safety that you gave me when we first became friends. We actually were still at the acquaintance stage when I felt, instantly and instinctively, your God-given gift of love and acceptance. I will always be grateful. Your courage, support, and love have lifted me up when I was well beyond despair. There are times when you didn't even know you did so. Believe me, if you think I saved your life, you have no idea how many times you have saved mine.

"I am thrilled beyond words that you and Myra are so happy. You deserve that happiness more than anyone I know. I do believe that your mission is blessed and guided by God every step of the way. I see His presence in your eyes and I hear His voice in your voice. I feel His courage in your heart. You will make a difference in this world.

"You are so dear, XXX Janic"

At long last I can honestly say, "I'm glad I'm gay." I recall attending a PFLAG meeting in which one of the women asked the group, "If there were a pill you could take that would make you straight instead of gay, would you take it?"

Several immediately replied that they certainly would take that pill. I'll never forget, though, what one member confidently stated: "No, I wouldn't take the pill. I like myself the way I am."

At the time I was shocked by her words. She actually liked being gay? I stared at her trying to fathom what she meant and couldn't figure it out. Surely she didn't mean that! Who would want to be gay if you could be straight? I spent most of my life wanting to be straight. I would have paid any amount of money to have had a pill to keep me from being gay, to make it possible for me to love a man. But now that I have become comfortable with myself, with who and what God made me to be, I finally understand her feelings. If someone were to ask me that same question today, I would say, "No way would I take that pill. I like who I am."

[In the end of the story about Adam and Eve] *God with his own hands makes them garments of skins and clothes them. It is the most moving part of the story. They can't go back, but they can go forward clothed in a new way--clothed, that is, not in the sense of having their old defenses again behind which to hide who they are and what they have done but in the sense of having a new understanding of who they are and a new strength to draw on for what lies before them to do now.*

Listening to Your Life, by Frederick Buechner, p. 70.

ENDNOTES

1. Mel White, <u>Stranger at the Gate</u> (New York: Simon & Schuster, 1994, p. 284.

2. Ibid., p. 287.

3. Ibid. p. 293.

4. Ibid., p. 239.

5. Source Unknown

6. White, p. 147. (Mel White's words and thoughts are liberally sprinkled throughout my book, not all appearing in quotations. In personal correspondence with him, he gave me permission on February 18, 2008, that he was not worried about footnoting or giving credit.)

7. Bruce Bawer, <u>A Place At The Table</u> (New York: Touchstone, 1993), p. 89.

8. Philip Yancey, <u>What's So Amazing About Grace?</u> (Grand Rapids, Michigan: Zondervan, 1997), p. 232.

9. Ibid., p. 230.

10. Ibid., p. 230.

11. White, p. 236. (Reference to interviews conducted by Bette Greene in preparation of writing her novel, The Drowning of Stephan Jones.)

12. Rembert Truluck, http://www.truluck.com/html/six_bible_passages.html.

13. Ibid.

14. Ibid.

15. Bawer, p. 133.

16. Ibid

17. Ibid

18. Ibid

19. Ibid. pp. 133-144.

20. Ibid. p. 134.

21. Ibid. p. 140

22. Ibid. p. 141

23. Walter Wink, "Homosexuality and The Bible," an article which appeared in the Christian Century Magazine copyright 1979, Christian Century Foundation. Revised version copyright 1996., p. 12.

24. Ibid. pp. 12-14.

25. Dorothy C. Bass, editor, "Practicing Our Faith: A Way of Life for a Searching People," John Wiley & Sons, Publishers, page 101.

26. Report of the Committee on Baptist Integrity, September 28, 1999. Distributed at BGCT (Baptist General Convention of Texas) annual meeting in November 1999.